Captaincy

Captaincy

Graham Gooch
with Patrick Murphy

Stanley Paul
LONDON

Stanley Paul & Co. Ltd
An imprint of Random Century Group
20 Vauxhall Bridge Road, London SW1V 2SA

Random Century Australia (Pty) Ltd
20 Alfred Street, Milsons Point, Sydney 2061

Random Century New Zealand Limited
PO Box 40–086, Glenfield, Auckland 10

Century Hutchinson South Africa (Pty) Ltd
PO Box 337, Bergvlei 2012, South Africa

First published 1992
Copyright © Graham Gooch 1992

Set in Linotron Sabon by
Deltatype Ltd, Ellesmere Port, Cheshire

Printed and bound in Great Britain by
Clays Ltd, St Ives PLC

A catalogue record for this book is available
from the British Library

ISBN 0 09 175018 0

Contents

Acknowledgements

So many have been helpful and supportive to me over the years but I must pick out three. Keith Fletcher, my old Essex captain, has been the biggest influence on me as player and captain. Any practical knowledge I have picked up on the game has been largely due to Keith. Doug Insole, another great servant of Essex and England, has also been a major influence on my career, a wise counsellor, full of common sense. Doug was manager on my first senior England tour and he has been tremendously helpful to me at all times. He and Keith have been constant factors at Essex during my time with the county and I count myself very fortunate to have enjoyed their friendship and support. With England, Micky Stewart has been a tremendous help to me, both before I became captain and throughout my time in charge. As England's cricket manager, he has been dedicated and conscientious. A wise confidant, Micky has always been there for me as a sounding board and he has never stopped encouraging me or helping with my own game.

Finally, my grateful thanks to my collaborator on this book, Pat Murphy. We have been friends for many years and that made it easier as we enjoyed each other's company from Adelaide to Brentwood, working on this book. My particular thanks to Pat for following me up and down England's motorways for a few hours' work on his tape recorder, and for his tolerance as I started yawning in mid-evening!

Photographic acknowledgement: the author and publishers would like to thank Patrick Eagar, AllSport and Graham Morris for the use of their copyright photographs.

1
What makes a captain?

The ideal captain just doesn't exist. How could he? What human being could possibly combine the qualities of tactical guru, sergeant-major, thoughtful counsellor, supreme man-manager, excellent player, diplomat, inspirational gambler and consistent motivator, skilled in media relationships and overflowing with luck? That animal has never existed, and it is part of cricket's charm that all captains try to conceal their weak spots while hoping that their positive virtues will paper over the cracks and get their players performing to their full potential.

I freely admit that I still fall down in certain requirements of captaincy. I tend to be rather intolerant of players who don't do themselves justice: I expect them to show the same dedication I bring to my cricket; I am still learning how to get the best out of spinners in the field; my inability to reach an understanding with David Gower in recent years must indicate a man-management problem; and as for relationships with the media – well that is something that doesn't keep me awake at nights. To me captaincy is fundamentally about commonsense, about influencing your side's style of play in a positive manner, building up team spirit so it isn't found wanting at crucial times and setting the right example in terms of fitness and attitude to your profession. It's also important that the captain actually *enjoys* the job.

If pushed to make a choice, I would admit that I prefer batting to captaincy. That's what I'm best at and so it follows that if I'm playing well, that helps my side. I'm also totally responsible for my successes or failures, whereas the captain has to carry the can at all times. I never really coveted the job of Essex captain and certainly not the England leadership, because playing and enjoying the game has always been so important to me. The first time I captained Essex was in a John Player League game towards the end of the 1980 season and although I

1

worried about all the odds and ends, the senior players helped me a lot. In 1983, I was appointed vice captain to Keith Fletcher and the learning process really started. Yet I had always been interested in the thought processes of captaincy. Anyone who takes their profession seriously ought to watch how more experienced people go about their jobs and I was so lucky to be able to learn about the game's intricacies under Keith Fletcher at Essex and Mike Brearley with England. Most good judges would surely admit that they were two of the best English captains of the last twenty years – they had terrific tactical ability, they were dedicated to winning and would be ruthless when they had a side on the run, they were positive in approach, and they had that knack of being accessible to the players yet sufficiently detached from them to win their respect. Fletcher and Brearley exuded authority and I enjoyed trying to read their minds out on the field. I'd often wonder, 'Now why's he done that?' and consider the other options; more often than not, they'd chosen the right one.

I suppose it will always be a blot on my copybook that I gave up the Essex captaincy in 1987 because I couldn't handle the pressure of the job. My detractors said in later years, 'How can Gooch be England captain, he couldn't cut it with Essex?!' An understandable point, although that argument does ignore the fact that when we won the County Championship in 1986, we were led by a certain GA Gooch, so perhaps I wasn't that short of the necessary qualities. The truth is that in 1987 I had my worst season with the bat since I had become an established player, and whatever runs I did get failed to please me, because I felt my technique was all wrong. As one of our front-line batsmen, I wasn't contributing enough to the team effort – something that has always meant a great deal to me – and so I handed back the captaincy at that time because I was being distracted by worries about my form. I really thought I had lost for good that special spark that had made me an England player and believed that unless I concentrated more on getting my batting right, I would be letting the side down. With Keith Fletcher taking over the reins for another season, Essex weren't exactly landed in a mess and when I regained the captaincy full time in 1989, the fact that we finished second, second and first in the Championship over the next three seasons suggests that I might now be competent at the job. It is so much easier for me to captain now, because I'm not as worried about my form as I was in 1987; if you're playing well, that gives you greater authority when you demand total commitment from your side. It also means I can devote more time to the team's needs without fussing over my technique in the nets for hour after hour.

How important is it that the captain should be one of the best players in the side? That was never a problem to Keith Fletcher at Essex – he had scored Test hundreds and every season he made a stack of runs in the Championship – but that aspect of the job worried Mike Brearley at England level. Mike was a fine opening bat for Middlesex, but I believe it bothered him that he never scored a Test hundred, especially as his usual opening partner, Geoffrey Boycott, was not slow to point out who was the better batsman. Mike knew he could captain England superbly, but I'm sure he would have liked to score more runs to reduce the pressure on him. I saw it get to him in the dressing-room and that inner tension may explain his occasional explosions of temper which quickly faded away. David Gower's captaincy against the 1985 Australians was positive and sound and one of the main reasons for that was because he was batting so well that summer. He wasn't distracted by his form, he could concentrate on how to beat the opposition and his personal confidence was shown in the way he led us. Yet if you *are* an outstanding captain, there is a case for your retention regardless of performance to an extent, because motivating the team and maximizing its potential are priceless assets. I have often wondered how David Hughes saw his own position as player at Lancashire in recent years. How did it feel to bat at number nine and not bowl? I really enjoy contributing to the team effort as a batsman, but Lancashire did well under Hughes' captaincy because they have good players and he brought out the best in them. On that basis he was the best man for the job. The Brearley syndrome at county level, if you like.

Ian Botham's experience as England captain suggests that the best players aren't always the ideal captains, even though in terms of inspirational quality they would qualify. The genius in Botham – that maverick approach – meant that he couldn't lead lesser mortals sensitively. I believe he didn't really understand what the players needed as individuals, he lacked that knack of fine tuning that coaxes the extra couple of per cent out of someone. Ian's attitude to the disciplines of the job meant that the only time he would try to lead by example was out there in the middle. His desire to remain one of the lads eroded some of his authority because he could never be someone like Brearley or Fletcher and keep his distance at the right time.

Ian had many excellent qualities that he brought to the job of captain. He was fearless, he'd never ask a player to do something on the field that he wouldn't also try to achieve and he had many bold, positive ideas. Even as a young player, Ian had an excellent cricket brain. When you stripped away all the bravado, there would be a great deal of sound tactical sense. On the field he sized up situations very quickly. But Ian was also unlucky, a trait that hampers unsuccessful captains. He was unlucky to come up against a magnificent West Indies side, some of whom were still good enough to be playing Test cricket against us ten years later – Marshall, Haynes, Richards and Greenidge for example. On that basis, he did well to lose just three Tests in two back-to-back series. With a little luck, we would have beaten them at Trent Bridge in 1980 (Ian's first Test as captain), instead of losing by two wickets. In the other Tests against them in that period, we were never in a position to force a win, but at least we competed, and there was never a hint of those two awful 5–0 series defeats we suffered in the mid-eighties. Mike Brearley's detractors are entitled to ask how he would have fared against the West Indies after clocking up impressive wins in a Test period weakened by defections to Kerry Packer. I believe Brearley would have struggled against those West Indian fast bowlers and that may then have affected his captaincy, but in tactical terms I'm sure he would have remained excellent and he would have got more out of Ian Botham than Botham did out of himself when he was captain.

Brearley was lucky to have Botham in his prime – the most talented English cricketer I have seen, a genuine matchwinner. He also had some superb bowlers at his disposal – Bob Willis, Mike Hendrick, Chris Old, John Lever, Derek Underwood, John Emburey and Phil Edmonds. They could bowl at a high level of performance and *maintain* that standard at any stage of the day. However tactically astute you are, the captain is dependent on his bowlers doing their job properly. You need the tools for the job. Clive Lloyd and Viv Richards have been lucky enough to profit from a production line of excellent fast bowlers, Ian Chappell enjoyed the devastating combination of Dennis Lillee and Jeff Thomson, Keith Fletcher has profited from the skill and stamina of John Lever (the best county cricketer of my time), while at Essex I have been fortunate to enjoy the services of Neil Foster, who so often makes vital early breakthroughs.

So the successful captain *must* have good players. An experienced, tough skipper can be very adept at avoiding defeat, a damage limitation exercise, but unless there are matchwinners in the side, he can't be expected to win trophies or Tests. He is like the soccer manager: if his players perform to their capabilities, he is a miracle worker, otherwise he is a candidate for the chop. I agree with Mike Brearley's comment that there is too much extremism attached to assessments of captaincy. There seem to be no shades of grey – it's either 'Gower's Goons' or 'Captain Courageous' and the next day, it's 'Captain Cock-Up' in the tabloid headlines. The captain can be out in the field, racking his brains, tapping into the experience he has picked up, he tries something just for the sake of it and if he gets lucky, the media call it 'an inspired change of bowling'. Once a captain has got the side he wants, ensured they are solid in morale and teamwork, high on self-discipline and ideally prepared – there's nothing he can do if they get bowled out for 120. He can't stop his best batsmen from smashing half-volleys straight to cover or his opening bowlers spraying the new ball down the legside. What he *can* do is change the side if the players show no signs of fulfilling their potential. I can cajole my bowlers in between overs ('drop it shorter at the left-hander'), replace them after a time, but I can't bowl the ball for them. It's just like the soccer manager in the dug-out; he has told them the tactics needed, he has marked each player's card, but he can't do the passing, running and tackling for them. As England captain, I would never tell one of my batsmen *how* to play. When Graeme Hick struggled in his first series against the West Indies, I couldn't take him to one side and say, 'This is how you play the short-pitched ball.' I believe each batsman has to do it his own way, the method that suits him best. I was there for Hick with advice about coming to terms with the Test Match atmosphere, how to cope with a bad run and how to approach an innings, but he had to sort out his own technical shortcomings with hand-picked technical advice from someone he respects. It's the same with bowling. I'd never tell my bowlers how they ought to run up, how to deliver the ball and at what speed – but I'll tell them *where* they should be putting it and where the batsman likes to have it bowled at him. If those players under my charge continue to let themselves and the team down, then they have to be dropped. No captain can turn a bad side into a good one overnight.

What he *can* do is influence the way the side plays, set the tone of its approach. This is one aspect of captaincy that particularly interests me. The way you play is more the concern of a county side, because Test cricket is fairly stereotyped; you are hoping to win the toss on a good wicket, bat the opposition out of the contest and then pressurize them, picking up twenty wickets in the process. There is much more scope in the County Championship. When I took over at Essex, our chairman Doug Insole – a wise counsellor to me over the years – told me that one of the advantages in being captain was that you could impose your own style, choose the tactics you would like to adopt, try to make things happen your way. Not everyone might agree with you, but you call the tune. To most senior players that creative challenge is attractive, but it mustn't be an ego trip. The job as county captain shouldn't go to someone simply to prolong their career, to keep them interested – you have to believe in your ability to do it, be aware that it can be an awful hassle, but want the chance to put your thoughts on the game into practice. I have always loved cricket, enjoyed talking about its complexities. Over the years, I've learnt a lot about the game in the bar at close of play – exchanging titbits of information with the opposition, talking about who has improved, who doesn't fancy the quicks any more. All that is part of your cricket education. As a youngster I listened quietly to what the senior players had to say and gradually built up my knowledge.

Eventually, when I settled down into the job, I came to enjoy putting my views over to the team. Keith Fletcher once told me that it took him two full seasons before he got the hang of county captaincy; until then he didn't really enjoy it. I can see what he means. When I first took over in 1986, I was glad to have Keith out there with me; I struggled at the job the following year and it took me some time to come to terms with all the various responsibilities and be able to impose my standards on the squad. I had been highly influenced by Fletcher and Brearley (to my great pleasure), but I knew that I had to be my own man when it came to my approach to the job.

I believe very strongly that a captain must expect to win every match. A positive approach rubs off on the others; that is one of the reasons why I rate Mike Gatting's captaincy so highly. Like myself under Fletcher, Mike learned his trade at Middlesex under a great captain in Brearley and I think it's no coincidence that Essex and Middlesex have been the top two teams in the Championship over the last decade. Both go out there *expecting* to win, provided that they play up to their capabilities. When I sit down and talk about prospects for the next day, I make sure the word 'defeat' is never mentioned. Negative thoughts such as avoiding defeat are just not a factor. I talk about how we will win if we play well and we pick the right eleven. In the course of the match, you can ensure you don't lose (for example, you'd be unlucky to lose a Championship match lasting three days if you score 500), but at all times I think positively. It's the same at Test level – winning boosts your confidence. When we beat Sri Lanka at Lord's in 1988, many said 'So what? It's only Sri Lanka.' What would those cynics have said if they had beaten us? 'England's Day of Shame!'? After a 4–0 hammering from the West Indies that summer, it was important to me as the new captain to stop the rot and try to rebuild the confidence of our players. It had been a miserable summer for English cricket and ignominious defeat at the hands of Sri Lanka would have been a cruel finale. Three years later, when we again faced Sri Lanka, my job as England captain was a different one. We had just beaten the West Indies at the Oval to square the series and many were on a high after a great achievement that had made me very proud. Yet there was still another Test to be played before the summer was over and I impressed that on the team very forcibly. We were expected to win – given our respective abilities, that was only right and proper – but I told them not to rest on their laurels, that we must work hard against a good batting side. We did and we won, to my satisfaction, after a dodgy first couple of days.

You can never get complacent about winning, because there are many days when you deserve to lose, and do so. As captain, my job is to minimize those bad days. Even when the odds are firmly against you, it is important that the captain still talks up his side's chances. I have never forgotten that astonishing Test at Leeds in 1981, when we turned over the Australians thanks to amazing performances from Bob Willis and Ian Botham. What sticks in my mind from that final day was the positive approach of Mike Brearley. We had very little to defend and everything pointed to a comfortable Aussie win, but Mike said, 'You just never know on that pitch.' He was right. Willis bowled fantastically, but it was Brearley who instilled that will-to-win in us. Ten years later, when we were up against it in the Perth Test, I made a point of mentioning Leeds '81 to the players before the final day. Australia only needed just over a hundred to win, with nine wickets left, but there were widening cracks on the pitch and if we bowled tightly, it could have been touch-and-go. We bowled loosely and they ran out easy winners, but I still think I was right to hark back to a Test Match of ten years earlier – not least of all because only one other player at Perth survived from that Leeds game and I just knew that Allan Border would be warning his side about the dangers of batting carelessly.

For me, the wrong attitude is far worse than a lack of ability. This is the nub of my disagreements with David Gower about the way the game ought to be played. Now David to me has always been a magnificent player and I have never felt he should be shackled in the way he goes about his batting out in the middle. He is a free spirit and I love seeing him at his best. Yet David's approach to the game isn't the same as mine: I feel the game at the highest level now demands so much more dedication and preparation. The ones who prosper nowadays are those who know their game plan and how to get the best out of themselves. As I've discussed with David Gower many times, there's a bare minimum involved and that's not to do with running five miles a day or sweating buckets in the nets. Under my captaincy for England, I believe David hasn't shown a good attitude or given enough to the rest of the team. The younger ones quite rightly look up to him and respect what he has achieved but he needed to set a better example to them and he didn't, especially in Australia. Now I am well aware that many cricket fans all around the world cannot understand why David can't get in the England side, and I know I must sound like an old gramophone record with the needle stuck when I go on about the need for dedication, but I recall a very good quote from the West Australian coach, Darryl Foster: 'When your attitude drops five per cent, your performance drops twenty per cent.' I think the way Australia has improved under Bobby Simpson and Allan Border since 1987 shows how much can be achieved by hard work and professionalism. I was very impressed at the way they went about their Ashes campaign in England in 1989. They looked as though they were enjoying their pre-match training sessions, they had a game plan out in the field and they looked a good, solid unit. They deserved to beat us because they put more into their preparations. They also looked as if they were good pals. It's amazing how the breaks go your way when you're all pulling together and helping each other out; the way the Australian tail-enders batted so valuably in the 1990–91 series underlined the importance of a good team spirit. Gary Player's famous quote, 'The harder I practise, the luckier I get' kept coming back to me on that tour, as I came to terms with my failure to motivate my players.

Setting the right example is one of the best ways to earn the respect of the players, a vital ingredient in making a success of the job. Some first-class cricketers are perfectly happy when it rains; they think, 'Oh good, a day off,' but you mustn't think so passively about your career. You don't get runs or wickets sitting in the pavilion and I expect my players to enjoy all aspects of the game. You have to be straight and honest with them; they may not like what you tell them, but you owe it to them to talk honestly about their career prospects. They must be told why they've been dropped. I recall the occasion when Essex stood Keith Pont down after he'd scored a hundred in the previous match – he had to make way for the good of the side and it had to be faced openly and honestly. The captain must know instinctively the right time to console a player and when to climb into him with justified criticism. Sometimes – inevitably – the chosen moment and the words are wrong. I still regret my inability to rouse some of my players on England's tour to Australia in 1990–91, how I failed to make them realize the highest honour in the game was theirs. You never stop learning.

On that tour, I was amazed that so many people kept coming up to me to say, 'Well done'. I was frankly embarrassed at that, because I didn't see any cause for congratulation. I had batted well at Adelaide yet we lost badly at Perth after I'd recovered from my hand injury. We had failed to compete at vital times in the Tests and, overall, our approach was simply not good enough. For that I was ultimately responsible. I would have been ducking my responsibilities as captain if I had happily taken the praise as batsman and not the criticism as skipper of an outfit that at times looked a shambles. A few months later it was a matter of great pride to me that we competed hard with the West Indies in all five Tests, even when we lost two of them. At no stage were we ever truly out of the game and that is what I expect from England players.

I want players under me who are mentally hard and expect to win. I can take defeat, but not if it was avoidable and has happened because of a lack of backbone in my team. My players should be hungry to succeed but not to the extent of being selfish. If I suspect a batsman is playing for himself, I come down hard on him. That happened at Essex a couple of years ago when John Stephenson and Nasser Hussain contrived to miss out on a fourth batting bonus point when it was there for the taking. I had a quiet, but firm word with them afterwards – pointing out that the first landmark when a county side bats is usually four batting points, and also that one missing point can cost us the title, as it proved for Kent in 1988. It's not my style to blow up at someone in the dressing-room but they were told in no uncertain terms that this was not the Essex way. They were looking to get us past 400 and a big lead but those full bonus points were more important. Championships are won on all pitches, in varying environments and with valuable contributions from everyone at various times, with a full haul of eight bonus points whenever possible.

I think it helps if the captain is one of the older ones in the team, whether at county or Test level. Sometimes there can be a little resentment towards a young captain from senior players and it does help if the captain has experienced most of cricket's unlikely scenarios to give him the depth of experience to take decisions on something more substantial than a hunch. That experience also allows the captain to sift through the advice that ought to be coming his way out on the field. I like every player to be thinking about what's going on out there, but I only want about three players to channel thoughts through to me. Otherwise the over-rate would be down to twelve an hour!

The captain owes it to his players to care about them. He must never forget he's dealing with human beings of differing temperaments, some of whom feel insecure. In a crowded county season, the strain of living in each other's pockets can be intense, while on England duties abroad, there are always a few players who are fated to miss out on the Tests and are liable to bouts of homesickness and depression. A player out of form should not be a happy man, he should be striving hard to regain his touch. The captain should be able to recognize those who need the arm around the shoulder and a quiet meal together to talk things through. He should have no favourites, and be accessible to everyone in the squad. I believe the family atmosphere we managed to engender in the England squad before we left for the West Indies in 1990 had much to do with our encouraging performances out there – and we got that feeling back when we did well against them in the summer of '91. An element of selfishness is an ingredient in the make-up of any top sportsman, but in team games like cricket, the captain just *has* to get his guys playing for each other.

Despite all the disappointments and the hassles, the captaincy of England has been a great honour to me. I enjoy the responsibility of getting the players behind me, that unique feeling of pride when I lead the side out and – particularly in the 1991 series against the West Indies – to feel the crowd willing us to do well. My main motivation as a player has never been to attain status. If that was the case, I would have accepted gladly the offer of the England captaincy when I was first asked if I would be interested in the summer of 1988 against the West Indies. Mike Gatting had already lost the job for disciplinary reasons, it then passed to John Emburey and when it was clear that the off-spinner couldn't be picked to play at Leeds where the conditions usually favour swing and seam bowling, Chris Cowdrey was asked to take over. I was already committed to Western Province for that winter and I felt that with the selectors looking towards the winter tour of India, they ought to establish a captain during the summer, so he could feel more sure of himself in the job later that year. I acted in good faith throughout, made myself unavailable for India because I felt I couldn't break my contract with Western Province. So Chris Cowdrey captained England at Leeds and when he was subsequently injured, they turned to me for the final Test at the Oval.

I was pleasantly surprised at how much I enjoyed the job, how helpful Micky Stewart proved in taking a lot of the off-field pressures away from me – and more importantly, at the response I got from the side. We competed on equal terms for the first four days and although we eventually lost easily, I had thoroughly relished the challenge and the experience. When Western Province kindly released me from my contract, the way was cleared for me to lead the side to India in the winter of 1988–89, but political issues led to the cancellation of that tour. I certainly wasn't playing England off against Western Province, I just felt that I owed it to WP to fulfil the contract I had already signed before the captaincy issue arose. If I had really been consumed with desire for the England captaincy I would have made that known during the summer of '88 and before Cowdrey's injury forced the selectors to turn to me. My main motivation in cricket has never been status, to see my name up in lights and to have people staring at me in the street. For me cricket is about batting well, thereby helping my side, and as captain, to help my players to do better. I enjoy it when we play well and I enjoy getting a positive reaction from them when we don't play well; the thankless times come when you feel you are making no progress.

Seven months after leading England to victory over Sri Lanka, I was deposed as England captain, without playing another Test. I wasn't surprised at the decision, because the new chairman of the England Committee, Ted Dexter, had his own ideas and that was his prerogative as the new man in charge. I feel I ought to have had an interview with the Committee, though, even if it was simply a formality, because I was nominally still the man in charge – England hadn't played a Test since the Sri Lanka one. I know Mike Gatting and David Gower were formally interviewed, whereas all I got was a phone call from Ted Dexter, underlining his wish that I would be playing in the forthcoming Tests. I think it all might have been handled better but that experience has helped me, as I now always try to locate a player if we have decided to leave him out of the England side. You have to care for your players.

Several months before he had deposed me, Ted Dexter had made it clear what he thought about my captaincy credentials. In his newspaper column, he wrote that I had all the charisma of a wet fish. Now, as the new chairman, he had to act as he saw fit. I can't deny that Dexter's description of me hurt. He was commenting on my statement that a captain is only as good as his team and that if they struggle, then so does he. Dexter wrote that I was talking rubbish, that a captain should dictate and make things happen. I think there's truth in both arguments but Dexter has never really discussed his 'wet fish' quote with me, which is certainly the tactful option. I can confirm we have enjoyed a good working relationship since I became captain! Yet there was bound to be a good deal of mischief-making in September 1989 when Dexter replaced David Gower with me. The press gleefully pulled out the 'wet fish' quote and enjoyed the fuss, while pointing out that I was the wrong man for the job. I can honestly say that I wasn't bothered by the criticism, because pleasing the press has never been my main motivation. Since my Test ban for going to South Africa in 1982, I had become wary and suspicious of the media and I certainly wasn't going to be swayed by their opinions. I was well aware that I wasn't the 'right sort' – whatever that means. England's selectors have often looked for the right background in appointing their captain, presumably in the hope that a public school education or a university degree helps you to inspire the players more and keep the media happy with a few cosy platitudes and dollops of charm. Of course that cut no ice with me; some blokes can do the job, others can't and it has nothing at all to do with your background. You can only pick from who's available, evaluate their captaincy skills and pick the man. Is he up to it? By September 1989, I thought I was good enough and had no intentions of captaining the side in ways that would please the media. Getting the players right was the urgent priority, not coming up with quotes that might haunt me. I also had one major consolation: at least I was worth my place in the side as a player, provided my form was good enough.

England have had too many captains since Mike Brearley in 1981. All the chopping and changing has sapped morale; there seems to have been no long-term strategy, no continuity of selection, so the players can't perform with complete confidence. As a result our Test record in the eighties was poor when you consider the talent we have had at our disposal. We needed to return to an atmosphere where the players weren't looking over their shoulders, wondering if they'd get another chance, or if the press were about to push another flavour-of-the-month. Since I took over as England captain, the management has been determined to lay down a sensible policy of selection and preparation, where forward planning wasn't derided by the fans of flair, and flair alone. We had decided we had to approach international cricket in a different way. In the end, the captain has to stand or fall on his own instincts and I knew that if I failed, they would wheel on someone else. What did I have to lose?

2
Forward planning

Professionalism seems to be a dirty word in some people's opinion. Many suggest that I trot it out simply to justify hours and hours spent in the nets, then working out like some fitness freak, and demanding a monastic attitude to socializing and getting to bed. Turning the players into robots, clones of each other, squeezing the individualism out of them. All untrue, short-sighted and very unfair. I like a drink as much as anyone, I have been known to laugh out loud in public and I have always been a great admirer of flair players like David Gower and Ian Botham. Yet I think I'm entitled to use my practical experience of playing for England since 1975 as a base from which I can try to give us a better chance of winning more Tests. Having observed the ways in which we prepared for Tests over a decade ago, I now believe we owe it to ourselves and our country to be in better shape – both physically and psychologically – than we used to be. The talent is there – so it should be, with the number of players we can choose from – but we have to ensure it flourishes in the right atmosphere. That means we must think more about our game, about the opposition, about our attitude to fitness and any technical problems, and about gelling as a unit. From my experience over twenty years with Essex, I feel that a happy side has a greater prospect of success on the field. If the long-term strategy is right and the players are fully integrated, you've got a good chance of competing with anybody. In some quarters that approach is described as 'a joyless regime': well, I can think of many a joyless day from my time with England when we were being soundly thrashed because it was felt that flair and big-match experience would suffice, that if you were good enough to play for England, you automatically knew how best to prepare yourself. I don't like losing if it's our fault, through a lack of heart or application. We are in a profession and we have to be more professional, because the stakes are now higher. The all-round competition is much stronger at inter-national level than when I first started, the financial rewards are so much greater, so what could be more logical than putting in more time and effort to achieve more? Any successful businessman would be astonished that I even have to put the question.

When I took over the England captaincy in 1989, I knew I had to do things my way or I had no chance of success. If my way didn't work, they would get someone else. The tour to the Caribbean lay four months away and none of the pundits gave us a chance. That suited me fine – we would work quietly away at our preparation while the media talked about the might of Viv Richards' team. Before the West Indies tour we were due to spend six weeks in India, playing in the Nehru Cup, a one-day international tournament. That competition was derided in many quarters as a waste of time, but not by me. I saw it as an ideal chance to mould team spirit, to see which of the guys coped best with the pressure of playing in front of those volatile crowds. A tour to India is a good place to foster team spirit, because there are fewer social distractions than in places like Australia or the West Indies. So we talked cricket together for long periods, discussed how we could revive our international standing and how to prepare for tours in the future. We played well and only lost in the semi-final to Pakistan through an innings of genius by Salim Malik; and the gains off the field were enormous. We talked at great length about how we would approach the West Indies tour. The general feeling was that the West Indies batsmen love fast bowling and they like to play it off their legs; balls on the off-stump are pinged away through the legside with just a roll of the wrists and when they are going well their batsmen can be unstoppable. So we decided to bowl just outside the off-stump, a nagging line at fast-medium pace. Ball after ball in an area of about a foot and we would then let them decide if they would be played through leg. We hoped that after a time, they'd get impatient, play a loose shot and get caught in the slips or drag one into their stumps. That's exactly what happened several times in Jamaica – when we won the First Test – and in Trinidad, where we nearly won. We needed the bowlers to be accurate enough for this plan and we had them in Angus Fraser and Gladstone Small, with David Capel a reliable back-up. Our wild card would be Devon Malcolm – not as accurate as the others, but a good foil because we expected the West Indies batsmen to take him on when he bowled bouncers and there was always the chance that they'd get themselves out. We got the breaks we needed in the first two Tests and I was delighted at the comment from one of their batsmen, Carlisle Best, in Jamaica. He said it was obvious that we had hit on a good plan and it was working. I took that as a compliment and a justification for all the hard thinking we had put in before we arrived in the Caribbean.

So hard tactical thinking and also hard physical work were needed. We simply had to be fitter for long, arduous tours than previously. I remembered the England trip to the West Indies early in 1981; you could've turned up for that tour without doing a stroke of work for three months and then be expected to compete with a great side in gruelling conditions. A player would say he had been to the nets in his local area three times a week and nobody could disprove that. I had been concerned about such situations for some time and when I was named as captain for the Indian tour of 1988–89 I was hoping to institute some system of preparation. I had talked it over with the England manager, Micky Stewart, and we agreed that the tour party should gather at the National Sports Centre in Lilleshall for some intensive physical and technical work. When I mentioned this to my great friend, John Emburey, he looked horrified – Embers' idea of keeping fit has always been to go to bed early! When the Indian tour was called off, the Lilleshall experiment was also left in abeyance. A year later, it returned with a vengeance to the top of my agenda. We all gathered there for a hard week's training just before leaving for the West Indies in January 1990. I was pleased with the results. The guys were certainly fit and the physical tests we had at Lilleshall also instilled a competitive spirit in the squad. The reaction of Eddie Hemmings particularly pleased me. Now Eddie is a good old pro, but he has a mind of his own and I wondered if this new-fangled insistence on physical training might jar with him. On the contrary; he said when he first started twenty-five years earlier in county cricket, the players would run round the boundary a few times in early April, then go to the nets for long sessions. He'd then just bowl himself fit to bowl long spells. He preferred the new way, believing that it would help to prolong his career. That's what I wanted to hear from a man whose experience and opinion I respected. Even Wayne Larkins, a man of the old school didn't complain! He got stuck into his training and made it quite clear that he could adapt to the new regime.

So I was satisfied that we would be the fittest England side to go on tour. That would hopefully mean we wouldn't be wilting when the pressure was on and the ball whistling round our ears or disappearing out of the ground. But would our batsmen be technically equipped to cope with the fast, short-pitched delivery, the stock ball of West Indian fast bowlers over the last fifteen years? Our younger batsmen had to know what was in store for them; it wasn't enough to acknowledge that they had faced most of them in county cricket, this would be far more taxing, as they would keep coming at us, hour after hour. So we enlisted the help of Geoffrey Boycott. That caused a stir in some quarters, especially as Geoffrey was then beginning to forge a career in the media, talking about the game in his usual forthright way. I wasn't unduly worried about that; we had a mutual respect from our days as England's opening partnership. He wouldn't let me down with ill-judged comments about our chances. Micky Stewart was a little concerned about unfavourable publicity but he had the original idea of approaching Boycott to tap into his expertise, so we decided to go with it. Those three days we spent in the indoor nets at Leeds were invaluable. We told the fast bowlers to pitch it short at the batsmen from a distance of eighteen yards, to test the speed of their reactions, and they all took blows to the body. They stood up to it manfully and I'm sure they gained much from the advice of Boycott, one of the most courageous and skilful players of fast bowling I have ever seen at close quarters.

It helps if the England captain and the cricket manager see eye to eye in matters like forward planning. I have been very lucky to have had Micky Stewart by my side during my time in charge. He is not the favourite of the media, partly because he acts as a buffer between them and the players to take some of the pressure off them and also, since he doesn't always agree with what is written or said, he won't fit in with cosy theories dreamed up in the press box. Our relationship works because we don't get in each other's way – I'm responsible for our style of play and he takes much of the strain off me by carrying out those policies. He takes on a lot of the chores that can drag a captain away from his main tasks and he never stops encouraging the players. Sometimes he rubs a player up the wrong way with his sergeant-major style but that is just his way; he genuinely wants each player to do well for his country. Micky has worked tirelessly for the good of England's cricket and he has certainly made my job as captain easier. We both feel that England has under-achieved at Test level and Micky has some gruesome statistics that suggest we haven't been particularly impressive since the end of the First World War! Useful facts to have at your disposal when the media react to our latest Test defeat by saying that it's the worst England side of all time.

Micky and I both strongly believe that you must feel that you are going forward, that your strategy is clear, that you have created an atmosphere conducive to getting the best out of your players. We had been equally impressed by the attention to detail and professionalism shown by the Australians in 1989, when they beat us 4–0. No one can ever convince me that our players were all that inferior in terms of quality and practical experience of Test cricket; we just weren't cohesive enough, we drifted on the field, we didn't get stuck into them, or show enough resilience. Nor did we prepare for each Test in the same hard way as the Aussies, though they were lucky to have two days clear before each Test, while we were still tangled up with our respective counties. Something had to change and I was privileged to be able to do something positive about the situation when I was appointed captain for the Nehru Cup and the West Indies tours. The first practical task was to pick two touring parties on the day I was appointed. That didn't exactly leave me too much time for researching all the player options and I rang Keith Fletcher during our selection meeting to sound him out. Ted Dexter, Micky Stewart and I eventually took the decisions on selection and, right from the start, we made two controversial choices. There would be no Ian Botham or David Gower.

I've heard it suggested that I was presented with a *fait accompli* over David and Ian as soon as I walked into the room, the 'new boy', with little time for preparation. Some have also hinted that I was responsible for their omission. The truth is a mixture of both. Ted and Micky had clearly decided that new blood was needed for the tour and that both these great players might find it difficult to fit into the new style that I was going to introduce. I didn't disagree with that point: I had no intention of wasting too much time trying to persuade Ian and David to throw themselves into the fitness training I would demand from everyone. They were set in their ways and I wanted a fresh, dynamic attitude from all my players on that tour. Keith Fletcher, although a fan of both players, agreed with me. In cricketing terms, Botham didn't deserve to be selected after a mundane season by his previous standards. He also had a poor record against the West Indies, much to his annoyance, but he had given little indication in 1989 that he could recapture the success of his great days. David was different. Despite enormous pressure on him during that Ashes summer, he had batted well. He was still a tremendous batsman at the highest level and a very fine player of fast bowling. Other matters came into consideration, though. I felt that David wouldn't throw himself into the preparation that was needed, he would go his own way, leading to the danger of splinter groups. Obviously everyone in the touring party had to be seen to be pulling in the same direction, helping each other through the bad times, working hard in training and in the nets. That has never been David's style and even though he has always been deservedly popular (with me as well, incidentally), I thought we were better off without him. The door was not closed on him – as it transpired a year later – but for this particular tour, and bearing in mind what I wanted, he wasn't picked. I talked to him the following morning to explain the decision and it wasn't a pleasant conversation. He clearly expected to be picked and I'm sure to this day, the decision still rankles, but sometimes a captain has to make harsh decisions if he believes in what he's doing. Every top England player of my time has been dropped at some stage: there is no automatic passport into the final eleven. I knew the media would have a field day over David's omission, but looking back on it, and remembering what we achieved in the West Indies, I think we were right. After failing to get through to David on the Australian tour a year later, I was even more convinced we were right. As for Ian Botham, I rang him up and told him that his form hadn't been good enough. I said that a captain must have the squad he wants on tour and he understood that, as a former England skipper should. He blustered a little but vowed he would fight his way back into the side. Two years later, he did and I was pleased to have him back. But in 1989, there was a big job to be done and I wanted it done my way, without any distractions.

There was never any doubt in my mind when I saw them as young players that Gower and Botham had that extra quality which suggested they could make it as Test cricketers – but how do the selectors assess that potential? Whenever I play away from Essex, supporters, committee men and players drop hints that so-and-so has the right stuff in him. The selectors get a lot of criticism and I would be the last to suggest their methods are foolproof. Certainly under my captaincy, we have made mistakes but we have tried to get some consistency into the selection process. There is no infallible method in assessing someone's international potential, but you have to talk to good judges, observe how the player conducts himself on and off the field and try to assess his character. Does he love the game? How hungry is he to get to the top? Does he think you can simply coast through a career? How does he take his team's defeat? How does he react to being out of form? Does he actually watch the game from the dressing-room when his team is batting or does he prefer cards, or the sports page or finding out what's for lunch?

You cannot be sure about someone's Test aptitude until he gets there and is tried out. Graeme Hick knows this from the bitter experience of 1991 against the West Indies. He of all people looked good enough to bridge the gap between county and Test cricket – his batting record had been massively impressive, his dedication to all aspects of his profession was unquestionable, and he deserved to be picked as soon as he became available. Yet he failed. Graeme lacked the all-round game to cope with the West Indian style of bowling and he lacked the experience to cope with Test cricket's unique pressures. I feel that Graeme has the ability and the attitude to step up that final grade but he knows he has to adjust, get mentally tougher. There is no substitute for practical experience and that is why the England selectors sometimes get accused of playing safe. The problem in England is that there are many players of a similar standard and a vast pool of them to choose from. That sometimes clouds the issues and in that sense the selectors in Australia and the West Indies have an easier task, because they don't have a lot of players to look at. So they tend to trust in class and experience – not a bad stance to adopt.

If it's a one-day squad, we will assess the opposition, discussing if they're likely to play any spinners, or pack the side with seamers, or if they have many dangerous, attacking batsmen, the kind that can put the match beyond your reach very swiftly. During the one-day series, we'll consider how the opposition played our bowlers last time, where the next game is to be played and if the ground has any special characteristics, and decide whether to play the second spinner instead of the fourth seamer. When it comes to a Test squad, the opposition is a minor issue at that stage although the horses-for-courses thought is never ruled out. If a player invariably does well against a certain country, that becomes relevant (for example, Peter Willey against the West Indies), but usually you go for your best team and assess each player on his merits. There are three of us – the captain, cricket manager and chairman of the England Committee – and that does help to simplify matters. I like to write down the players who are definite in my mind, then fill in the gaps in the squad of twelve or thirteen. We will all have our own ideas about various candidates and Micky Stewart and I will already have talked them through over the phone before the meeting. The discussion isn't formal: we sift through what we have seen for ourselves recently, what our regional scouts have to offer, and also the input from respected senior players. I have made a point of asking the likes of Mike Gatting, John Emburey, Phil Carrick and Peter Willey for their current thoughts. These are guys I've played with over the years whose advice I value and who I know will give me straight talking, without pushing anyone from their own counties. I also talk to one or two umpires, the fellows who are in the best position of all to judge whether a player has the right qualities. I have to be careful how many I ask, though, because you can get a wide range of opinions. In 1990, I asked about the Yorkshire wicket-keeper/batsman, Richard Blakey. One umpire said he was a very good bet, another said he was a goodish keeper and the third said he couldn't keep pigeons! So it's important to remember that your source might have seen the player have a good or a bad day at the appropriate time, so you use the input as a sighter, not as gospel. If the same names keep cropping up from all sources, then your job of selection is that much easier.

Is there bias against certain counties? I'm sure the followers of say, Glamorgan, Gloucestershire, Somerset and Derbyshire would swear it exists. Peter Parfitt, the former Middlesex and England batsman tells a very good after-dinner joke that revolves around a list of Middlesex players' names and after mentioning each player, he pauses and adds 'and England'. Certainly if you look at the England players that have come through from Middlesex over the last two decades, you would conclude that playing at Lord's in front of influential people has been a distinct advantage. They have also been a winning side for a long time as well, which suggests good players, but the detractors do have a point. It must also help if you play for the same county as the England captain and Middlesex have provided three of them since 1977. When we plumped for Nasser Hussain as the young batter to go on the 1990 West Indies tour, it was suggested that he was lucky because he played for Essex alongside me. Well, that final place was between Mike Atherton, John Stephenson and Nasser, all fine young players. Mike and John had both been blooded in the Test series against the Australians while Nasser had been twelfth man at the Oval. It was close, but I was keen on Nasser, having seen him score a magnificent hundred against Kent on a dodgy pitch at Southend. The following game at Southend, he steered us to victory against Yorkshire, when it looked as if we could lose on another tricky pitch, the one that led to us being docked twenty-five points, the ruling that cost us the Champion-ship. So I knew that Nasser had great fighting qualities and I was obviously influenced by that when we picked the tour party. At that stage, I hadn't seen enough of Mike Atherton and that's a problem when you're thinking about players from your own county. You have to guard against unconscious bias that might simply stem from the fact that you've seen more of your county colleague. It clearly helps if I've seen players from other counties do well under pressure against Essex. That's not a case of bias, simply an awareness of being impressed at close quarters and filing the name away. When we didn't pick Mike Atherton, it wasn't because we wanted to shield him from the West Indies fast bowlers, to avoid sacrificing his England prospects early on – none of the three candidates had done anything special over a consistent period, so we went on the captain's hunch over Nasser Hussain. And Nasser was far from disgraced in the Caribbean, showing the fighting qualities I expected from him, including playing in two Tests with a broken wrist.

It's hard for the captain to keep fighting against an unconscious prejudice for or against certain players during a selection meeting. Yet I think it's right that the captain has the decisive say because he has to go out on the field with that group of players or tour with them on the other side of the world. He has to take responsibility if the team does badly, so he should get who he wants. It was me who stuck out for Wayne Larkins for the Australian tour. I've always rated Wayne highly as one of the most talented English batsmen of the last decade but with an average career record. I wanted him for the West Indies and he did quite well, showing he could bat for long periods under pressure from top-class bowling. After an injury-hit season in 1990, he seemed right out of contention to most good judges, until he hit 207 for Northants against Essex in September, with yours truly standing at slip for long periods. When the Australian tour party was picked a week later, a great deal was made of that Larkins innings, suggesting that it got him the trip. It didn't. He was dropped several times and it wasn't relevant because I knew how he could play. I believed in him and asked for him. Wayne didn't come up with the goods in Australia and that was a pity. With more application and dedication, he could have been an outstanding player. He got a poor report after his first England tour, to Australia in 1979–80, and I'm sure that counted against him in later years. He was disillusioned when his opening partner Geoff Cook got the batting place ahead of him for the 1981–82 Indian tour on the strength of a hundred in the NatWest Final, and that led to his trip to South Africa under my captaincy and his subsequent ban from Test cricket. Perhaps he lost his best years to that ban, I don't know, but in the end it was sad for him, not to come up to the highest standards.

I was happy about pushing for Phil Tufnell for that Australian tour, despite our disagreements about his attitude and application. In 1990, Tufnell was the best slow left-arm spinner I had faced that year, but just to confirm my assessment I rang up several of my contacts and asked them to compare him with Richard Illingworth, the other candidate. They all said Illingworth was a very good, tough cricketer, but that he doesn't bowl many sides out when the ball is turning – he gets three or four wickets at around 2.5 runs per over, not six or seven at the same rate. We knew the ball would turn in the Sydney Test and that would be a big opportunity for us to win, so we went for Tufnell, the more likely matchwinner. On the basis of backing class, we were vindicated, whatever my reservations at the time about other aspects of his cricket.

The selectors were criticized for not taking Hugh Morris to Australia as first choice instead of Larkins, because he had scored 2,000 runs and was obviously in prime form. So were many other batsmen in the summer of 1990, that season of suicidal bowlers and dead pitches. When I had seen Morris in previous seasons, he hadn't looked all that special. I was well aware that a batsman can suddenly sort out his game and crack on from there but I admit I was wary of Hugh's credentials. Many umpires I talked to considered his opening partner, Alan Butcher, to be a better player, even in his late thirties. Alan had finally worked out the way he wanted to play and he had become very consistent. I needed to be convinced that Hugh had finally discovered the way to score runs consistently. A year later, Hugh was given his chance to show what he could do in two Tests against the West Indies and while I was very impressed by his guts and competitiveness, I'm still waiting to see if he can make it.

Although I believe in a long-term strategy for the England team, there are times when you have to pick a team with a specific game in mind. It happened in Australia in 1990 when we had to drop Jack Russell, the world's best wicket-keeper, to allow us to play Alec Stewart, thereby leaving us clear to play five bowlers. We needed five bowlers for the Adelaide Test for two reasons – we were two down in the series with just two to play and Angus Fraser was only about eighty per cent fit. If Angus broke down early on, we would be struggling to bowl Australia out, so we needed cover. That's why Jack had to go. Even though Jack was a far superior gloveman, Alec Stewart's batting meant our tail wouldn't be too exposed. Although Alec did well behind the stumps, our experiment couldn't be said to have succeeded – but it worked at the Oval later in the year. We were 2–1 down against the West Indies and we needed to win the final Test to square the series. So we took the gamble of again dropping Jack Russell and bringing in Alec Stewart to stiffen the batting. The press had a field day, pointing out that Stewart had only kept in limited-overs games in 1991 and that Russell was one of our few world-class players. True – but I had this feeling that Alec Stewart could cope with the pressure and wouldn't let us down. Snide comments about his father having a decisive say were too pathetic to bother about and I was more interested in the fact that Alec has a combative attitude. His tough competitiveness would mean he would do his best to make up for the absence of the Russell polish behind the stumps. On top of that, Alec's determination with the bat meant he could fill in easily enough at number six, giving us the chance to bring in an all-rounder to bat at seven. That all-rounder was Ian Botham.

Genuine all-rounders are worth their weight in gold and Ian's presence gave us a nicely balanced bowling line-up, with attacking bowlers. I didn't think Ian could be judged as a banker at number six in a Test anymore, but one place down was ideal for him. He had been close to selection for the previous Test at Edgbaston, but we settled on a different line-up. It wasn't a case of judging whether he was ready or not, because he had been in pretty good form – it was simply that we had to attack at the Oval and Botham was ideal for the side's balance.

We continued the attacking philosophy by bringing back Phil Tufnell, although I didn't consider that such a great risk. He had been taking a stack of wickets for Middlesex, the extra bounce at the Oval would obviously suit him and he was again proving he was the best of his type in the country. He had been omitted after Australia because of his general attitude to his cricket. In the field his concentration wasn't good enough. In my opinion he was spending too much time thinking about his own bowling, thus letting himself and his team-mates down. By August Mike Gatting and John Emburey reported back to me that there had been a marked change in his attitude and he was back in the England team. He then became a hero, bowling out the West Indies cheaply in the first innings and helping us enforce the follow-on. We won a memorable Test, English cricket won back some pride – and the selectors could for once feel satisfied with themselves. I don't recall too many bowls of humble pie being eaten by the media, though!

I can understand why the selectors get so much criticism, it's a national pastime, isn't it? All summer, the press had been on at us to pick David Gower against the West Indies, conveniently ignoring the fact that at no stage did he score a first-class hundred. We had made mistakes, of course. At Edgbaston we had expected the ball to turn for Richard Illingworth, but it went straight through for him. The wicket played up and down for the seamers and if we had picked a fourth

Perhaps I should bowl myself more, but it doesn't always end up as happily as this!

David Gower knows the feeling – would that fielder please stand exactly where the batsman is going to hit the ball?

Playing the sweep shot that proved so successful in the World Cup semi-final in 1987 against India. That hundred was one of the most satisfying innings of my career because I had thought out the specific way I wanted to play

Merv Hughes and the rest of the 1989 Australian tourists really impressed me with their dedication to preparing for the Tests in England. They enjoyed the hard work and at all times looked the part. Their example certainly influenced my thinking when I became England captain

Allan Border has set a great example as captain to the Australian side in recent years

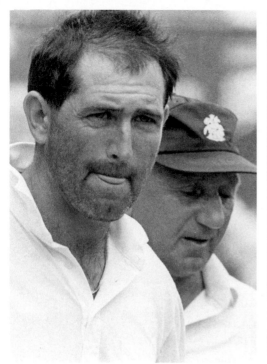

With Micky Stewart, my invaluable guide as England's cricket manager since I became captain

How did England captains cope before the mobile phone? But will he be fit for the Test?

Sometimes the press have to search for my dry sense of humour, but it does exist!

With Mike Gatting, one of the best captains I have known – popular with the players but tough when necessary, a positive leader and a very fine batsman who leads by example

'That's more like it, Tuffers!' More than most bowlers, Phil Tufnell needs encouragement to keep his confidence on a high

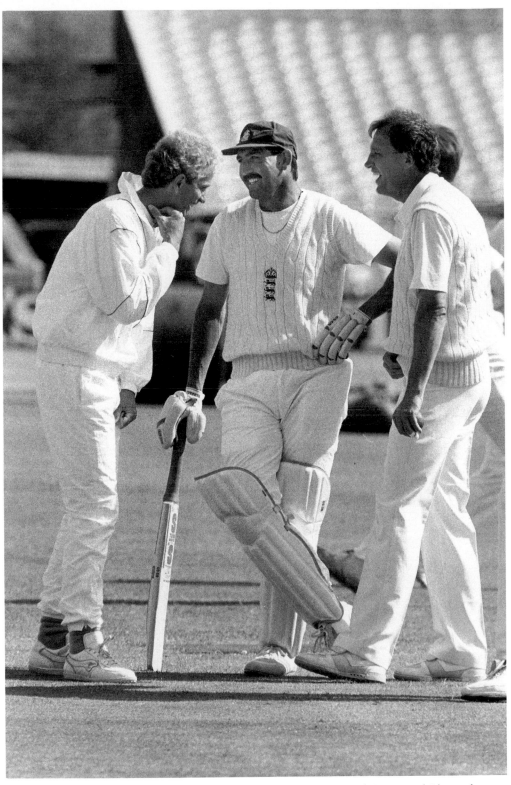

Despite our occasional differences of opinion on cricket matters, David Gower and I have always enjoyed each other's company

On my way to a hundred in the Benson and Hedges Final against Surrey in 1979 – a momentous day for Essex. We won our first trophy and that gave us the confidence to start winning consistently. Winning the big games became a pleasant habit

On Essex duty with Geoff Miller (centre) and Keith Fletcher, the man who has taught me more about the game than anyone else

Attending to press duties on tour – this time at Antigua at the end of the 1990 Test series

David Gower and I both know from harsh experience that there are some days when everything the captain tries rebounds in his face

Reflecting on the day ahead, after practice with Micky Stewart

Keith Fletcher and John Lever – two major reasons why Essex have been a force for the past decade. Fletcher, the master tactician and fine batsman, Lever the best bowler in championship cricket during my career

Mike Brearley setting the field during the final stages of the 1981 Headingley Test. With so few runs to play with, Brearley's calm assurance, positive attitude and attention to detail were a godsend to us

Ian Botham and Mike Brearley were good for each other. Brearley was lucky enough to have a matchwinner at his disposal but he had the qualities of man management to get the best out of his brilliant, young all-rounder

accurate seamer, the pressure exerted throughout from both ends might have brought us victory. Some felt that Graeme Hick ought to have been dropped after a third successive Test failure and that Mike Atherton was lucky to survive all series. It's all a matter of opinion, and there's no chance that the selectors will always get it right. The press love to say 'I told you so', but they conveniently forget about their touting of a certain player who then fails for England; by then they have picked up on a new favourite. Selecting eleven players for Test cricket is a good deal more complex than a gentle scan through the latest first-class averages.

I am very keen on giving players a fair crack of the whip once they've been selected for England. I think three Tests is the least they deserve. Look how the West Indies kept faith in Carl Hooper and Gus Logie till they blossomed and the Australians did the same with Steve Waugh. I think loyalty cements team spirit and the fact that we only used eighteen players against the West Indies in 1991 was a factor in our improved performances. I like a more stable basis on which to select players than simply good figures in county cricket. The temperament of the player is very relevant. We gave Neil Fairbrother a decent run in 1990, not just because he was scoring a stack of runs for Lancashire, but because we hadn't seen him in Test cricket for a while and it would be interesting to see whether he had toughened up in his approach. I felt he was worth his place and I told him he'd be in for at least two, possibly three, Tests against the New Zealanders. I wanted him to feel confident, to understand I was backing him. Yet Neil was unsure of the way he should bat and he asked my advice. I had a problem about that because I hadn't seen a great deal of the way he was scoring his runs in county cricket, yet I felt he should play the way that had brought him success with Lancashire. I can't do it for the player, he has to work it out for himself and I'm afraid Neil fell between two stools for England. After he had been dropped, he made a scorching hundred against us at Colchester, having a dart at everything. The Lancashire lads told me he'd been playing like that all summer, which explains why he had asked me how he should play for England. He knew that if he played his natural attacking way in the Tests and screwed it up, he would have been exposed to all sorts of criticism. So he opted for a typical tight Test Match approach and didn't do himself justice. At least he was given the chance, though.

One way to try to ensure England players *do* get the chance to give of their best has at last been adopted. For some years now, I have envied the opportunity the visiting country gets to be settled in the Test

Match environment two days before the game actually starts. In contrast, we would turn up on the Wednesday afternoon, after finishing a county game the day before. We would be tired after driving a few hours in holiday traffic, dodging the motorway cones, in no state for a meaningful bout of practice. So we would don a tracksuit, lope around the boundary edge, hit a few balls in the nets, turn the bowling arm over, then retire to the dressing-room, in some cases to get treatment on wearied limbs. I felt it was just a cosmetic exercise, done partly to keep the watching media ranks happy. In contrast, the opposition would have trained and netted for two days in a row and would be better prepared than us for the Test Match. When we played abroad, our preparations were better for the same reason, so in 1991, Micky Stewart and I at last managed to get our players with us a day earlier for meaningful practice. Some of the counties were unhappy that some of the Championship fixtures had to finish on the Monday to accommodate the England camp's desire to have two full days with the players and I can understand their objections. That summer I used to get confused about which day the Championship matches were due to start, but the gains to me as England captain were great. Initially some of the media tried to suggest it was another of Gooch's obsessional schemes to get his players netting and running around all day, but even they eventually realized the value of it. The main idea was to get two days' break from playing, to recharge the batteries and get the mind in gear for the Test. Two days before, it would be a case of a gentle run around the ground, some catching practice, a net for those who wanted one and that was it. That night we would have an informal dinner together, all very relaxed, a few drinks and cricket discussed if anyone wanted to – otherwise general banter and gossip. We want the lads to get to know each other, because we're part of each other's lives for the next week and I want the chemistry to be right between us. When I turned up at Edgbaston on the Wednesday for my Test debut in 1975, I only knew Keith Fletcher and felt rather on the outside. After the team meeting, I didn't have a drink with anyone and just drifted off to bed. Now I want a family atmosphere, where newcomers are made welcome. If you are relaxed at the right times, then you play better.

After a relaxing Tuesday, we work hard at the ground the next day – both in the nets and in fielding practice. That night we have our team talk, then dinner. The team talk is conducted professionally and taken seriously, in contrast to some of those from my early days with England, when sometimes there was too much frivolous complacency.

I tend to start off outlining why we're here, crystallizing the attitude I expect from them, reminding them that if the opposition are 200 for 1 the following afternoon, we still have to keep battling away, still believing that we can pull things round. I try to focus their minds on the task ahead and then Micky Stewart goes through the opposition. He has notes on every player we are ever likely to face; he has compiled the dossier ever since he took the job in 1986 and before a team meeting, he will go through the dossier and affirm what he wants us to know. Having played a long time now, I tend to remember how certain cricketers play, but I'm happy for Micky to mark the cards of our less experienced players. I believe a captain should know how the opposition play, because if you don't then you're not very good at your job. I prefer concentrating on the strengths of my own players and building up their confidence rather than harp on about the opposition, but there's no doubt that the Stewart dossier has been valuable at times.

Our attention to detail had a lot to do with our encouraging display in 1991 against the West Indies. Against their accurate fast bowlers, we knew that we'd get little in our half of the wicket, inviting the drive off the front foot! So we didn't expect many 'four balls' as we call them – even more important then to steal as many singles as possible and to turn ones into twos with intelligent, positive running. I had never been very good in that department and I said that we all had to run between the wickets as if we were playing a one-day match. Watching the Australians stealing so many runs off us had spurred me on to look at a part of my game that I had neglected, and it worked against the West Indies. I also impressed on my players that a Test against the West Indies is not a very long game, because they take such a time to bowl their overs and they can bowl fast and accurate for long spells. That's why they are so difficult to beat. So the batters had to steel themselves for a lot of chest-high deliveries, wait for the odd bad ball and put it away without risk. It's not enough just to be an occupier of the crease against them because you can play excellently for two hours and end up with fifteen. That's why Allan Lamb has been so valuable against them because he goes for his shots; his hundred in Jamaica was a vital part of our victory because he scored his runs at a good speed. I was sorry Allan couldn't find his form in the 1991 series, because his usual quota of runs might have made a big difference.

Our batting wasn't wholly convincing in that West Indies series, I agree, but I was pleased with our bowling. The previous series in 1990 had confirmed to me that they were a little vulnerable if you tried to bore them out and so it proved. We told Derek Pringle we wanted a solid, reliable job from him and he did us proud with his nagging accuracy and that extra bounce. The quicker bowlers, as expected, didn't cause them a great deal of trouble, but Pringle was just the right pace and length to keep them guessing – and he swung the ball just enough. At the Oval, when I told Viv Richards that Derek was unfit, he paid him a high compliment. He said that when he first played against Derek, he had no worries about him 'but now he's a class bowler, he's never quite there for the drive.' That's just the way we wanted him to bowl at Viv and the rest. Phillip DeFreitas was even more impressive. His line around the off-stump was impeccable, his pace lively, he moved the ball around and his stamina was exceptional. Pringle and DeFreitas demonstrated what you can achieve if you *think* deeply about what you must do in a Test Match.

All the forward planning is geared to ensuring everyone is in the right mental groove for eleven o'clock on the first morning of the Test. For me there is nothing to match that first morning, especially in England. I'm a light sleeper so on that first morning, I'm usually awake by seven o'clock, anticipating the build-up. My mind will be racing through the various scenarios and when I get to the ground there'll be that special feeling of expectancy. The buzz on that first day is unlike any other day because the slate's clean and there are questions to be answered. Who's won the toss? Who's been left out? What's the wicket look like? What's the weather forecast? On other mornings, there's the previous day's play to discuss but at the start of the Test, the 'don't know' factor touches us all. As captain I will have a lot of tasks on that first morning. There might be a dilemma to resolve on fitness and gambles to be weighed up. At Melbourne in 1990, we wanted David Gower to play, but we were worried about his injured wrist. David had been in these sort of situations before as captain and he conscientiously told us he was about eighty-five per cent fit, that he would struggle in the field but should be alright with the bat. We decided to take the chance on him and he scored a beautiful hundred. In the end you have to go on the player's word and trust in his character. For all my strictures about David Gower, I have never doubted his courage or awareness if he could do the job, and the same applies to Angus Fraser. When Angus told us he had no chance of playing at Sydney or at Perth, that was enough for us because he is such a great-hearted cricketer, but when we took a gamble on his fitness for the Adelaide Test, he knew he couldn't let us down and he kept going heroically. I was desperate to have Robin Smith playing in the

Edgbaston Test against the West Indies despite his broken finger and we left the decision open until the very last minute. It hadn't looked good for his chances for a week up to the Test but I eventually told him that even if he was only eighty per cent fit, I'd go with him as long as he felt he could bat satisfactorily. He had to be happy in his own mind and in the end, he ruled himself out. He was right to do so; the player is the one who makes the final decision, no matter how keen his captain is to see him play.

Fielding practice is an important part of the pre-Test preparations, as it is on every morning if the team's being run on professional lines. Meaningful and enjoyable fielding practice is the aim and we want the opposition to think we mean business, just as I thought when I watched the 1989 Australians prepare each day. We start with a warm-up for about ten minutes, then the slip catchers will have another ten minutes, swapping the bat around so that everyone has a go. Then we'll have long catching practice – a fielder is nominated to run, dive and catch the skyer, then whip it into the keeper by the stumps. If it goes wrong, we do a bit extra. I like the keeper to have a baseball glove so that we can really ping in the returns and it seems to improve the accuracy of the returns as well. Fielding is one of the skills of the game and we practise daily because I want us to improve those skills, not for cosmetic reasons. If you don't move for a catch hit in the air during practice, what chance do you have in a match situation? It's far better to put the fielder under pressure in practice, making him sprint thirty yards for the catch or running full pelt twenty yards to your left to get to the ball and hurl it back accurately. If you do five of those in a row it sharpens you up, and puts you under pressure – just as in a match. Leisurely fielding practice only gives you a sighter, and is no preparation for the real thing.

Our increased perception of the importance of quality fielding practice has paid off at crucial times. When Devon Malcolm ran out Gordon Greenidge on the first morning of the Jamaica Test, that vital breakthrough stemmed from hard work by Devon at practice, leading to that bullet throw under pressure. Devon is not a naturally agile fielder but he has a powerful throw and he had improved his accuracy greatly by the time we got to Jamaica. Who knows what would have happened in that historic Test if Greenidge and Haynes had been able to put together one of their large partnerships? The next time we beat the West Indies – at Leeds in 1991 – our fielding played an important part. I was pleased to hold on to three good catches, but we were inspired by some brilliant work by Mark Ramprakash on the second day, when he caught Phil Simmons and ran out Carl Hooper, just as they were beginning to get near our small first innings total. Those two marvellous moments were the complete justification of our insistence on proper, meaningful fielding practice.

By the time we have finished running, diving and catching around the outfield, I will be getting near to tossing the coin with my opposite number. Before that, we have to declare our eleven and it is sometimes as late as 10.15 before a decision is made on that. Usually the die has been cast the night before and the players informed, but if the weather is unsettled or the pitch difficult to read (will it turn?), then the options are kept open. Invariably it comes down to a spinner or an extra seamer, but it would be a boring game if we always got the final selection right. I fully supported David Gower's decision to put the Australians in at Leeds in 1989, because the conditions were ideal for swing bowling in an area that traditionally encourages that type of bowler. It wasn't David's fault that we bowled so badly that they ran up over 600, but he took the flak for putting them in. In my first Test Mike Denness consulted the weather oracles, decided to ask Australia to bat, and then after just one over of our first innings, it rained. In those days, the pitch wasn't covered during a day's play, so we were caught on a wet wicket against Lillee, Thomson and Walker and we were rolled over. I got a 'pair' and Mike Denness got the sack.

So after I have broken the news to the twelfth man, it's time to toss the coin, negotiate a quick television interview out in the middle, then pick my way back to the dressing-room, politely declining autographs because I really do need those twenty minutes with my players. If we're batting, I shall have a cup of tea, thinking about my game. I won't mind if there's a lot of noise in the dressing-room: I find it helps to ease the tension and builds up intimacy between the players. You should be mates, supportive of each other, in this together. If we are due to field, I like to go round each of my players just before we go out. I'll shake hands with each one, wish them luck and tell them to get stuck in. I look each player straight in the eye, letting them know instinctively what I expect from them. It's a personal gesture from me, a form of bonding, an awareness that it now only involves the eleven of us. I want them to realize we're doing it for our country, that we are the honoured ones, this is special, a Test Match, the ultimate for any cricketer. I don't want to see anybody slumped in the corner at this time, they should be on a high; I want a buzz of camaraderie. All the hard work, the planning, the talking – it's been channelled into this moment. It's time to go over the top.

At county level, the captain doesn't have to work that hard to develop the right blend, because he ought to know most of his players very well. He has probably grown up with many of them through the second eleven and hopefully they will know what is expected of them once they are established in the first team. I have always thought the second eleven captain has a very important role to play in developing young players. Keith Fletcher does a tremendous job for Essex in that capacity; his task is to nurture the players, telling them what they ought to be doing and why. He tells the youngsters how to play on certain pitches, he helps set their fields for them, and he talks cricket in the bar with his usual sound commonsense. It's so useful actually to have Keith out there in the middle with them, because a word in the ear at the right time can be priceless. It's a vital part of county cricket to bring players through the ranks and Keith lets them know what's expected of them and what they can achieve. At Essex, we tend to think that if someone in his mid-twenties hasn't broken through, we'll let him go. If your aim is to win the second eleven title, then you'll hang on to such players, those who've played a few times for the first eleven – but we feel the priority is to train them for the first team, and be indoctrinated in the Essex way of things. If you're taught those principles right from the beginning, then you don't know any other way. Essex players take great pride in our county and I like to think that's because young players get their chance. They're eased into the first team in stages, they bat down the order and are given time to get used to the new atmosphere. It's hard on the capped player in his early thirties who has to give way to the nineteen-year-old with potential but no real track record, but how will we know what the youngster's like unless we try him out? That is where the future lies, not in the experienced capped player whose career has stood still. When we replaced Brian Hardie with Nadeem Shahid halfway through the 1990 season, it wasn't because Hardie was playing badly. He had made a lot of runs early on, but we thought young Shahid had great potential and we wanted to see how he fared in the higher standard. Brian's career was winding down – he wasn't going to get any better – and the youngster couldn't get in the side any other way. So he took Brian's place and justified our faith by scoring over 1,000 runs that year. The experienced guy wouldn't let us down but we took a long-term view for the good of the side's future. For years, in soccer, that has been the Liverpool way – easing new players into a team that's playing well and can absorb the tinkering around. I don't think it's done Essex any great harm either.

Generally I don't think enough thought goes into forward planning in the English game. I'm no revolutionary, but at least I've tried, with the help of Micky Stewart and Ted Dexter, to improve our chances at Test level. That extra day's preparation has been so important in allowing the England players a chance to rest and get themselves ready to play for their country. At last we seem to be enjoying the benefit of the experience of some fine coaches and former players like Geoff Arnold, Alan Knott, Norman Gifford, John Snow, and Keith Fletcher. I have made no bones about asking Geoffrey Boycott for advice, because I consider him a deep thinker on cricket. Some take exception to his blunt way of talking but that never bothered me when we played together. I think he has things to offer and our ideas tend to run along similar lines. He was very supportive of me when I went to see him for a day after the Australian tour of 1990–91. I was depressed at my lack of success in motivating some of the England players and I had decided that from now on, only those with a deep commitment to the cause would get my support. We bounced a few ideas off each other in his home, discussing what went wrong in Australia, and although I didn't agree with everything he said, he did help me formulate my thoughts on our next stage of development. Boycott is very knowledgeable about how Test cricket should be played, if you just take the trouble to ignore some of the bluntness and listen to what he really has to say. That day up in Yorkshire, Boycott confirmed to me that my vision of how English cricket should progress was the best one for my style of captaincy – and it was also the way he would have tackled the job if he had been captain. The modern game demands greater attention to detail than we have given it.

3
Batting and captaincy

There is no doubt in my mind that I am now a better captain than when I first took the job for England back in 1988. Although I had enjoyed first-hand experience of playing under two excellent captains in Mike Brearley and Keith Fletcher, I still had to learn the ropes about setting fields and tactics – the 'hands on' element if you like. I have become more confident in my captaincy and the main reason for that is my consistency with the bat. With me, the two are complementary. Batting well is a major motivation for me – it's what I do best in cricket and I feel a responsibility to my team in that area. When I fall down consistently in that department I feel I am letting the team down. My decision-making abilities as captain are then affected and I don't do the job as well as I can.

I'm gratified that my Test batting average has doubled since I regained the England captaincy in 1989. For some time I had been disappointed with an average in the low thirties; I had missed out on too many hundreds, getting out in the seventies through a lack of concentration or poor shot selection. The extra responsibility of captaincy undoubtedly helped me get my game in order, so that since 1990 I've been playing more consistently than at any stage in my career. I'm sure that I am less exciting to watch, less flamboyant and unlikely to reel off many hundreds before lunch, but I've been churning out the big scores. To me a 'big' hundred is 150 plus and scores like that (provided they don't take too long) can't fail to help your team. I know I'm not particularly pretty to watch – I'm more of a bludgeoner than a deflector – but I have learned to stroke the ball in recent years, rather than smash it. I was pleased with the way I batted against the Indians in 1990, not simply because I scored so many runs but because their style of bowling (medium pace, teasing you with a bit of late swing) has exposed my footwork – or lack of it – in the past. In that series, I decided to bide my time, avoid committing myself too early, and caress the ball rather more. The runs never stopped flowing that summer for me and even though the conditions favoured batting, I was happy to cash in.

A year earlier I had been sorely troubled by Terry Alderman's late swing in the Ashes series – so much so that I asked to be left out of the Trent Bridge Test because I wasn't worth my place in the side. I knew some fine tuning was necessary to stop me falling over to the offside and getting unbalanced at the crease but it's difficult to put those things right in a crowded English season. Geoffrey Boycott put me right during our three-day session at Leeds before we went to the West Indies. He reminded me that when we batted together for England I had a simple method of going back or forward, without moving across the crease. I'd fallen into the trap of getting too far across the offside to play the ball through legside. My head was too far over to leg compared to previous years when my body and head had been lined up in a straight line in relation to the stumps. Boycott reminded me that my body movement ought to be negligible and that advice paid off. It was only a minor alteration but significant. I still play the ball through legside a fair amount, but I fall over to the offside much less now. My footwork is more decisive, I'm not so prone to shuffling around my crease, prone to lbw appeals.

Every batsman experiences technical problems at some stage in his career and you just have to get through them, hoping that there's someone of the calibre of Boycott around to spot the defects. This is where a batsman/captain can be useful. I can relate to the problems Graeme Hick experienced against the West Indies and those Robin Smith endured a few months earlier in Australia. When I talked to them, I could tell their attitude was right, they were determined to battle through it and that was commendable. A batsman in the same side must be careful about telling another how he should play – everyone has his own method – but I do recommend getting hold of a video of when they are playing at their best. For a start that would boost their confidence and, more importantly, they could observe what they were doing *right*. Batsmen of the calibre of Hick and Smith don't become bad players overnight and they had to realize that fine tuning can overcome what may seem to them an insuperable technical flaw.

A county captain having a bad season with the bat still has to show character and set the right tone for the rest of his players. He owes it to them to remain positive and supportive because he is charged with the responsibility of their careers. In 1987, I'm sure I fell down on the job in several ways, not least of all my lack of accessibility to my players at Essex. I was so preoccupied with my poor form that hardly anybody bothered to come up to me and talk about the usual things that concern players in a season. They could see I was distracted, morose and uncommunicative. That is no way to lead a side. We weren't playing very well anyway and, although I felt responsibility for that, I should have been able to shake myself out of my depression, rally the team and show that I was there for each of them if they wanted to talk. I failed and that's why I resigned the captaincy. That sort of thing stays with you for a long time; it's an albatross around your neck and I know that when I sometimes failed after I regained the captaincy, people would say that I wasn't suited to the job anyway, I lacked the bottle and the personality to come through the bad times. It suggests a weakness of character, an unsuitability for the job. To me it was a simple case of priorities.

Right from the start of the 1987 season, I felt out of sorts with my game, picking up two separate 'pairs' in one week alone. Everything seemed wrong with my batting – footwork, the way the bat was coming down, my concentration. I just couldn't get my mind right when it was time to go out and bat. As an opener, I need time to organize my thoughts, to think about the bowling, the wicket – generally to compose myself for around twenty to thirty minutes before the umpires walk out. Instead I was rushing to get ready because I was having to deal with things like practice, having a word with the twelfth man to explain why he wasn't playing, handling too many organizational matters before I could get my pads strapped on at 10.45. I'm a meticulous person in all areas of my life and when it comes to batting – what I do best – my equipment and approach have to be right. (I have pairs of batting gloves numbered one to five, so that when I want a replacement brought out to me, the twelfth man knows which one I need. I never change the right glove unless it's falling apart, the left one gets the wear and tear because that's the one I grip tighter against the handle.) My experience of 1987 led me to ensure I got on the ground early enough to have my net, otherwise the responsibilities of captaincy mean you start rushing around and can't find the right amount of time. Now I expect to be left alone for twenty minutes or so as soon as possible after 10.30. All the other aspects of the game are now out of my thoughts.

In 1987 I was just too distracted. I wasn't doing enough for the side in my best category and although I enjoyed leading the side in the field,

I felt I could do more for Essex by getting my batting right. It was a great honour to be captain of a club that had always treated me so well and I felt a keen responsibility to get it right. The fact that the reigning county champions managed just two wins in 1987 and finished nowhere in all the other competitions suggests that the leadership wasn't all that special that year. I didn't play in any of the Tests – quite rightly – and although I scored a hundred in the Bicentenary game at Lord's, I wasn't fooled by that one swallow in a miserable summer. I honestly wondered if I had lost whatever secret ingredient makes you a Test batsman; I started to think that at thirty-four, I was perhaps on the wane. Resigning the captaincy would at least give me the chance to see if my batting could recover sufficiently to prolong the career I had enjoyed so much.

Keith Fletcher resumed as Essex captain and I played well throughout the summer of 1988. I got back into the Test team and showed I could still compete against them. Towards the end of the '88 season, Keith stood down to give the younger players a chance and I led the side. I enjoyed it and it was an honour and a pleasure to take over again in 1989. Keith was there, helping to organize things beforehand, which meant I could have my precious time alone before I went out to bat. I'm sure things might have been different for me in 1987 if I had been a number four batsman but my job was to lead from the front as opener and captain and I had failed on both counts. Like any other manager in other walks of life, I needed to delegate in order to do my job better. Thanks to Keith Fletcher and Micky Stewart, I was eventually able to concentrate on essentials.

Some years before my nightmare season, I had seen how the pressure of failing with the bat had got to Mike Brearley. By the time I returned to the England side in 1978, Mike was a mature, calm individual with a natural flair for captaincy. He had some superb bowlers at his disposal, we were a fine fielding side and we won a lot of Tests under his excellent leadership. But he was troubled at his inability to make enough runs. Mike had originally been picked as a batsman for England under Tony Greig's captaincy and when he took over in 1977, the fact that we were successful had a lot to do with him. The press wouldn't let go of the fact that Mike wasn't performing with the bat, though, and the tension did get to him at times. He was so popular with the players and so good a captain that we banded together behind him and made public displays of our loyalty that from this distance seem a little embarrassing. In 1978, Mike dropped himself down to number five at Trent Bridge against the New

Zealanders after four successive Tests in which he hardly got a run. The press were hot on the scent of that one, with some suggesting that England were playing ten men and a captain and there's no doubt that Mike felt the pressure. We were desperate for him to succeed at Trent Bridge and when he got to his fifty after more than three hours we were all out on the balcony leading the applause. I agree it was all rather out of proportion when you consider the Kiwis weren't much of a bowling side in those days, (apart from Richard Hadlee), but we were relieved for Mike. I'm sure that his fifty in his last Test innings at the Oval in 1981, which helped us save the game against the Australians, must have given him some quiet pleasure. He made nought in the first innings (just as he did at the start of his England career), but at last he showed what he could do. You don't make 25,000 first-class runs without being a good player and I can now appreciate Mike's frustration after going through the mill myself in 1987.

I think the opening position is a good one for the captain/batsman. I say that because I think it's the best place of all to bat. You get a great opportunity to bat throughout an innings; you know what the state of the match is and how long you can bat for and you can assess how the wicket is playing at first-hand. For me there is nothing better than turning up at the ground on a fine, sunny morning, winning the toss and getting calmly ready to open the innings on a good wicket. When you're down to bat at number five or six, you never know when you'll get in and I feel for a number three batsman, because he can be in for the second ball of the day or several hours later, so it's hard for him to relax. The down side for an opener is that he can get cleaned up for nought by a very good delivery with the new ball, but if you're a good player you can cope with that. I'd prefer an occasional nought to scratching around for two hours to get to twenty, then getting out to a bad shot. There is also the prospect of getting off to a flier, with men around the bat and gaps everywhere. Opening bowlers can be just as nervous as the batters when they have the bright new ball in their hands, and they can't help spraying it around.

The captain seeks particular goals from his openers. He wants them to score as many runs as possible as individuals, to get the team off to a good start and to ensure that the new ball doesn't expose the middle order. It doesn't really matter if the openers are a bit slow early on. I see getting through the first fifteen overs as an encouraging landmark, because by then the opening bowlers are due for a breather, if not before. By the way, it's wrong to assume that the opening batsmen have the best defensive technique in the side. Some openers end up there by chance (myself included) and others open because they are happier against the quicker stuff than spin. Someone like Mike Atherton bats number three for Lancashire, even though he is very sound defensively. Mike has enough quality to adapt to either role but I'm sure it will benefit Mike's career to end up opening for Lancashire because that's the best place to be, in my opinion.

I look for a supportive stance between batting partners. I'll never say, 'Don't play this shot', but I'll point out how I think the wicket is playing. Reassuring players is more constructive. To a methodical, calm player like Mike Atherton, I'll just say, 'Well played, keep going' – he doesn't need any strictures about concentrating hard. For a few years, I used to chivvy away at my Essex team-mate Paul Prichard because he kept getting himself out in the thirties through a lack of concentration that led to rash shots. I'd say, 'Come on, no mistakes. Play tight, if it's a reasonable ball, don't think you can score off it.' I would tell Paul that I'd be on at him before we batted and he didn't mind. He's mentally tougher now and more consistent. With all batting partners, it's important to shout encouragement down the pitch when a good shot has been played. If there's a bit of needle between batters and bowlers, I shout 'Shot!' approvingly as the ball speeds away: no bowler likes to hear that. At the end of each over I like to talk to my partner. That was something Geoffrey Boycott and I did a lot when we batted against the West Indies – you can feel a little lonely out there without a chat! In these situations, I focus on the positive, tell my partner he's going well and build up our confidence. Robin Smith needs that reassurance, even though he's highly motivated and a great fighter. He likes to be told the exact state of the match, what pace he should be going at, so he can concentrate on the mechanics of batting. With someone like Allan Lamb it's usually a case of 'Well played – where are you going for dinner tonight?' To keep myself pumped up at the crease, I talk away to myself, nothing too deep, just telling myself I can do well here today if I concentrate. Over the years, Malcolm Marshall has troubled me with his late swing and ability to jag the ball back at me for the lbw decision but I eventually worked out my own psychological method of combating his threat. Instead of thinking, 'He got me out last time,' I would recall the days when I scored hundreds against him for Essex and for England. When I tell my batting partners, 'You're a good player, believe in yourself' I mean it. Self-belief in top-class sport is essential.

Quick singles are now a vital ingredient in a side's batting attitude, in my opinion. I had been very poor in that respect until I saw how the

1989 Australians stole runs off us. Around that time, Micky Stewart shocked me with some facts about a typical innings from me. He showed me a chart that proved I didn't score off all that many deliveries. I managed a fair amount of boundaries that kept my runs-per-balls ratio high but I just wasn't picking up the singles. I decided to do something about it and now that I have improved so much, I feel justified in going on about quick singles in team meetings. They have many advantages – runs, irritation for the bowlers – and you can rotate the strike so that the bowlers can't settle on their line. We upset the West Indies with our sharp running in 1991 and it kept the scoreboard ticking over when there were so few loose deliveries around.

A good understanding with your partner is essential but it's now clear to me that if you are alert enough and run on the call, you will be unlucky to be run out. I used to think run-outs were an avoidable way of being dismissed, but it's simply a case of taking a calculated risk and being aware that now and then you *will* get run out. It only becomes a problem if it happens too often. In 1991, Salim Malik did for most of the Essex batsmen because he had his own style of calling – he'd hit the ball, run a couple of yards down the wicket and then call. If he shouted 'No!' it would be rather difficult for his partner to stop and turn when he was halfway down the wicket! There were no bad feelings about this in the dressing-room, simply a case of the lads saying, 'Who's next to be sawn off at the knees, then?' We soon got the hang of his personal style but it was just as well he was such a popular player and scoring so many runs. There *is* a danger of batsmen losing confidence in each other if there are a few too many run-outs. The worst thing is a stand-off where you miss so many runs because they won't go for the single or the second run unless they're sure of getting in. In that case, it's up to the captain to sort it out, tell them to behave like grown adults and to have confidence in each other. I'm glad I wasn't England captain when Ian Botham and Allan Lamb went through a spate of running each other out; it was just as well they were good mates, because the air was often blue when one of them was left stranded. To be fair to both of them, quick singles have never been high on the priority list of the strokemaker – until now.

Geoffrey Boycott had a reputation for pulling up the ladder on his partners but I never had any problems when we came together for England. In fact I ran him out more times than the other way round. By that stage in his career, Geoffrey's game plan involved a lot of ones and twos and I thought he was perfectly safe. He'd call loudly and early and that was perfectly simple. I really enjoyed batting with Boycott, particularly against the West Indies when I could admire his superb defensive technique. He was very courageous, never shirking the fight, and I learned a great deal from him. Don't believe a word of the rumour that Boycott didn't fancy fast bowling and that was why he dipped out of Test cricket for three years. He was a magnificent opening batsman.

Should the captain alter the batting order because a player is out of form? For me, hardly ever. I believe the better players ought to be able to score faster than the bloke who is sent in early to have a slog. I know it comes off now and then – Chetan Sharma did it to us in the Nehru Cup in 1989 and sometimes Neil Foster gets promoted up the Essex order because he's a fine striker of the ball – but I'm not generally in favour of tinkering around with the order. At Sydney in 1991 we had an outside chance of winning the Test if we could score at around nine an over, so I took David Gower in with me just to see if we could get anywhere near that total. Gower had scored a wonderful hundred in the first innings, he was an experienced left-hander and therefore a useful foil to me and my regular partner, Mike Atherton was out of form. It was a one-off situation as far as I was concerned, even if we had succeeded. Mike had the technique and the temperament for the opener's job, while David has been an ideal number four or five. If a player is out of form but still in the team, I expect him to show the character to play his way out of that trough, but as long as he is battling hard, I shan't complain. We all have bad spells – it's how you cope with them that is significant.

Sometimes, flexibility is needed in the batting order during a one-day game. In the World Cup Final of 1987, Craig McDermott was sent in early to galvanize the Australian innings against us and he slogged a few to get them moving again. Chetan Sharma's hundred at Cuttack was about the luckiest I have ever seen but good luck to him, his captain told him to slog us all around the park and he did just that. You need to be able to adapt, as Geoffrey Boycott discovered in Australia in 1979. At that stage in his career he was ideally suited to the pace of Test cricket but when Mike Brearley dropped him from a one-day international, he was not impressed. His nose was pushed out of joint and he came back into the one-day side and was a revelation, hitting the ball over the top and looking our best batsman in a form of cricket that was supposedly foreign to him. That episode underlined to me that your best batsmen are your best batsmen, whatever the type of game you are playing, and you mess around with the order at your peril. Mind you, Boycott did cause Keith Fletcher a headache on the Indian tour of 1981–82 when he discussed moving Chris Tavare away from the number three spot. Tav was not a fast scorer in the Test arena and Boycott was worried about the two of them getting stuck together if I was the first to get out. Boycott wanted to play at his own tempo, relying on the likes of me, David Gower and Ian Botham to smack the ball around, but Fletcher sensibly left well alone. When you consider that at times the Indian *spinners* bowled around nine overs an hour, there was very little likelihood of any of us getting the chance to play a devastating innings.

Batsmen get confidence from knowing where they're going to bat and dropping someone down the order except in extreme circumstances can be counter-productive. In 1979 at the Oval, Sunil Gavaskar almost inspired India to an historic win as they chased four hundred plus in the final innings. Gavaskar and Vengsarkar were together when the last twenty overs started and they needed just five an over, with nine wickets in hand. When Gavaskar was out for a magnificent 221, India promoted Kapil Dev to swing the bat when there was no need. They only had to pace the innings and they were home, yet they held back Viswanath, one of their best batsmen, a player perfectly capable of organizing the assault. Kapil was caught by me at long-on for nought and then India started to panic. We got away with an exciting draw, but I'm sure India would have won if they had stuck to their usual batting order.

I do agree that it's good to have a batting order that alternates styles. Sometimes you need a gritty player in between the strokemakers just to give the batting a look of solidity – look at the sound job Larry Gomes did for the West Indies during the eighties and in his later years, Allan Border has done the same for Australia. Perhaps we had too many strokemakers one after the other in the England line-up, when Gatting, Gower, Lamb and Botham were all in the side. You do need players with a steadying influence. That's why we split up Graeme Hick and Mark Ramprakash in their début series against the West Indies. The feeling was that someone like myself or Atherton would help Hick settle in, while Smith, or Lamb could shepherd Ramprakash along. It didn't really work but on paper it looked a well-balanced batting order. A left-hander is always an advantage and if you can have a left-hand/right-hand combination for long periods, that does frustrate a fielding side. The bowler needs to alter his line frequently, and the field keeps having to change over. It can be hard sometimes for the fielding captain to keep his players totally switched on.

Every batsman has his own aims when he goes out to the middle. When I first started in county cricket, Colin Cowdrey told me he takes ten runs at a time; ever since I first played club cricket, I've looked for twenty. That's the first landmark and after that I tell myself to keep going, you're on your way. If I get out, I'm obviously disappointed but the important thing is *how* you are dismissed. If it's a good ball, I can live with that, but not if I'm responsible for my dismissal, and I try to impress that on my younger players. Kenny Barrington, who was such a great influence on me in my early England days, used to tell me, 'If you're playing well, make it count because you could get nought next time and then another nought. You can never get enough big hundreds to tide you over the low scores.' Now that I'm senior partner to Mike Atherton with England and John Stephenson with Essex, I tell them both what Kenny had to say all those years ago. I keep reminding them to focus on their low scores if they've had a bad run, so that they'll really make it count when they get the chance.

When the run chase is on, the captain has a responsibility both as player – setting an example when it's his turn to bat – and as captain, communicating to the others what he wants without getting them too uptight. In one-day cricket most run chases are possible these days and in the first-class game, if you have wickets in hand, there is always a chance. So you can afford to take it slowly and sensibly at the start and then accelerate; keep a sense of proportion, attack the bowling efficiently *and take quick singles*! Once the opposition goes on the defensive, takes some of the close catchers out, thereby reducing the risk of being dismissed, then you are beginning to make progress. A positive state of mind is important: when you expect things to go wrong, they invariably do. Don't play a rash shot after four scoreless deliveries, play it away for a single, keep calm and look to punish the bad ball.

I feel it my duty to lead from the front in these cases and to go for the whizzbang if necessary. Many times I have gone out there for Essex, determined to play shots from the start against a stiff target because that is my job and I couldn't ask anyone else in the side to do it if I couldn't or wouldn't. If you don't play positively, then you'll never win a run chase. We almost won a thrilling victory at Eastbourne in 1986, even though the odds were very much against us. Garth le Roux and Adrian Jones bowled very tightly against us at the start and we were well behind the asking rate. I asked Keith Fletcher for his thoughts and he said we had no chance, but I thought Sussex were bound to try their spinners soon and then we could get after them.

When they came on, they went for over forty in a handful of overs and we were off and running. We finished just sixteen runs short with Allan Border getting a hundred, but at least we had a go.

We were more successful in 1984 when we won a crucial game against Middlesex that had a lot to do with us taking the Championship that year. We finally bowled them out after tea and that left us needing 210 in 33 overs against a fine bowling attack. I said I'd have a go, Chris Gladwin and I wellied it around from the off and we won by four wickets with yours truly getting one of the most enjoyable hundreds of my career. It was particularly satisfying because Essex and Middlesex never give each other a thing if we are in contention for the title, as we were on this occasion. They tried their utmost to avoid defeat and we got there because of the team's positive attitude. The teams that settle for a dull draw in a run chase, and call it off early to get on the motorway don't win the title. So much depends on the attitude of the bloke in charge.

One of the few pluses for me from our disastrous tour of Australia in 1990–91 came on the last days at Sydney and Adelaide when on both occasions we gave the Aussies a fright. If Allan Lamb had been fit to play at Sydney, we might have gone a little closer but at least we had them worried in the first hour of that run chase. At Adelaide, Allan Border rightly didn't declare until he was certain we couldn't win because he knew from our days together at Essex that I would give it a go. A target of over 470 was almost impossible, but there was a time, when Mike Atherton and I were doing well, that the Aussies got a little twitchy in the field. As we walked out after lunch, I said, 'Let's keep playing sensibly but just go up a gear.' In the morning we had taken what was on offer but it had been difficult against deep-set fields. After a few minutes into the afternoon session I decided to go for Greg Matthews and it came off for me. I said to Mike, 'Let's go for it' and there was just a sneaking chance then, with Gower and Lamb still to come, as we passed two hundred with all our wickets in hand. Geoff Marsh took a good catch in the gully to dismiss me and we couldn't get there in the end. But I took consolation from the fact that we had responded positively and given them a few worries.

Such successful run chases in Tests are very rare. Usually victory comes when a side outbowls the other and the successful unit has allowed itself enough time with an impossible declaration to winkle out ten wickets in the final innings. That was my strategy at Lord's in 1990, although the way those Indians batted that summer, I couldn't be certain they would fail in the chase. Luckily for me, they did.

Somehow it doesn't seem to matter if a captain's gambling declaration sets up a close finish in a first-class match and he loses, but in a *Test Match*! In some parts of the Caribbean, Gary Sobers hasn't been forgiven for the declaration which gave England the chance to go one up and win the 1968 series. When the Indian batsmen responded to Clive Lloyd's declaration in 1976 to score over 400 and win the Jamaica Test, the shockwaves rumbled far from the West Indies: Lloyd decided to adopt the tactic of using four fast bowlers after that Test and the strategy proved overwhelmingly successful at the expense of the spin bowler.

A run chase can be a long haul and the successful assault is a matter of stages. A good start is vital – wickets in hand are more important than five an over early on. The captain must keep calm in the dressing-room during the critical stages: he will have outlined what is needed if necessary, his batsmen will have been left in no doubt about what is expected and then it's a matter of keeping the lid on emotions if things get particularly tense. A twitchy, chain-smoking captain who strides up and down the dressing-room every few minutes is no use to anyone. If colleagues start to criticize the slowness of one of the batsmen he must talk constructively, pointing out that the player is doing his best and will break free soon. He could be out of form, but as long as he is seen to be attempting to be positive, no one can really complain, just hope. I do get annoyed if a good batter plays a rash shot and gets out, but I'll keep that to myself. If he does it again in the near future it'll be time for a quiet, stern word. The vital ingredient is the player's ability to cope with the pressure; some, like Allan Lamb or Derek Pringle, seem to be able to cope easily, others just shrivel. It's easier for numbers one to three in the batting order in these situations because they have more time at the start to set the tempo; numbers four onwards usually have to pick things up right away, manipulating the ball around for the singles and picking up fours without needing to slog. First-class bowlers are usually too good to be slogged for any length of time, so if the batters can manage to play correctly and still score at speed they are doing a great job for the side. I also look to their commonsense when they're caught up in the high pressure of a run chase. It may be necessary to keep out the class bowler, nudging him away for singles, while climbing into the weaker link at the other end. The likes of Curtley Ambrose don't often get hit back over their heads for six!

Bad light and/or rain can be a difficult one for the captain of the batting side. It's amazing how keen we can be to stay out there when you can't see your hand in front of your face if there's a good chance of winning a run chase, yet we scuttle off at the sight of a few dark clouds when the bowlers are on top. As a rule I tend to leave the decision to the batsmen because they are far better judges of the conditions than the captain sitting in the pavilion. If they're happy to stay out there, that's fine by me. The problem comes when a wicket falls and the new batter has to cope with hostile conditions. That's when the gnashing of teeth starts because you feel you've thrown away a wicket by staying out there. I felt for David Capel during the Trinidad Test of 1990 when, as the last recognized batsman, he had to decide whether to come off for bad light with about thirty runs needed for victory. The West Indies were taking so long to bowl their overs and the light was so bad that we eventually had no chance of winning and could even have lost it if we'd stayed out there too much longer. It was difficult to give a proper message to Capel, who was getting very frustrated at the lack of precise guidance. It was so dark that he could barely see us in the dressing-room and in the end we had to give him the one clear message – come in.

I recall one occasion when I decided to stay out there when there was every justification for coming off. At Leeds in 1991, Derek Pringle and I were battling away against the West Indies after Curtley Ambrose had whipped the early batting out and with spots of rain scudding around and the light poor, there was good reason for accepting the offer from the umpires. Yet their bowlers were tiring, the fielders didn't fancy being out there and we didn't see why we should come off to allow them to rest up and be fresh when play resumed. Derek and I decided to stay on, carry on playing properly and take every run we could. It was the right tactical thing to do and I feel our partnership of 98 runs was one of the decisive elements in our first victory over the West Indies in a home Test since 1969.

I think Derek's twenty-seven at Leeds was the most influential minor innings of the 1991 series. If one of us had got out early, I'm sure the West Indies would have gone on to win the Test and, having taken great comfort from winning in cheerless conditions, they would have been very difficult to beat when the sun started to shine. Derek performed the kind of back-up role I had asked for when we talked about the approach needed before the series started. I had been impressed by the resistance of the Australian lower order during the Ashes series, at the way Greg Matthews, batting for over eighteen hours in the series, had organized the tail to hang on in there and gather precious runs. In contrast our tail never lasted very long. I wanted that to change; I was conscious that the West Indian fast bowlers had wrapped up our tail in clinical fashion in recent years as we often declined from 150 for 2 to 215 all out. This time *everybody* had to think about their batting and the likes of Devon Malcolm, Steve Watkin and David Lawrence had a net every day. They were encouraged to show stickability because if numbers nine to eleven could get thirty between them, there was a good chance of the same amount coming from the other end if an established batsman was still there – plus all the inevitable extras you get when the West Indies are bowling. Every run was to be seen as a bonus from the tail and they did us proud throughout that series. The example of Derek Pringle and Phillip DeFreitas was also very encouraging. In the past they had got themselves out too often in Tests through a lack of concentration and poor shot selection. Now they simply had to discipline themselves to not playing loosely outside off-stump, to leave those deliveries alone, play up the wicket to the straight ones and flick away to leg those balls coming in at them. Both players were a revelation and it was Pringle who showed what could be done at Leeds with an intelligent appreciation of what Test cricket demands.

Another tester for the batting captain is getting the timing right over the use of the nightwatchman. I tend to favour sending him in for the last twenty minutes, unless quick runs are the priority, rather than risk losing quality wickets. The accredited batsman is on a hiding to nothing if he goes in late because he can't score many runs and the bowlers will find extra effort for a possible breakthrough. What I expect from the nightwatchman is that he takes the final over of the day. His job is to protect the front-line batsman and so he must accept the responsibility. My former Essex team-mate, Ray East, had an interesting attitude to his nightwatchman's duties. Once he was sure that there was no time for another over, Ray would do his utmost to play expansive shots and score more runs. 'My job's done now', he would say as he swept the spinner. Derek Underwood had a more professional outlook to the task. In the Sydney Test on the 1979–80 tour, he lasted till after lunch the following day, taking everything that Dennis Lillee could hurl at him. When he finally walked off, the respectful applause from the Aussie fielders spoke volumes for his guts.

When I made my 154 not out at Leeds against the West Indies, it was inevitable that it would be described as 'a captain's innings'. Certainly it was the most *meaningful* knock of my career in that I knew we had to get something over 200 to have any chance of bowling them out in the fourth innings. I hadn't been in very good form so far that season and I reckon I only timed about six strokes in the entire innings, so there was immense satisfaction in just staying there and instilling the same sense of purpose in the lower order. It was the first time I had batted all the way through an innings and it felt strange batting with Devon Malcolm at the end. The statisticians enjoyed themselves that day but I have to say that winning the Test was much more satisfying.

Other 'captain's innings' spring to mind, like Allan Border's battling efforts for Australia in the mid-eighties. It seemed at that stage that Border carried the fortunes of his team on his shoulders when he went out to bat and his was always the prized wicket. Significantly, he hasn't clocked up the big hundreds for Australia in recent years. I wonder if that's because there hasn't been the pressure on him to hold the side together. Border has always been the man for the crisis. David Gower scored a lovely hundred against the Australians at Lord's in 1989 when he and the side really needed it. David hadn't helped himself by walking out of the Saturday night press conference because he was going to the theatre, so the knives were out for him in the press box. He responded in vintage fashion on the Monday and if he hadn't, the Test would have been over that day and another ignominious defeat for England would have accelerated his fall as captain. He gave us at least a glimmer of victory, even though we eventually lost on the Tuesday afternoon, but when his side needed a major contribution from the captain, he provided one. That is the type of responsibility a batting captain has to take on if he is to maintain the respect of his players.

4
Captaincy in the field

It doesn't take all that much to be a good captain on the field: flexibility, the ability to read the pitch correctly, to choose the right bowlers at the right time, to read the batsman's mind, position the fielders in the exact spot, goad his bowlers into productive spells, hand out rollickings when necessary, take advice in the proper spirit, ensure his side is aggressive yet balanced and generally be an inspiration. And lucky. Nothing to it really.

ATTITUDE

One asset that's crucial for a fielding captain must be the belief that you can win, whatever the odds. Mike Brearley instilled that into the England team and it was never more vital than in the Edgbaston and Leeds Tests of 1981. To all intents and purposes we were dead and buried both times, yet Mike managed perfectly to balance the equation between getting ten wickets while defending small totals. He was ruthless in his bowling changes, his memory for batting strengths and weaknesses was faultless and he instilled in us a great sense of purpose. That win at Edgbaston was even more astonishing because Ian Botham bowled them out cheaply on a flat pitch after being told by Brearley to put his bowling boots on at lunch, because he was going to be bowling in the afternoon. Botham thought the spinners were our best chance but the captain insisted. He exerted great pressure on the Australian batsmen and they couldn't cope. The occasion, the frenetic atmosphere, Botham's inspiration and Brearley's intuition got to them. At the next Test at Old Trafford as they started out, trying to get over four hundred for victory, Kim Hughes their captain admitted to me, 'We've got a better chance of getting that than a hundred', and they did make a good stab at the target before losing. That admission by Hughes was significant, though – he knew that the pressure would get to them in tight situations.

Keith Fletcher was also brilliant at seizing a game by the throat and refusing to let go. He had a great memory for where batsmen like to play their shots, whether gully should be squarer, or if someone played in front of, or behind square leg. His vast experience enabled him to get the best out of his bowlers and he was capable of taking advice from a few players on the field, sifting through it and quickly deciding his course of action. I can still see him now, cajoling his bowlers, slapping them on the backside, clapping his hands at his fielders, darting quick glances all around him as the bowler ran in. No cause was ever lost when Fletcher was on the pitch. At Taunton towards the end of the 1986 season, we faced defeat as Viv Richards and Ian Botham smacked us everywhere. At one stage Somerset needed twenty to win, with five wickets in hand and two of the world's fiercest batsmen at the crease. I was captain and I was struggling for inspiration. Fletcher said, 'We've got to get Viv out or we'll lose. Bring up the deep mid-wicket into the ring and hope he holes out. Tempt him to go over the top.' He did just that. Then we had to get Botham out. We tempted him with the spin of John Childs and he holed out at long-on. We won by nine runs. It was poor batting by Richards and Botham but Fletcher's belief rubbed off on me and the rest of the Essex side. A week later we had won the Championship, with that victory at Taunton decisive.

Both Fletcher and Brearley would be the first to admit that you need good bowlers to be an impressive unit in the field, so luck plays an important part. That's why I was so impressed with the positive captaincy of Chris Cowdrey in 1988 when Kent came within a point of the title with an ordinary bowling line-up but a collective belief in the team that was obvious from their brilliant fielding. Generally it's the bowlers who win you the longer games. Fletcher had one of the great County Championship bowlers in John Lever while I have been lucky enough to have Neil Foster. Lever was amazing. He would bowl all day and you struggled to get the ball out of his hand. Spells of six overs were no use to Lever, he was just warming up then; I've often seen him bowl all morning and be just as dangerous as at the start. This ability to bowl for long spells and sustain a high standard is the hallmark of a top bowler – normally you can get about seven good overs from a fastish bowler but if a man can bowl twelve overs in a row without decreasing in quality, that gives the captain greater flexibility. John

Lever knew you couldn't get wickets fielding at third man and Keith Fletcher handled him superbly. Sometimes, if he thought John wasn't bowling as fast as he should, he'd tell our wicket-keeper to stand up to him. That usually did the trick!

Mike Brearley had the same knack of getting the best out of Ian Botham. Those who have only seen Botham trundling in off medium pace in recent years ought to realize what a brilliant bowler he was in his heyday. He could be quick, he had endless variety, the ability to swing it both ways – and he loved bowling. He was central to Mike Brearley's bowling strategy because he could keep going for a session if necessary. In the Bangalore Test in 1981–82 he bowled almost fifty overs when it was really hot and steamy; and in the Perth Test in 1979 when Brearley got it wrong by picking three spinners and leaving out John Lever, Botham bowled eighty overs in the match, most of them into the wind. In that three-Test series, Botham bowled 242 overs, as well as scoring a hundred and fielding brilliantly. Brearley did very well out of Botham; every captain wishes he had someone of his talent and hunger available to him. The young Botham was a phenomenal cricketer.

MOTIVATION

The first thing a captain must do before he takes the field is to try to get his players' minds switched on to the job in hand. To expect a handful of professionals to concentrate one hundred per cent over the next two-hour session isn't exactly an onerous demand, but we're dealing with human beings and we're all fallible. In my early England days under Mike Brearley's captaincy, I had a few rockets from him for dozing off in the outfield, so I'm no paragon. There *is* a danger of saying too much before we walk out and I do find that banging the fist on the table is something that should only be attempted rarely. Nothing wrong with saying that the next session must be better than the recent disappointing one, but there are ways of pointing that out. Mike Brearley used to talk to the team as a group, while Keith Fletcher preferred a quiet word with individuals, but the message should remain the same – be mean, miserly and give them nothing. That's the best way of getting the top players out. After I've said a few general words, I like to see the team walk out together, as if we mean business. That's partly cosmetic, because it's something that's noticed by the opposition and the crowd and underlines that we're keyed up. If the team dawdles onto the field, with hands in pockets, it looks as if they're lacking in zest and purpose. Now and then I'll gather the side together for 'the huddle'. This started in India during the Nehru Cup when I found that I couldn't give my final thoughts to the team because the opposition was next door in cramped dressing-rooms and there was no privacy. So we'd go out onto the pitch and I'd talk to them. The press photographers liked 'the huddle' and so did I. We had stumbled across it, but *it looked good*, it made it clear that we meant business – rather like the Haka the All-Black rugby team performs before each match. In that short chat in our circle, I wouldn't offer any earth-shattering thoughts, just a re-affirmation of what we were there for, the need to give a hundred per cent and to keep battling away. We adopted 'the huddle' several times in the West Indies and now and then, I'll go for it in England – like on the Sunday of the Oval Test against the West Indies. Its value lies in its rarity and also in cementing the feeling that we're all in it together.

READING THE PITCH

Once out in the field, the captain's job is to read the pitch correctly and to pick those bowlers he thinks will be successful at certain times in the session. At the start of the innings, it will be just a case of giving the new ball to the usual opening bowlers, but at any other time, I will have consulted and told the selected bowlers that they were straight on after the interval. They must be given time to work out their plans and be ready for action. I will also tell two other bowlers that they *might* be first change, but my options are always open on that because the situation is fluid. Once I think about a bowling change, I let the player know a couple of overs in advance, so he can warm up, think about his field and focus on the batsmen.

Sometimes it's a genuine dilemma about who to start with. On the final morning of the Oval Test in 1991, we needed early inroads against the West Indies, especially as Richie Richardson was still there. I asked advice and it was conflicting. Mike Atherton suggested giving David Lawrence a go from the Vauxhall End, because he was our fastest bowler and he'd have the wind behind him. I was concerned that they might get off to a flier against him and I thought about Phil Tufnell from the Pavilion End where he'd taken all those wickets in the first innings – and Richardson was known to be a far better player of seamers than spinners. In the end I played a hunch. Phillip DeFreitas had looked out of sorts bowling from the Pavilion End the day before but I put that down to the fact that he hadn't been feeling well. He had been our most consistent wicket-taker all summer and I decided to take a chance on him from the Vauxhall End. He took two wickets in that first over and the hutch was open for us. At the end of that over, Atherton smiled and said to me, 'Good job I wasn't captain!' but I quickly pointed out I often get it wrong!

Sometimes a bowler has to operate from an end that doesn't suit him. Generally one end is more favourable than the other on English grounds (because of a slope, a crosswind or poor footholds), and I've seen situations where a bowler has told his captain he doesn't want to bowl from a certain end. Yet someone has to do it, it's unprofessional to have rows like that on the field; it's also a waste of time. The captain must get his way on this one and hopefully if the spirit is good in the side, the unlucky bowler will just get on with it. At Lord's the choice of ends is a problem, because of the slope. There is a nine foot drop from the Father Time Stand to the Tavern Side and bowlers have difficulty in adjusting their line and length. The slope is quite apparent when you go out there to bat and when the bowler comes in from the Pavilion End, he's in danger of pushing it down legside to the right-hander. That end generally has assisted the quicker bowlers like Bob Willis and Curtley Ambrose, those who hit the deck and get the ball to move off the seam. There's also a ridge at that end, so if the quicker bowler manages to get his line right, he can be a nasty proposition. From the Nursery End, the ball tends to swing away from the right-hander, so people like Ian Botham and Malcolm Marshall prefer to come in from there. The wind tends to come across from the Father Time Stand, so that also helps the swing bowler operating from the Nursery End.

Knowing the bowling conditions at Lord's gives the Middlesex lads a big advantage because it can disorientate a bowler – Devon Malcolm struggled there against the West Indies batsmen, because he kept pushing the ball down the legside from the Pavilion End. In situations like that, the captain just has to work with his bowlers, asking them which end they prefer, but also telling them they've got to be flexible and that they might have to do a few from the end they don't fancy.

FIELD-PLACING

Field-placing can be another bone of contention between captain and bowler. It's always a problem balancing the number of close catchers against those who are saving one, yet you must remember that fielders saving one in the ring are just as likely to catch somebody as see him caught at slip. A lot depends on the captain's memory for the specific batsman's style of play; you shouldn't be feeding his strengths. Yet there are times when it's justifiable to cut off a batsman's favourite shot by getting him to play in that area. Terry Alderman bowled very cleverly at me in 1989, posting men in on the legside, trying to get me to play across the line in attempting to pierce that field. It worked: Gooch lbw Alderman for very little far too often. One up to Allan Border, he'd watched me closely during his two seasons at Essex. We all try to stifle good players, getting them to play shots they would rather not attempt. Leicestershire's James Whitaker likes to punch his drives either side of the bowler and to hit the spinners over the top. We have managed to quieten him down by placing a short mid-on and short mid-off, almost level with the bowler, and have another man out for the lofted drive. So if Whitaker mistimes one of his speciality punched drives, he could be caught. That tends to put doubt in his mind and he has to manufacture shots from elsewhere because he is aware that if he tries to go over the top, he could be caught on the boundary. It is very satisfying when you get things right like that because it's been done to me when I've been batting and you appreciate the thinking behind the strategy.

Good batsmen have to be *got out*, rather than be simply dismissed. A bowler needs a stock delivery against class batsmen – five out of six each over have to be on the right spot, on a good length around the off-stump. The length can vary, but not the line; two out of six isn't professional enough, the good batsman will just pick off the runs. Devon Malcolm and David Lawrence found out the hard way that the West Indies batsmen like the ball coming quickly onto the bat and if it's not accurate, the ball also disappears quickly. The quality bowlers like Lillee, Alderman, Hadlee, Fraser and Marshall keep plugging away around the business area and another twenty-five per cent is given over to variety. If you bowl middle to middle and off-stump in Tests, the quality batsmen will work you away on the legside and you will disappear consistently. If you bowl at a genius like Azharuddin, be prepared for him to play a different shot to two successive balls landing on the same spot. He is a great challenge in field-placing. After his brilliant hundred at Lord's in 1990 we tried to stop him playing that unique 'top spin loop' stroke that deposits the ball pitching outside off-stump in front of square leg. We posted two men at short mid-wicket to try to get him playing somewhere else, and also bowled a fuller length on his off-stump, because he's not normally a straight driver, he prefers playing square of the wicket on both sides. Somehow he still managed to pierce our fields: players of Azza's calibre have that knack!

HOMEWORK

You have to do your homework to have a chance of getting good players out cheaply. When they come in, you remember who's a shaky starter. Imran Khan is surprisingly nervous early on, while David Gower can be sketchy because he relies on timing rather than footwork. Gower hits the good balls to the boundary as well as the bad ones when he's going well. He isn't renowned for his straight driving, he prefers to play square with an open face. So you would think that it would be easy to set a field to him until your mind goes back to that day at Chelmsford in 1989 when he kept finding the square offside boundary, even though I had posted a square third man, two slips, two gullies, and a cover point. He was stroking the ball, not edging it and it was almost impossible to bowl at him.

When a class batsman comes in, he has to be attacked but in the right way. Don't feed him his most productive shots. Dean Jones loves to whip a ball on middle stump away through mid-wicket, while Allan Border likes to pull and square cut. There's a chance of getting him caught in the slips, sparring at one on or just outside the off-stump, as Angus Fraser has discovered a few times. Generally a good batsman makes mistakes through a lack of concentration and that's when you need fielders in the correct catching positions – the slips, deep gully, and bat/pad. It's important that he doesn't get off to a flier, so if you can bowl at least tightly at him, there's a chance he might do something rash. If his partner is more vulnerable at the other end, both bowlers can draw strength from the fact that at least they are being shown some respect. If the class player can be kept away from the strike so that the lesser batsman can be attacked, so much the better.

One of the reasons why we bowled so well against the 1991 West Indians was because we knew a fair bit about their batsmen and where they could be vulnerable. We had fresh memories of one or two incidents in the previous series just a year earlier and we sat down and talked it through. A few of their players were just as likely to be caught in the covers rather than slip because they like to hit the ball on the rise: Richie Richardson and Jeff Dujon both got themselves out that way.

Viv Richards was unlikely to be caught at slip, but his fondness for working the ball to leg meant he was a candidate for a leading edge and a skyed catch. Phil Simmons and Gus Logie both liked the square slash and we had Simmons caught at cover point at Leeds and in the gully at the Oval, while Logie was picked up at deep gully in the 1990 Trinidad Test playing that shot. Logie also likes to flick the ball in the air off the back foot, going right across his stumps and we had him taken at deep backward square leg in the one-day international at Edgbaston. For Desmond Haynes, we had a bat/pad because he always plays forward with bat and pad close together. For a back-foot player like Logie, the bat/pad position was a waste of time.

For most of their batsmen, we had both mid-off and mid-on squarer because they don't play in that area like the English. They tend to open the face and send the ball more in the extra cover region or whip it away to the left of mid-wicket. We would have a square cover for Haynes, Hooper, Richardson and Logie, because they like their skimming shots in that region and can get caught. Brought up on good, hard wickets they tend to play loosely outside the off-stump off the back foot when the ball is moving around – that's how Jeff Dujon was caught at short extra cover in the Leeds Test. I caught him in the same position in the Jamaica Test of 1986, when he mistimed a shot that is his trademark if the bounce is true and his timing working. Putting in a short extra cover for Dujon also had the added merit of making him think and consider where else he could get his runs if that productive area was blocked off.

Terry Alderman did the same to me a few months earlier on a slow wicket during the Melbourne Test. The catching positions were short mid-wicket and short extra cover, rather than slip, because the bounce was so low that there was a danger of the nicks not carrying. Terry also placed an inner ring for the drive – a short mid-on, a short mid-wicket and a man between mid-off and extra cover. He bowled a fullish length and tried to get me driving in the air. I was inhibited by the field settings and it made me think hard about where I could get my runs.

The important thing about bowling to the 1991 West Indians was to remember to bore them out. The dependable bowlers like Derek Pringle and Phillip DeFreitas went for under three runs an over in the series while the quicks went for around five an over. Sideways movement at a slower pace was the best tactic: make them play half-forward, rather than back, but not half-volleys. I would have been happy if the weather had stayed unsettled every time we played a Test in 1991, because the softish, seamer's pitches just didn't suit their batsmen. What they would have *loved* would have been the sight of Devon Malcolm and David Lawrence in harness in a Test, because that sort of fast bowling can be meat and drink to them. It would have been a different situation against New Zealand or India but I didn't want to let Viv Richards and company off the hook. Tight, attritional bowling is the method against them, not meeting fire with fire.

CATCHERS

As fielding captain, I tend to have too many catchers, rather than be cautious. I work on the assumption that my bowlers will put it in the right place and that the risk of conceding a few boundaries to a top batsman in the hope that he might get caught at gully or third slip is worth taking.

Sometimes I have to compromise with three slips and a deepish gully, saving one – a position where a lot of catches are taken, especially in the one-day games off the full-blooded slash. We call it 'the Sunday League position' and Essex put our best fielder (Nasser Hussain) in there, because he's agile, quick to the ball, sharp with the throw and a good catcher. Chris Lewis does it for England in one-day internationals; he has all the necessary attributes.

With mid-off, I sometimes have a problem with the faster bowler when I'd prefer to have someone in a catching position instead. I want my opening bowlers to bowl line-and-length, not halfway down the pitch, wasting the new ball, and if I take away mid-off they might drag the ball down a little and bowl too short. A mid-off will encourage them to pitch it up further (without being a half-volley) and it also means the batsmen don't get singles for safe little pushes, rotating the strike and frustrating the bowler. So you try to boost the bowler's confidence that there'll be no easy runs in the mid-off area, but if you take away the gully or slip to accommodate that position, and the batsman nicks one through there to the third man boundary, what do you do next? If that keeps happening you just have to install a third man at the expense of the gully and stiffen the off-side cordon, saving one – or carry on attacking and post two gullies and two slips. All very taxing and frustrating, especially if the batsman who flirted through the slip area early on goes on to make 150.

THIRD MAN

Third man is another dilemma for the fielding captain. Now I know that older players and the commentators on radio and television bemoan the fact that so many runs go down in that vacant area, but who do you take away to send down there? If I had ten fielders at my disposal rather than nine, I'd have a third man all the time, but otherwise you're having to take out one of the slips, the gully, the man at bat/pad or the mid-off, all vital attacking positions in my eyes. If a tail-ender comes in and there's a bit of bounce in the wicket, I'll do away with mid-off and have third man, because he's more likely to get runs down there than with proper shots off the front foot.

I'm a great fan of the man at bat/pad on the legside. Over the years I've seen a lot of catches go there, yet it's invariably the first position many captains dispense with once the first attacking ploy is over. On the offside, it's the pressure position, trying to get the batsman to play differently, but on the legside, there are a lot of catches from the one that nips back, takes the bat, then the pad and lobs up. John Lever got a stack of wickets there, bowling left-arm over the wicket into the right-hander. You need a brave man in there and it doesn't always follow that the best man for the job is a young player. If the youngster's no good at it or doesn't fancy it, take him out. Brian Hardie fielded there for Essex for most of his career and he was a brilliant reaction catcher, particularly brave during the pre-helmet days, and in fact his specialist skills in that area kept him in our side at times. I think it's essential that fielders close in should be allowed to wear helmets, even though there's an argument that this gives them an unfair advantage.

The way people play these days means it's essential to have a man at bat/pad. You get most tail-enders propping forward competently enough, with bat close to the pad, resisting the temptation to slog the spinner up in the air – so what's wrong with putting them under pressure with a fielder close in? It's also a good position for a bowler who wants to sow doubts in a batsman's mind. The position is usually filled by a batsman, because you can't take the chance of one of your bowlers being injured. Robin Smith does it for England and although he's brave and willing, I know he's not keen. He doesn't do it for Hampshire, sensible chap: nothing wrong with pulling rank when necessary! I finally found myself in there at Folkestone in 1991 after avoiding it for almost twenty years. I wasn't physically afraid but I admit standing at slip is more pleasurable – the captain looks more masterful directing operations from there than turning his back every now and then!

Neil Foster and I often have disagreements about the bat/pad position. Now I usually allow an experienced bowler to have the final say on field-placing, but I do tend to dig my heels in over this one position because it leads to so many wickets. I had the last laugh over Fozzie once at Canterbury when he wanted to take out the bat/pad for his first over at the left-hander, Simon Hinks. I said, 'No, let's leave him in – he doesn't play that far forward usually but this might make him play differently.' He was caught there off Fozzie's first ball and I looked rather smug for a time. Yet he still thinks he doesn't get many wickets in that position. So often I decide against my better judgement to take away the bat/pad and the ball flies in the air shortly afterwards. You kick yourself and that's why I err on the side of aggression.

In the Trinidad Test of 1990, we were on top when Jeff Dujon came in. I suggested a silly point for him to my vice-captain, Allan Lamb, standing alongside me in the slips. 'He doesn't play it there,' Lamby said, but I just had this feeling that he might be perturbed by it and he'd play back, rather than forward. He did – and Gladstone Small had him lbw for a handful. I'm sure that wicket stemmed from the pressure exerted from silly point's presence. You don't always expect a catch from a man in a catching position, you're hoping that he'll make the bloke play in a manner foreign to him. It's such a pleasure when you manage to out-think a batsman and that's why I get annoyed at times when a captain has just opted for a standard field after the first fifteen overs and he gets wickets through loose shots, rather than his own tactics. We all have a tendency to follow the ball, and it can be very frustrating when one of our own batsmen obliges, hitting one straight down a fielder's throat when he has just been moved. As I tell my bowlers – you can't set a field for bad bowling. So it's frustrating when unimaginative tactics gets wickets.

SPINNERS

Captaining the spinners sympathetically is an art and I admit it's something I'm still working on. When you've grown up with the likes of Lever, Botham, Willis, Hendrick, Old, Foster, Pringle and Fraser; when you've batted against great performers like Holding, Roberts, Lillee, Hadlee and Marshall; you tend to have a healthy respect for the faster stuff. My detractors say that I'm unsympathetic towards spinners because I play them pretty well. Mike Gatting gets a similar label. That's untrue because I respect what a class spinner has to offer. It's not my fault that so many things are weighted against him in modern cricket – the flat wickets, heavy bats and the way tail-enders just block them. I always enjoy captaining the side when the spinners are on. There are more overs, more variety of strokeplay, you have to think differently, get the field placings exact, and the batsmen often go for their shots. Spinners mean a greater interest for the players and spectators and if you have a helpful wicket, they can be matchwinners because some front-line batsmen don't play them so well these days on turning pitches. The West Indies batted very badly against Phil Tufnell in that famous Oval Test. There was no magic about his spell, even though he bowled very well. The West Indies haven't picked too many of the twirly boys in recent years and some of their batters played as if they'd never seen a slow left-armer. Significantly, they played Tufnell better in the second innings.

Spinners need the right wickets for their particular skills and then they can do just as good a job as the seamers when the conditions favour the faster forms of bowling. It's so easy to write, 'Once again Gooch failed to use his spinner,' but you can only act as you see the conditions and gear your plan towards what is best for the side at that particular time. I don't rotate the bowlers just to give the press some variety to write about, I do it to take ten wickets as quickly as possible. When I used John Childs very early in Derbyshire's second innings late in the 1991 season, it was because I thought he'd do the necessary on a wicket that aided the spinners, even though he had a new ball in his hand. At the Trent Bridge Test of 1990, I brought on Eddie Hemmings after just eleven overs on the first day, because it was such a slow, nothing pitch that the New Zealand openers were just lunging forward and any edges weren't carrying behind the wicket. I thought Eddie might turn it and he tested them out. Later on in the day it quickened up a little for the faster bowlers and I brought them back again. All I was doing was being sensible, trying to read the pitch and choosing the right bowlers accordingly.

I know Eddie Hemmings thinks I'm too negative about spin bowling, that I go on too much about 'keeping it tight'. As I told him when we discussed this, I see that as an *attacking* philosophy, rather than a defensive one. As a batsman, I don't like to be tied down, I feel pressurized if I can't get the ball away and I was surprised that a spinner of Eddie's vast experience couldn't see that. When Kapil Dev hit him for four successive sixes at Lord's in 1990, I kept encouraging

Eddie to bowl normally at him, because he could easily hit one up in the air. Eddie was the right bowler for Kapil at that time, because there was a chance he would get over-dosed on adrenalin and try one ambitious shot too many. All credit to Kapil – they were magnificent shots – but keeping Eddie on was hardly the action of a seam-obsessed captain.

In that same series, I tried Mike Atherton's leg-spin at the Oval because I genuinely thought he could get Azharuddin, who was playing very rashly at the time. Whenever I'd seen Mike bowl in county games, he looked very useful but at the Oval it was just a diet of long-hops and full tosses. I couldn't keep him on, going consistently for seven an over. On the day, no captain can do much when the spin bowling can't reach the necessary standard, surely?

My biggest tactical error as England captain came on the day when I over-bowled the spinners. It came at Sydney in 1991 when I declared behind on first innings to give us a chance of victory, with us two down in the series and three to play. There was no point in being level on first innings because that would have taken too long. The wicket was turning and we needed to bowl them out in their second innings as quickly as possible. It went well for a time and we had them just over 200 ahead, with only three wickets left and enough time left to get them. Carl Rackemann came in, a negligible batsman, and I thought he'd fall to Phil Tufnell or Eddie Hemmings pretty soon. I was wrong; he hung around, padding the spinners away and I took too long to bring Devon Malcolm on. Devon had a bad back, yet I told him he had to come out to field, otherwise he wouldn't be allowed to bowl. I was concerned that a couple of loose overs from Devon might set us back twenty runs and the time-to-runs equation would be tilted the way of Australia. Also the spinners were bowling tightly and in my experience they are usually too good for the likes of Rackemann. When I finally brought on Devon, he bowled Rackemann in his first over, by which time we were too late to force a victory, despite having a good thrash when we batted. So that was one day when I chose the wrong option – but at least I came down on the side of the spinners.

When I first bring on a spinner, I try not to attack too much because it's so important that he finds his line, length and confidence. For a slow left-armer, I'll have a slip if it's turning, possibly also a gully and – of course – a bat/pad once he has settled into his groove. I like to have someone slightly to the left of extra cover (on the perch, we call it at Essex). That means I can push back the mid-on and mid-off for the lofted drive and hopefully they'll also stop the single. There'll also be a square cover in the absence of a gully and a deep square leg. No third man, hardly anything should go down there if the spinner's bowling properly. The first man to go if the ball's turning will be mid-on, and I'll be hoping that the batsman will be tempted by that gap and play across the line to the turning ball. For an off-spinner, I'm looking for a line on or about six inches outside the off-stump for a right-hander. If he bowls too straight he can be played through legside, so I'll have five on the offside – usually slip, silly point, three in the ring – and on the legside, bat/pad, mid-wicket, mid-on and deep square leg. That leaves the off-spinner vulnerable to the little tickle down to fine leg, but if he's bowling the right line, that's a risky stroke and if it's turning, he might get a catch at bat/pad.

If the batsman is adept at the sweep, I'll expect my spinner to vary his length, to drop it short or bowl it fuller to keep the batsman guessing. The good length ball is the ideal one for the sweep and you can usually tell if the batsman is going for the shot by the way he sets himself and his footwork. The bowler must persevere, but extemporize in the same way as the batsman is trying to mess up his line. The reverse sweep is even more frustrating for the spinner if he continues to concede runs with that shot; then he has to take a fielder out of his offside ring, or even lose one of his close catchers. I'll want my spinner to bowl straight if I think the reverse sweep is on, because it's a safer shot when the ball is pitched outside off-stump, with the angle not so narrow. It's harder to get a bat on it if it's straight. All very taxing and enjoyable for the captain and bowler – but different from the standard deployment of seam bowler's fields. For all I know, it may have been easier to captain spinners twenty years ago, when batsmen played them more conventionally!

On good wickets, spinners are generally played better nowadays. Some batsmen look to dominate as soon as a spinner comes on, so the bowler and captain have to keep their nerves. It's hard to keep a bowler on when he's going for eight an over, even though he's not bowling badly – as I found out when Mark Waugh got after Phil Tufnell, playing him superbly, in the Adelaide Test. I don't like taking *any* bowler off after a couple of overs, so it's a case of encouraging the spinner and looking to the other fielders to do the same. Spinners do get tired and if they start to drop it short, they probably need a rest. A lot goes into the delivery and after a two-hour stint, the fingers get sore and they start to just *put* it there, rather than bowl it. It's a fact that spinners have to bowl more overs for their wickets than faster bowlers of equal quality – the spinner looks to winkle batsmen out, rather than get wickets straight away – so they need to be handled with patience and understanding. I'm still learning how it's done but I think I'm getting there.

NEW BALL

How much latitude can the captain allow a fast bowler who is wasting the new ball? If he's an experienced performer, you persevere a little longer, but a younger bloke might have to be taken off after three or four overs and brought back later. You need to assess how much damage is being done by exposing him to prolonged punishment, and hope you're not putting too much pressure on him by saying 'try one more'. Someone like Devon Malcolm or David Lawrence needs around six overs minimum because it takes them at least three overs to get firing properly. The captain must guard against conceding eight an over too often, because there's no pressure on the batsmen, they're just picking off the runs. At such times, it's a good idea for the captain to station himself at mid-off, saying things like 'keep going, you'll get it right.' Show the bowler you understand. You gain the respect and confidence of your players by not shouting or bawling them out when the pressure is on. I prefer a quiet word on the field and a firmer word afterwards if I think he's let the team down but as long as the chap's trying his best, I can accept that he's simply bowling badly. If he continues to bowl on Chris Broad's legs instead of trying to slant it across him, that is bad cricket and the bowler should be told so.

When we faced Richie Richardson, our bowlers knew that he liked the shortish ball, because his best strokes are off the back foot – so they had to bowl a good length and give him very little width outside the off-stump. You expect such discipline from international bowlers. If the class player is scratching around and he looks edgy, that is the time to keep the pressure on him. He can easily regain his timing after one good shot and he'll be on his way. Give him nothing that will boost his confidence.

The second new ball can be a boost for the batsmen if taken at the wrong time. It's rarely a factor in county cricket unless it's a four-day game, but the stock situation in Tests comes when you're near close of play and you can have two darts with the new ball – in the last ten overs of the day and first thing in the morning. Yet if the batsmen are well set and the bowlers are tired, there's a case for delaying the second new ball. It usually goes quicker off the blade when new, the field is usually fairly attacking – so there are more gaps – and if the batters are established, they can easily cash in. You may find yourself on the defensive, with just two slips and a gully, so it might be best to re-group next morning with fresh pairs of legs, and the batsmen having to start all over again. During the Oval Test in 1991, the second new ball was available to us in their second innings but Phillip DeFreitas and Chris Lewis didn't want to take it. The old one had kept its shape, it hadn't gone soft and the two bowlers and Ian Botham all said, 'Hang on to this one, it's still swinging.' Lewis in particular was moving it around, beating Richie Richardson several times outside the off- stump. Every now and then I kept querying their suggestion, but they stuck to their guns and I backed down. After our third discussion, with the new ball due twelve overs previously, I prevailed over my bowlers. I just felt we now had to try something different and go for the extra bounce. There's no happy ending to this tale – we didn't get a quick wicket!

Sometimes it's obvious that you must take the new ball but it's strange how some fast bowlers are more dangerous when it's a few overs old and some of the shine has gone. Malcolm Marshall and Waqar Younis for example, and I've seen Wayne Daniel hold the ball *across* the seam to avoid pushing it down the legside. Andy Roberts used to do the same when he bowled a bouncer. He didn't want to hit the prominent seam on a new ball because that would make it bounce too high; his aim was to hit the flat part, so the short ball would skid through and stay on line. I can confirm that Andy bowled a very mean bouncer!

THE BOUNCER

The bouncer should be used for shock purposes and – if the batsman doesn't fancy it – as a means of systematic intimidation within the laws. Graeme Hick was worked over by short-pitched bowling from the West Indies, while the bouncer was cleverly used now and then, just to keep him on his toes. His dismissals came via the ball coming through at chest height, or if he dragged it on when he was expecting to be pinned on the back foot. Clever bowling. Malcolm Marshall uses the bouncer cleverly at me, giving me one off the first ball or in his first over. He's trying to get me out of my normal groove, trying to force me onto the back foot – then jagging one back at me for the lbw. He knows I'm vulnerable in that area and he's got me several times by breaking up my rhythm of play.

When a batsman loses confidence against the short ball, it quickly gets around the circuit and the faster bowlers ought to capitalize on it. Clive Radley was never the same player after Rodney Hogg hit him on the head at Adelaide in 1978, while my Essex opening partner, John Stephenson, has been in a quandary sometimes, not knowing whether to duck or go for the hook after taking a blow or two on the head. It's the fielding captain's duty to use every *legitimate* means at his disposal when an established batsman no longer fancies the short ball. With the tail-enders you hope such ruthlessness won't be necessary but if they hang around for a time, with all their protective equipment on, they can't complain if they start smelling the leather.

I like my bowlers to *mean it* when they deliver a bouncer. In the West Indies in 1990, I asked Angus Fraser and Gladstone Small to bowl one every ten or twelve balls – to make them know they meant business and to vary their attack – and they also put their backs into bowling the bouncer. Derek Pringle, now a medium pacer, bowls one now and then and that's good thinking because some batters take him on at that pace, hit too early and glove it. John Lever used to try one towards the end of a limited overs game, realizing that he needed something different against a batsman who was in a groove and expecting either good length balls or yorkers.

The temptation to overbowl your faster bowlers is often very hard to resist and many captains have been guilty of this. I am no different and both Mike Gatting and Kim Barnett (as county captains) have criticized me for extending Angus Fraser and Devon Malcolm too far. Take Angus first. He is such a fine bowler, such a competitive character, that any captain would be delighted to have someone like him who just loves to bowl and bowl. Like John Lever, he's a captain's dream – 'Had enough, Gus?', 'No, one more.' I agree he's someone you have to protect for his own good but having said that, he needs to bowl his quota of overs to get wickets. Gus doesn't blast men out, he nags away at them till they finally get exasperated. I got a lot of stick for giving him thirteen overs on the trot on the second evening of the 1990 Old Trafford Test, but he *did* take three Indian wickets that night and he was going to have an overnight rest. He looked dangerous, he wanted to bowl and I think it was tactically correct to keep him on.

In Australia a few months later, he injured his hip in the Melbourne Test, but we took a chance on him in the next one-day game because we had a chance of getting to the final and we needed our most reliable bowler. Gus was happy to give it a go, but it messed him up for the tour and the rest of 1991, as it turned out. We played him in the Adelaide Test even though he was only eighty per cent fit because we were two down in the Series with two to play. It was kill-or-cure for Gus and he was more than willing to try his best. On the fourth day at Adelaide, he bowled twenty-six overs even though not fully fit, but he knew that Phil Tufnell had been ill and was now lacking in confidence and he knew that he could get by at a reduced pace. He also knew that he wouldn't be playing in the last Test at Perth, so this was his swansong. None of us had any idea that his hip injury would prove so serious, but I can't believe it stemmed from bowling a fair quota of overs under me. Mike Gatting isn't the only captain who missed Gus Fraser in 1991 – imagine how he would have pressurized the West Indies batsmen.

Devon Malcolm isn't like England's premier fast bowler of a decade ago, Bob Willis, who was usually fast and accurate from the first over. Devon's best overs are invariably numbers three to seven, and sometime even later than that: he's a big, muscular guy who runs a long way and needs to ease himself into a spell. In Australia Devon did more bowling than I would have liked because Angus Fraser was injured for a time and Gladstone Small disappointed. Devon thrives on confidence and you can see the effect it has on him if he gets an early wicket. On the other hand, he gets down very easily and I like to encourage him by giving him a few overs to get him firing properly. I'm a big fan of Devon – he has the raw material, the stamina and the strength to be a consistently hostile, genuinely fast England bowler – but he knows that you can rarely take five wickets in fifteen overs in an innings against top batsmen on good Test wickets. You can't get wickets unless you bowl.

TAIL-ENDERS

There are many frustrations just waiting for a fielding captain, but one of the biggest is when the tail wags. A lot of them are useful players who know how to defend, there aren't many like Les Taylor and Jim Griffiths around these days. Somehow bowlers *press* too much when they're trying to mop up the tail, instead of bowling in the way that dismisses the good batters. They can see the finishing line, the cup of tea in the dressing-room, yet subconsciously they feel it's a formality. Often the number eleven isn't good enough to get a touch, but he survives and the frustration increases. In the end, you've got to make them *play* at the ball, just like any batsman.

I clearly remember the over Dennis Lillee bowled at me on the Saturday night of the Leeds Test in 1981 – he knew I was on a hiding to nothing and I was looking to leave anything, but he made me play at every ball and finally had me caught at slip for nought. The same principle applies to tail-enders: they're not usually sure where their stumps are, so they mustn't be allowed to leave a ball. Against the better batsmen, you're conditioned to struggle for your wickets, but it's much more aggravating if a tail-ender hangs around.

The greatest innings I have seen came in the company of a tail-ender when Javed Miandad got a double hundred against Essex on a turning wicket at Colchester. Robin Hobbs batted with him for eight overs, *and he didn't face one ball*! The fifth ball of each over would be hit for six or four, then somehow Javed would pinch a single off the last one. As the bowler delivered it, Hobbs would be running and they got in each time. The first ball Hobbs faced saw his dismissal. It was a phenomenal innings by Javed and it was interesting to see him go over the top off the fifth ball, with the field brought in for the quick single. Each time it worked and it was a masterful effort to judge the quick single so surely.

I once saw David Acfield deal equally calmly with the problem of taking a single near the end of the over. David didn't fancy facing the bowler at the other end, the fearsome Sylvester Clarke, the Surrey fast bowler with a reputation for disposing of any tail in ruthless fashion. In his cultivated tones, David announced, 'I'm not coming down Sylvers' end this ball, next ball or any bloody ball!' In the end they had to take Sylvers off and wait till David *was* on strike before unleashing him.

OFF DAYS

There are some days when – for all your cajoling – you just can't get it right on the field and dejection sets in. That happened to me on the second day of the Sydney Test in 1991, the worst day of my career. We were shocking in the field that day, a total embarrassment. Our bowlers were cut and pulled far too often, the throwing was poor, the ground fielding sloppy and the crowd laughed at us. Clem Driver, our scorer, a man I have known at Essex for years, told me he was embarrassed to be in the job that day and so was I as captain. It was my fault because I had picked that side to tour and I'd failed to get the right response from the start. There was simply no excuse for the lack of enthusiasm and I told them so afterwards.

Just occasionally I blow my top on the field and I try to ensure it's not too visible from the boundary edge. I got very annoyed on the field in a match for Essex against Somerset in 1991 when we collectively fell asleep for a while. Nothing was happening, the fielders were wandering around listlessly and the bowlers going through the motions. Luckily a wicket fell and I gathered my players together to give it to them straight: 'Do you want to win the Championship or don't you? Wake up, there's no urgency in our play!' It was all the more effective because that's not usually my style, but it was the captain's responsibility to get the team working again. And it paid off.

If Essex aren't challenging for the Championship, it's my job to find out why. I like to see everyone supporting the bowlers in the field with vocal encouragement. It's important to keep the players motivated so that the fielders will dive and stop certain fours. That gives the bowler a huge boost. The Australians under Allan Border became past masters at vocal aggression, shouting things like 'Let's take this guy into lunch with us, fellas,' but I don't mind that, it's all part and parcel of a hard battle out there. As long as it's not provocative and everyone keeps quiet when the bowler is running in, that type of balanced aggression doesn't bother me.

Sometimes a bit of kidology is necessary to get the best out of your bowlers. If Ian Botham wasn't firing properly, Mike Brearley would call him 'an old tart' and suggest that Chris Old was a quicker bowler – that usually did the trick! We call Angus Fraser 'Hand-Brake' if it looks as if he's not running in with his usual verve – as in, 'Come on Gus, slip the hand-brake!' You have to talk positively to the team, keep motivating them, telling them a breakthrough can change it round.

Keith Fletcher used to say to me, 'It doesn't matter that you've lost the toss and you fancied batting, you've now got to get out there and make things happen.' Ray Illingworth would tell his England players, 'It's you guys who can now turn it round for us.' You may be on the rough end of the situation, but if you don't concentrate and let things drift, the opposition will control the game. Against the West Indies batsmen, one bad session can lose you the game because they usually get around a hundred playing normally; if the wheel falls off, they can be devastating when they're in command. That's why Pringle and DeFreitas were so vital to us in 1991 – they were never collared. We gave them a good fight even when we lost, and that was important to me after the lack of guts shown in Australia.

THE LEFT-HANDER

The captain mustn't allow his bowlers to be upset by left-handed batsmen. I have troubles at Essex getting through to our medium-pacer, Don Topley, who just doesn't believe he can get them out. If they lose the strike it's a relief to him, even though he's only giving himself a fifty per cent chance of getting a wicket. At his pace he ought to be able to bowl with accuracy at them, but he can't. In my experience most left-handers are good offside players, whereas I'd say at Test level most right-handers favour legside. Most of the bowling is pushed *across* the left-hander, so he doesn't get much chance to play off his legs if the line is right. In 1990/91 we managed to restrict Mark Taylor in Australia by going round the wicket, slanting the ball in at him, making him play more at it. In 1989, he had looked a very well-organized player, a good leaver of the ball outside his off-stump and limiting himself to three or four shots. Once we started bowling *at* him, that tied him up, made him unsure about whether to leave the ball and he started nicking a few to slips and gully. Left-handers are there to be dismissed, there's no point in being paranoid about them because in the main the fielding positions are the same for the right-hander. The slips, for example, always take their positions from the wicket-keeper. So much of it is commonsense, there's no mystique about getting your side to look a cohesive outfit in the field. The example has to come from the captain and if the team spirit is high enough, so much can be surmounted. I see no value in getting perturbed by the presence of a left-hander, a dropped catch or a bad umpiring decision. You've just got to get on with it, play for each other and try to pull it around. An impressive, successful, happy side in the field doesn't come together by accident.

5
Limited overs captaincy

I like one-day cricket. I've grown up with it and although Viv Richards was right when he said it's the hamburger to Test cricket's steak, it's invigorating and exhilarating. Everything is more compressed compared to the longer game – by a certain stage the outcome of every ball is crucial and the fielders are diving around, the bowlers desperately trying to concentrate as the captain tries to keep order, while the batsmen are wondering where they can pinch a single. No matter how professional the side, human fallibility can lead to good cricketing habits going straight out of the window. No wonder spectators love a tight finish in one-day cricket: they can regularly see hardened pros make fools of themselves and play like inexperienced club cricketers.

In one-day cricket, you can get by on limited resources provided you do the simple things often and well. The team – and the captain – who handle the pressure more easily will win more games than lose them, but it's important to remember that anything can go wrong in limited overs cricket. It's how you react to these mini-crises that determines your calibre. You're never really out of a one-day match: a couple of quick wickets changes the situation within a few minutes, or some successful slogging sets you back in the field when you thought you were cruising. That's why it's exciting and so draining. A tense limited overs match takes a lot out of you mentally and physically and they can be particularly gruelling abroad when you have to play a couple back-to-back in the heat, with travelling thrown in.

It would be wrong to be too purist about one-day cricket. Success in these games can easily lead to better performances in the longer matches. You can't do much more than win a cricket match in impressive fashion and winning becomes habit-forming if your players gain confidence from those successes. After our débâcle in Australia, I was greatly encouraged to win all three Texaco Trophy matches against the West Indies at the start of the 1991 summer. We won the three games in contrasting ways and I was especially pleased with the gritty way that Richard Illingworth and Mike Atherton battled through to a one-wicket victory at Edgbaston. The enthusiasm and desire to win bubbled through during those few days in May and stood us in good stead when the more relevant stuff started at Leeds a fortnight later.

Our achievement in getting to the Nehru Cup semi-final in 1989 may have been largely ignored back home, but the effort and teamwork we showed out in India stayed with us for most of the Test series in the West Indies a few months later. We caught them cold in Jamaica and nearly did it again in Trinidad and there was an element of Caribbean complacency there, because they hadn't realized how much value we had got from the Nehru Cup. There is no doubt in my mind that Australia's resurgence up the international ladder dates from the day they won the World Cup in 1987. Allan Border took heart from that win, realized he was at last on the right lines after many disappointments and stuck largely with those players that brought him the trophy. Confidence comes from all areas of cricket and when it's flowing, you are automatically a better team.

The one-day game is now almost unrecognizable from the original version that saw the light of day in England in 1963. Now batsmen take what appear to be outrageous risks, fielders slide along boundary lines and the whole thing is pumped up. The approach to batting is now much more scientific compared to those days in the sixties when the likes of Tom Graveney, Ted Dexter and Colin Cowdrey played the same way as they did in the longer forms of cricket. It's now clear to me that although it's advantageous to score boundaries in one-day cricket, it's more important to score off as many balls as possible. The bowlers at county level are difficult to score off when they're on a tight line, with the field properly positioned, so you have to try to grab singles by just dropping the ball in front of you and running. The odd bad ball will eventually come along and you'll look to put that one away, but if you are scoring singles off the good deliveries, the innings won't lose its momentum. It's not all about hitting the ball into the crowd and bowlers get really annoyed when the strike is rotated. You get a psychological boost from getting away with a daring single, it's almost as enjoyable as hitting a four. The bowler thinks he's got through you as the ball nips back, you get a glove or a bit of pad on it, you call for the run, get in comfortably and the bowler is thoroughly fed up. There are countless safe singles to be taken at all levels of the game, yet so many are missed. I have improved my running between the wickets by at least fifty per cent and I was very happy to hear Viv Richards complaining about our work in that area during the Texaco Trophy match at Old Trafford on his last tour. He said to me, 'For someone so slow to move, you get down the wicket very soon,' in other words he thought I was close to sharp practice. I just laughed and said, 'I've improved, I'm quick now!' I was delighted that Viv started moaning at the umpires; he didn't seem to realize that if you are two or three yards down the pitch when the ball is delivered, and you remember to stretch and ground the bat at the other end, then you only have about eighteen yards to travel before you're safe. You have to accept that occasionally you'll be run out, but that only happened twice to me in all games in the 1991 season and I picked up a lot of runs for the risks involved. It helps if you have a regular opening partner and in recent years, Mike Atherton and John Stephenson have built up a good understanding with me; a prompt call from your partner is the key to sharp singles. This is an area of the one-day game that I have become rather dogmatic about because there is very little the fielding side can do if you run instantly on an early, clear call. The exceptions are if you hit it straight back to the bowler, or hard to a fielder close in.

Now that you have to include four fielders inside the 30 yard circle, there are many more gaps than there used to be in the days when captains would just line the boundary edge and restrict the batsmen to a couple of runs. As a result any target is feasible now in a limited overs match. If you get a four off the first ball and then five singles, that is a comfortable nine an over, without taking undue risks. Even at international level, I think ten an over is gettable, provided you have wickets in hand. I'm looking for a solid start – around sixty off the first fifteen overs with no wickets lost – then it's a case of accelerating as fast as possible, depending on how many overs are left. Keith Fletcher reckons that a chasing side should always look to reach the target with two or three overs to spare – don't budget for going right down to the wire, leave yourself a bit of slack. There's good sense in that because things can go wrong as the nerve ends get shredded towards the climax.

As opener/captain, it's easier for me in the run chase because I can set my stall out and hopefully have more time to launch the assault, without taking too many risks early on. It becomes difficult for me when I'm out and I have to watch the last desperate overs helplessly from the dressing-room. I mustn't get dragged into personal criticism at such times, when a player is struggling to get the ball away and some of the lads are saying, 'What's he playing at?' I realize that to keep the trust and respect of my players I mustn't get sucked into back-stabbing so I'll seethe inwardly, say something like 'He's doing his best' and remember that you just can't switch on timing, inspiration and luck like a light switch. All sorts of things can go wrong – like the opener who bats through the first half of the innings for forty, then gets out a few overs later for fifty, instead of going on to a hundred and anchoring the innings. That is a waste of all that consolidation.

I've never sent out a message to someone to 'get on with it or get out' but the guy who is stuck and doesn't get out is a worry. You're dependent on the batter giving his par performance, to ensure that not too much is left to your later batsmen. If you don't keep the score moving and it's climbed to eight an over for the last ten, it can be a very tall order if you then lose a couple of quick wickets. From the tail-enders you can only really expect a quick fifteen, rather than fifty spread over a number of overs. Mike Brearley and Geoffrey Boycott left the later batsmen with too much to do in the 1979 World Cup Final when they played well to put together a century opening stand, but they were too similar in styles and the West Indies were happy to let them accumulate. With Wayne Larkins coming in at number seven, we had a lot of powerful batting available, but when I walked in at number four, the asking rate was up to seven an over. In those pre-circle days the field was scattered, and against the quality of the West Indies bowlers, there were very few loose deliveries, so singles were about the only runs we could pick up. In the end that big opening stand was our undoing, because it took too long – there were only twenty-two overs left when Brearley was out.

In general, I've stuck to our original batting order in a run chase because I feel our best batters represent our best chance. Now and then I'll put Neil Foster in early for a slog for Essex – he has a good eye and times the ball well – but you have to instill confidence in your main batsmen that they can do the job. I was on the receiving end of a spectacular slog at Cuttack in 1989 when India promoted Chetan Sharma to number four in a Nehru Cup match. You rarely see a man chance his arm like that and get away with it for so long and we didn't bowl badly – but Chetan got a hundred that was lucky but great for his side. I tried everything, we all had a bowl, but he kept whacking the ball out of the ground. I knew then how Kim Hughes must have felt when Ian Botham took the Australians apart at Leeds; that day, I was sure Botham would hit one up in the air and get out for about sixty, but his luck held and he made 149 not out.

In the field, the captain *must* keep calm under pressure. The tension gets to everybody. Kapil Dev had the winning of the World Cup semi-final against us in Bombay right there in the palm of his hand but he hoisted Eddie Hemmings to the deep square leg boundary just after Gatting had positioned himself there. Bad cricket, the pressure got to Kapil when all he had to do was knock the ball around to win it. The captain has to get as many people as he can into the right positions as the game draws to a climax – that's why Gatting was right to go out on the boundary at Bombay, because he has such a safe pair of hands. If Devon Malcolm has to run from one end of the field to the other in between overs, he will have to do so because that means I want one of my best catchers at long-off. The players are under pressure when the ball goes high in the air because they are expected to catch it – they do it all the time in fielding practice, don't they? In the Refuge Cup Final of 1989, Franklyn Stephenson hit one miles up in the air, it had snow on it as it came down to me at mid-wicket. I didn't have to move, but I didn't really fancy it: I was right, it went straight through my hands and hit me on the head. It looked comical but it was an example of how an experienced player can just blow it in the pressure of the moment. It's so easy to lose your bearings and end up diving for the ball after you've steadied yourself for the catch. Somehow that seems to happen more in a one-day game when the adrenalin is flowing.

It's astonishing that so many limited overs matches come down to a couple of runs needed off the last ball, almost as if the human failings of the players have stage-managed the finale. The handful of runs you have missed becomes crucial; so do those fielding errors that gave away a couple of overthrows. If they need a run a ball in the final over, I'll get as many fielders in as I can to stop the single – deep gully, short extra cover and mid-wicket a couple of yards closer in than usual. Third man will be in on the edge of the circle, but they'll get one to him. You just can't afford to give them singles because one bad ball that disappears means they're close to ten that over. A couple of scoreless deliveries gets the batters fretting. In the last over, I shall ask my bowler where he plans to aim the ball. If it's going to be a yorker or slower ball, then long-on and long-off will be right back in case the batsman connects with it. Mid-wicket will be closer in case he just manages to get a bat on it, squeezes it out and looks for a single. If it's to be bowled on the legs, fine leg will be pushed back, because there's a chance of an inside edge. For a good length ball, mid-on and mid-off will both be up and third man and fine leg back in the event of a nick towards the boundary. Third man goes finer near the end because edges tend to go there, especially off a quickish bowler like Neil Foster. It's all about covering yourself and trying to stop the gaps being exploited and the singles stolen. An experienced, reliable bowler in this situation is a godsend.

I suppose the last over in the Benson and Hedges Final of 1989 just about sums up the classic dilemma in a one-day game. Nottinghamshire needed nine to beat us, with wickets in hand. It really was a toss-up, one of those situations when the fielding side thinks, 'How are we going to stop them getting nine?' and the batters say, 'This is going to be tough.' One boundary off any of those six balls would give the cup to Nottinghamshire, but my consolation was that the final over was to be bowled by John Lever, the perfect man for the moment. His first five deliveries were ideal and they could only get a single off each one. That left four needed to win, with Eddie Hemmings to face. John and I must have talked about the options for that last ball for at least two minutes, with the crowd roaring at us to get a move on, but I needed to be sure my bowler was happy with what we decided. Usually Eddie Hemmings plays 'inside out', backing away to leg and hitting through the offside, and he likes to guide it down to third man, but a few overs earlier, he had surprised me by whacking a couple over mid-wicket, not his usual scoring area. So we decided to post a deep mid-wicket just in case, because John had decided to bowl a yorker onto Eddie's pads and he might have nudged it through legside. We brought up Brian Hardie from deep cover to backward point on the edge, giving us four on the offside, along with extra cover in the circle, and long-off and third man. On legside we had long-on, deep mid-wicket, deep backward square leg and in the circle, myself at mid-wicket and short fine leg. John bowled the yorker on the leg-stump, Eddie was ready for it, he got a thickish edge to send it square on the offside. Brian Hardie gave chase from backward point but it rolled away and Nottinghamshire had won. Fair play to Eddie – he had set himself for that shot because he knew we had nobody in that area on the boundary. With his experience, he also worked out that John would try for the leg-stump yorker. If it hadn't been for Eddie's earlier shots over mid-wicket, I would have put a man on the square offside boundary, or put long-on or long-off out there, but then there was a risk of Eddie driving the attempted yorker down the ground to a vacant boundary.

I felt so sorry for John on his last appearance at a Lord's Final because he had bowled magnificently. For days afterwards, I agonized about what I could have done. I think it was right to have Brian Hardie in that backward point position, because although not quick, he's a good diver and stopper of the ball and the boundary is the place for the younger ones near the end of a one-day innings. If I'd taken a man over from the legside, that would have left gaps and it's a shortish boundary on that Tavern side of the ground. Maybe a bouncer might have been a better idea for that last ball, but Lord's isn't a very big ground and there's always the chance of a top-edged hook. A bouncer might have surprised Eddie, especially if we had put only two men out at fine leg and backward square leg, as from that field he wouldn't have expected the short ball. We could have brought up either long-on or long-off and put square cover back on the ropes to let him think we were expecting the ball to be played through the offside. Bluff and double bluff! There was also the danger of the bouncer being called a wide and Eddie getting an extra ball and another run. All this talk about one ball: John Lever bowled the right delivery and yet we still lost. Lord's finals are great occasions when you win.

Four years earlier, the same two teams played out another desperate finish at Lord's, in the NatWest Final. This time it was Keith Fletcher's responsibility to keep the side calm as Derek Randall looked like pulling off an astonishing win. Nottinghamshire had needed thirty-seven off the last three overs and eighteen off the final one, but when Randall took sixteen off the first five balls of Derek Pringle's over, it looked all over. I was down at deep square leg, wondering what Derek was bowling: I found out later he was spearing it in on leg-stump and Randall was making room for himself to smash it through the offside with some brilliant improvisations. Keith Fletcher didn't alter his field once in that final over and he looked so calm as Pringle ran in to bowl the last ball. Randall followed a ball going down legside and scooped it to short mid-wicket and we had won by a single run. It took a lot of nerve for Fletcher to stand his ground and stick to the field he had established at the start of the over before Randall started to threaten. He was that sort of captain.

In those days our Essex bowlers used to bowl the last over or so right up into the blockhole and by and large that was the best method when the slog was on, but now I think more variety is needed. You have to keep the batsman guessing, so the pace and length should be varied. The good length ball, the blockhole ball, the slower one – the bouncer. I recall Derek Pringle bowling a bouncer at Joel Garner in a tight finish and he got away with it. It was a good piece of thinking and if you can surprise the batsman when you're both under pressure, you deserve to come out on top. I like to see such imagination in my bowlers, but I get very uptight when they bowl no-balls, especially in limited overs games, because that is simply a waste. I have some lively discussions with the bowlers about their inability to land the ball of their foot behind a line. I'm sympathetic to 'effort' bowlers like Devon Malcolm and David Lawrence, but why do bowlers feel the need to go that extra six inches when the ball is to be delivered to a point twenty yards away? Does that extra few inches make that big a difference? If you practise hard to get it right, why slip back into bad habits? John Lever only bowled two no-balls in his entire career and Ian Botham has hardly ever bowled one in all his overs. It's slapdash and unprofessional in my view and in limited overs games, it gives an advantage to the opposition. If I were Viv Richards, I'd have been furious at the amount of no balls the West Indies sent down in the Texaco series of 1991. At Edgbaston, when we won a low-scoring game by one wicket, extras made up a quarter of our score. Hard work in the nets, coming in off the full run, should cure the problem, but I don't expect many fast bowlers I know to agree with me.

Captaining slow bowlers in a one-day game is very challenging. The knack is to get them on at the right time, and unless the conditions favour the seamer, keep them on for one long spell. One-day cricket doesn't help the art of bowling batsmen out with flight and spin, you're looking for containment, a bit of variation but above all, accuracy. The last *flight* bowler to play consistently in one-day cricket was Vic Marks, although I think Phil Tufnell will be very successful once he plays regularly and works out just how he wants to bowl.

It's very difficult for the spinner to switch from one mode to the other, from trying to get players out in the championship to containment in the one-dayers. He has to switch from off-stump line to middle and leg, and not think about giving it any air. In these circumstances it's hardly surprising that you can lose the knack of being a *spinning* spinner, you just run up and fire it in. Most of the successful one-day spinners learned their trade a long while ago and they were lucky enough to work alongside spin bowlers on the county staff who had nurtured their skills when there wasn't so much one-day cricket. That was certainly the case with John Emburey, the best of the modern spinners in the one-day game; he picked up an immense amount at Middlesex from Fred Titmus. Today, it's the one precious commodity in the game that's in short supply and the younger ones just aren't pushing the older spinners. Apart from Tufnell, the best are all nearing or over forty.

I'm sure the demands of the one-day game are responsible for the decline in spin bowling quality, because too often the spin bowler is brought on at the wrong time, and can't settle against batsmen who are determined to smash him out of the ground before the seamers come back. This is where John Emburey is so good. He can take the onslaught, keep bowling *his* way and still come back later on, with confidence still high. He has such a good control of line and length that batsmen in one-day cricket tend just to 'milk' him, rather than try to get after him. Embers is that rarity, a spinner who bowls in the closing overs and with his yorkers, the occasional quicker one and immaculate control, he is a great challenge. I thought of his self-control often on our tour to the West Indies in 1990 when Keith Medlycott struggled against punishment. Keith has talent as a left-arm spinner, but every time he was hit for six in our practice games or in the serious matches, he showed his disappointment, kicking at his footholds and looking the picture of despair. I had to tell him that he shouldn't let the batsman know he was so disappointed, because then he has the bowler over a barrel. So a spinner needs sympathetic handling in a limited overs match. Don't be too dictatorial about field settings, let him have his way, give him confidence. With Essex, I like John Childs and Peter Such to have a big say in setting their own fields, because they know where they're looking to bowl. Such, in particular, has thrived on one-day cricket. He was capped by Essex in 1991, largely on the strength of his one-day performances and you could see what it did for his confidence, not only with the ball but in the field, an area where he has been weak for most of his county career.

The spinner often represents one of the recurring one-day dilemmas: whether to give him that extra over. Although a captain likes to stick with a spinner for his allotted overs once he starts his spell, it's important not to be too rigid. If you give him another over when he's being punished and the first ball goes for six, then you are starting to have a problem or two. You want to show confidence in your bowler but if the batsmen keep getting off to a flier at the start of every over, it's difficult to claw it back. It's handy then if you have a sixth bowler at your disposal and can fiddle a few overs out of him while waiting for the storm to blow over. Sometimes it's a case of bowling someone all the way through when you would normally use him at the end. You just have to take a chance on one of the lesser bowlers at the death.

At Edgbaston in 1991, I took a chance against the 1991 West Indians and didn't use all of Derek Pringle's overs. I bowled out my opening bowlers (Chris Lewis and Phillip DeFreitas) from one end and kept myself and Richard Illingworth going from the other. I decided to keep them quiet instead of taking a risk at bowling them out for 140 when they were 121 for 8. Illingworth bowled tightly at the end and they only got 173 for 8 in their 55 overs but it's just as well that Illingworth helped to shepherd us to that narrow win – otherwise I would have had some deserved stick for not trusting my two opening bowlers to wrap up the tail in harness and for leaving the reliable Pringle four overs short.

So many captaincy decisions can go wrong within a couple of deliveries out there in the frazzled atmosphere of a one-day game. When Mike Gatting kept me on for one more over in the 1987 World Cup Final, it made sense. I had gone for around twenty in my seven overs and the Australians were getting bogged down. When Craig McDermott was sent in early to up the tempo I said to Gatt, 'Do you still want me to stay on?' and he said yes. I decided to bowl a fullish length to McDermott, but he slogged me around the park. I went for twenty, the Aussie gamble succeeded, Allan Border carried on the good work and they ended up with a formidable total that eventually proved too much for us. Would another bowler have been hit so successfully? Who can say – it was a difficult decision either way and the captain takes the flak if it goes wrong.

I think Kapil Dev might have been a little more flexible in his tactics on the day I scored one of the most satisfying hundreds of my career. It was at Bombay in the World Cup semi-final of 1987 and I went out to bat with a preordained plan that worked like a dream. Having looked closely at the pitch the day before and noticed it was rather worn, I knew that India would be banking on their two left-arm spinners, Maninder Singh and Ravi Shastri to do the damage. It would be a slow wicket, so I didn't fancy playing the front-foot drive in case the ball stopped on me and I decided not to go down the pitch to them, because there was a real chance of the ball turning away from the bat and getting me caught behind or stumped. The way to play them was with the sweep shot, sweeping at the length not the line; I'd put my left foot just outside the off-stump, so in theory I wouldn't be out lbw in case the ball straightened a lot. It worked perfectly and it was all the more satisfying for the fact that I had practised the lap shot in the nets the day before, with some locals bowling slow left-arm at me. Mike Gatting helped me add over a hundred in quick time, adopting the same method, and it took a long time for the penny to drop with Kapil Dev. Eventually – when I was past my fifty – he took one out of the offside cordon of five and put one in at short fine leg, but by then we were well set. I swept four out of every six balls an over, and the fielder at deep cover point touched one ball throughout my innings. I was delighted that their captain didn't make any real effort to combat my sweep shot and even more pleased he didn't bring on a seamer, just to get me playing differently. In any game of cricket, the fielding captain should try not to let things drift, that listlessness soon spreads to the fielders.

The one-day game has certainly accelerated a few retirements in recent years. If it weren't for the fielding demands of this type of cricket, the likes of Geoffrey Boycott and Dennis Amiss could still be playing. I struggle now with the day-to-day demands of fielding and it's a problem where to place fielders like me in a one-day match. I'm still a fair catcher, and can dive and stop a ball, so I tend to find myself at short mid-wicket. Another place for a safe catcher who isn't all that mobile is mid-off or mid-on. Fine leg and third man are other options, provided the batsman doesn't keep taking you on; then it can be a touch embarrassing. Towards the end of the innings, I put my whippets out in the deep, at deep cover or deep backward square leg, where their task is to turn possible twos into ones and possibly pick up a run-out. Deep gully is a very important position. It's a catching position when the seamers are on, because the ball flies through there off thick edges and genuine cuts. The fielder needs good hands, mobility and the agility to cut off that little dab on the offside, where the batsman looks for a run. Early on, it's a major run-out position. It's also a very hectic place to field, with a lot of leaping around and stopping to be done. Some sides tend to put their slow fielders in there because they're covered by third man and deep cover if it goes past them on either side, but I don't agree with that. At Essex we see it as a wicket-taking area and we put Nasser Hussain in there because he's our best fielder close to the wicket. Chris Lewis is also very good there for England.

Although the one-day game has spawned the 'bits and pieces' cricketer, the useful player not really good enough as a specialist batsman or bowler, I think the best players in this type of cricket are the best players in all forms of the game. In his heyday, Viv Richards was a truly magnificent player, able to win you a one-day game if he stayed in long enough. I'll never forget the way he dealt with the last ball of the West Indian innings in the World Cup Final of 1979. He was already well past his hundred and he was looking for something spectacular to close on as Mike Hendrick bowled him a low full toss just outside the off-stump, a good ball in the circumstances. Viv deposited it over the square leg boundary for six!

Desmond Haynes has been less spectacular but just as valuable for the West Indies in one-day games, clocking up the centuries and holding the innings together like a responsible opener. I rate Derek Pringle highly in these types of games. He bowls intelligently and bravely, with variety, and he is particularly effective with the bat. He's capable of hitting the ball a long way, he can also manipulate it around to find the gaps and for a big fellow, he runs well between the wickets. They tend to bowl straighter in this country in the one-dayers, and Derek's forte is that flick off his legs. He doesn't panic in a tight situation, keeps his eye on the scoreboard and is a very cool character.

Of all the players to choose from, I would pick Allan Lamb as the best one-day player of my time. He paces his approach so well, he never seems to be worried by an asking rate that seems impossible at times. He rarely gives it away or plays a rash shot, but carries on batting properly, picking up the singles and stroking, rather than slogging the boundaries. There is a big danger of hitting across the line towards the end when the pressure is on – not with Lamby. At Gujranwala in the 1987 World Cup, he played an astonishing innings in the most trying conditions I have ever experienced. The heat and humidity were almost unbearable but he guided us to victory against the West Indies, when we needed thirty-five off the last three overs and thirteen off the last. He never flapped, accumulated calmly and when the crunch came, he accelerated. That's the true test of a top one-day batsman – when he has to do it to win the game, as distinct from playing well when you bat first. With Lamby, ten an over is perfectly possible because of his calmness under pressure and his ability to bat properly, whatever the tension surrounding him.

It can be hard to come back from the strains of a Test Match to an important one-day game for your county the day after, but for me the special demands of limited overs cricket bring their own appeal. Scoring a hundred for Essex gives me as much pleasure as getting one for England and I find that if you're sufficiently motivated, you look forward to being on the ground at 8.30, ready for another hair-raising day on the limited overs merry-go-round. Any county can win a one-day trophy because it's essentially a simplistic exercise, where keeping one's cool is sometimes more meaningful than applying superior ability. A run of four or five good games can bring you a limited overs trophy, whereas in the longer brands of cricket, consistency over a long period is more relevant. Experience counts, because you're looking to repeat the same thing ball after ball; that's why bowlers like Paul Pridgeon, Jack Simmons, Ian Botham and John Lever have been so successful in recent years. Limited overs cricket is just that – limited. But I find it fun and stimulating, even though I'm sure its pressures are responsible for my hair loss!

6
Captaincy on tour

The captain's area of responsibility lasts for a long time when on tour. If things start to go wrong – results, form, morale, discipline – the downward spiral can be swift and decisive. The fortunes of the touring party are then cast in stone, no matter how much effort goes into retrieving them. I know this to my cost from the tour to Australia and New Zealand in 1990–91, a stark contrast to our trip to the West Indies a year earlier. The failure of a tour is the captain's failure because he has chosen the players, worked on the strategy and tried to foster team spirit. If he can't get the players pulling all the way *with* him that's his fault. That is why I was baffled why so many people Down Under and back in Britain sympathized with me over our performances in Australia. I didn't deserve any sympathy. The buck stopped with me and my good batting form when I recovered from injury was an irrelevance.

Somehow it didn't feel *right* before, or at any stage of that tour. Between the end of a long domestic season and our departure in October, 1990 we only had four days together at Lilleshall. The guys looked jaded and the commitment didn't seem to be there. The practice was of negligible value because we'd just stopped playing but the atmosphere was more downbeat than I would have liked. I put it down to a long, hard year of international cricket, starting in January in the West Indies, and hoped that we'd be galvanized when we got out to Australia. All year, we had performed well internationally, beating India and New Zealand at home and competing hard in the West Indies. I was looking for revenge for that 4–0 thrashing by Australia and was convinced that our better preparation and attitude would run them close this time. Yet at times we were as embarrassing as we had been in 1989. Although we had some good sessions in the series, we buckled at the vital times and the greater competitiveness and self-discipline of the Australians won the day. Before each day's play they *looked* impressive in their training routines and their established players were desperately keen to hang onto their places in the side. They were hungrier than us, it seemed to mean more to them to perform to their utmost.

On that basis, I have to carry the can as captain. My powers of motivation were clearly not powerful enough, even though we had team meeting after team meeting, as I tried to find the spark to ignite the lads. Some of them felt I was pushing them too hard in practice, that they weren't getting enough time off to rest. My attitude then was that we were proving to be so poor at the basics that we *had* to keep working and practising, in the hope that our grasp of the necessary disciplines would return. It was the worst fielding side I had played in throughout my first-class career, yet they were looking for days off, instead of trying to improve. Maybe we were wrong to push them so hard, but when the Australians came to England in 1989, they had their first cricket-free day *after* winning the Ashes at the start of August. Their wives even had to stay in separate hotels! That was a bit extreme to me, but at least it showed that they were in England to work, to represent their country and try everything to do them proud. Some of my players didn't seem too perturbed at losing and it was the *way* we were losing that annoyed me so much.

Excuses were on hand, but I wouldn't offer them. Injuries to myself, Allan Lamb, Angus Fraser and David Gower were a setback but the quality of a team comes when they overcome such problems. It's funny how the successful teams seem to be lucky – but could it be that they make their own luck? When we beat Australia 5–1 in 1978–79, that was a false margin, we weren't four Tests better than them; but we were a happy, professional squad of players and Mike Brearley out-captained his opposite number, Graham Yallop. So our débâcle was fundamentally my fault. We couldn't complain too much about the itinerary, because the Aussie players also had to do it. When we flew from Adelaide to Perth for the last Test, landing at one o'clock in the morning, the Aussie players were on the same plane as us – and a few hours later, they were practising hard on the hottest Perth day on record. This after winning the series. I couldn't inspire that same pride in performance from all of my players. In my opinion they didn't want it badly enough and at the end of the tour, I said publicly that each player had to look at his own performance and ask: was he satisfied with it? The answers the individual came up with would determine whether he had an England future.

I also pondered whether I should carry on as England captain. I was aware that I had made tactical mistakes – particularly not bowling Devon Malcolm earlier on the last day of the Sydney Test – and I could at last see that perhaps I had been a little dogmatic about extra practice, but I felt I still had something to offer in the job and I still considered it an honour to captain England. I would put Australia down to experience and think very hard in future about the character of every player picked for England under my captaincy.

A year earlier, it seemed as if we had got most things right for the West Indies tour in terms of preparation and stomach for the fight ahead. The two things were inter-connected in my view. We had three months to prepare ourselves for the Caribbean and when we finally gathered at Lilleshall before the tour, the atmosphere was exactly right. Everybody had worked hard at their fitness, they were all thinking deeply about their techniques and it seemed that we would not be lacking in character when the fast bowlers started to ping it round our ears or when Viv Richards started to take our bowlers apart. Gradually I felt our play would improve in all aspects and the motto 'If you fail to prepare, prepare to fail' rang very true. At our press conference before we left Lilleshall, I was asked by a BBC television reporter, 'If you fail in the West Indies, will all this sort of thing be dropped next time?', a question which showed a complete lack of knowledge of the point of the exercise.

It was our professional preparation that contributed greatly to winning the Jamaica Test and the lack of it which hampered us on the Australian tour. It's much more beneficial if the players can have a month off after a season's cricket, then build up for a tour two months away. I prefer going from a winter tour more or less straight into an English season and then having a fair amount of time off in the autumn before gearing up for a January departure with England. That way you get time to recharge your batteries – mentally and physically – in the autumn. The alternative is a month off before an October departure, then another month off before returning to your county in the spring and I don't think that gives you enough time to rest properly. A measured build-up before a tour gives the players time to get to know each other, it builds up morale, gives them time to work on technique, and it instills a common purpose.

As I found to my cost on the Australian trip, picking a tour party can be an exercise that comes back to haunt you. Sometimes your hunches don't work out. At Northampton in September, 1990 I told Wayne Larkins I wanted him for Australia even though he hadn't made many runs that summer, because he had done pretty well for me the previous tour. 'Don't let me down,' I told him, yet it didn't work out. These things happen. If you get runs or wickets in the last month of the season, it's uncanny how that seems to influence the selectors. It shouldn't because good figures in May ought to be just as relevant and it's not as if impressive form in September in England is going to be transported to Adelaide in November. Yet human nature seems to determine that a player finishing a season flushed with success has at least a good chance of tour selection if he's good enough.

Personal success in the NatWest Final in September has had a disproportionate effect on a player's prospects of touring that winter – one thinks of Roland Butcher in 1980, Geoff Cook in 1981, Chris Cowdrey in 1984, all good players but grateful for the nudge. Yet a good performance in a one-day game is hardly the best advertisement for a guy's qualities when the pressure is on thousands of miles away a few months later. When Phillip DeFreitas bowled out Northants in the 1990 Final, we didn't take that into account when picking the side for Australia. It was a green wicket, helpful to the seamer early on, and an England bowler like DeFreitas ought to have capitalized on the favourable conditions. So he wasn't in the original tour party. I think the 'horses for courses' policy is more meaningful than being guided by a one-day final. This is particularly applicable for tours to the Indian sub-continent and the Caribbean. Good players of fast bowling and doughty fighters like Peter Willey and David Smith have been taken to the West Indies, yet managed only one other senior tour elsewhere between them.

David Steele scored a hundred against the West Indies in the 1976 series yet wasn't picked for the winter tour to India because it was felt he didn't play the spinners all that well. The same thing happened to Chris Broad in 1984 – yet he had the satisfaction of playing very well against Abdul Qadir in Pakistan three years later. Yet Tim Robinson, his opening partner at Nottingham, got the India trip in 1984 because he was the better player of spinners at the time – and he did well out there.

In England, our selection committee gets around the country to get an overall view of who's performing consistently and find out about their characters and ambitions. They are encouraged to get away from predetermined opinions on a player, in search of that special quality: has he got the drive to succeed when the pressure is really on? In September, 1991 all the observers were asked by Micky Stewart to write down who they thought should go to the World Cup and the

New Zealand Test series, and the 'A' tour to the Caribbean. Two squads of players with seemingly endless scope for dispute. The six observers, all good judges of a player, all covering different parts of the country, came up with ninety-nine per cent of the same names. The 'A' tour is a breeding ground for our younger players – not a second team for England – so it's not as if the observers simply went for the understudies to the seniors. They plumped to send those to the Caribbean we wanted to know more about. And we all came up with the same players. Now that either indicates that we are all terribly narrow-minded and unimaginative or that there isn't perhaps the depth in quality you might expect from a pool of seventeen counties, with input from overseas cricketers on the decline.

In my experience, choosing a tour party of sixteen comes down to discussion about two or three places, once you have settled on your automatic selections. For the World Cup in 1992, we wanted Ian Botham in cricketing terms and the only discussion before the selection meeting concerned his other commitments. Alec Stewart's success against the West Indies and Sri Lanka solved the problem of the second wicket-keeper. David Gower was quickly ruled out because of his poor form all season, his known antipathy to one-day cricket and also because I felt happier at that time without him in the squad. Usually at least one young player is taken on tour for the experience, bringing them along quietly, helping them to bed down away from the home glare of publicity and hype. Yet the youngster is not there for the ride, he is one of the sixteen and I expect them all to be competing for places. Nasser Hussain got into the Test side in the West Indies, Chris Lewis would have been close had he not gone home through injury and Martin Bicknell just missed out in Australia. Towards the end of the tour, he would have played in a Test or two if he hadn't been injured. If they're good enough, their tender years ought not to matter.

Newcomers on tour also bring a social advantage – they have to entertain the old hands at the initiation party! Every new tourist has to put on a show in the team room early on in the tour; it can take the form of a sketch, a song or a monologue and it invariably features sideswipes at the management. On my first England tour, John Emburey, Clive Radley, David Gower and I had the duty and Gower was excellent at coining the appropriately disrespectful phrases. It's all harmless fun, designed to relax the newcomers and make them realize they're with a supportive group of colleagues.

The tour captain must get the party he wants because he is responsible for the cricket performances over the next few months. He will be highly praised if the players come back with enhanced reputations (look at Mike Gatting and the OBE award soon after Australia in 1987) and he will be blamed when the tour goes wrong (Mike Gatting again in Pakistan and Australasia in 1987–88). So he must be sure in his own mind about who's going with him. When I sat in on my first tour selection meeting as England captain – for the abortive trip to India in 1988 – I got what I wanted, even though new to the job. The other selectors were leaning towards Kim Barnett as vice-captain, but with respect to Kim, I wanted him to get to grips with Test cricket first, rather than have to worry about extra responsibilities.

It would have been an unfair burden on someone who had just got into the England team, irrespective of the impressive way he had been captaining Derbyshire and the understandable desire of the selectors to look towards the England captaincy in the future. I wanted John Emburey as my vice-captain, not because he's my best friend in the game, but because of his experience of India and his acute cricket brain and because he was sure to play in all the Tests. I won the day over that one. The fourth pace bowler was the other difficult decision. We were only taking four because three spinners were essential for India and Neil Foster and Graham Dilley were two certainties. We opted for David Lawrence, because his extra pace might be a variation and we thought Phil Newport's ability to swing the ball would be important in India. Gladstone Small and Derek Pringle were the unlucky ones to miss out – despite Gladstone playing in a one-day international a week earlier and Pringle being our most consistent bowler in the home series against the West Indies. It was hard on them, but there *are* only sixteen places available and the captain has to make unsentimental, practical decisions that he believes will serve him well. Every England player of my time knows what it's like to miss out on an England tour that he felt he ought to have been on.

The early weeks on tour are very important in setting the tone of the operation, building on team spirit and ensuring that the senior players are *seen* to set the right example to the younger ones. That worked in the West Indies but not in Australia, where our early form against the State sides was awful and things never really improved, apart from a good session now and then in the Tests. Some of our players seemed to think they could coast during the minor games and turn on the tap when it really mattered but the game isn't like that anymore. In my early days in Test cricket, you *could* ease yourself up a gear as the tour progressed but now I believe more commitment and dedication are needed. The older you get, the more difficult it is to hang onto form, unless you're prepared to work at it. That's why I was so disappointed with David Gower in Australia, because he didn't set the right example as a highly-respected, senior player. It wasn't enough to play well in the Tests, he had to do more off the field: younger players lacking his wonderful natural ability needed a more dedicated example from him.

Certainly it's more difficult to keep the players together as a tight, disciplined outfit when you tour Australia. There are many social distractions, the locals are generous, and there are so many English friends also out there on holiday that it's easy for an England cricketer to take his eye off the ball and forget he's out there doing his job. In that sense it's easier to keep team spirit up when you tour the Indian sub-continent; you stick together out there, because the culture is different and that togetherness is often apparent when you're out there on the field. It's getting like that in the Caribbean now and so we were an intimate group out there in 1990 for a long time. We were the underdogs, the only ones to fancy our chances and that suited us fine.

Early on, we had two meetings that were particularly valuable. My vice-captain Allan Lamb and I sat down over dinner and talked to the bowlers one evening and then our batters soon afterwards. The idea was to hammer home the disciplines needed to give us a chance. The bowlers *had* to stick to a controlled line just outside off-stump, to chip away at the West Indies' batsmen, giving them nothing loose. Devon Malcolm would be our wild card and we hoped his extra pace would profit from any uneven bounce. If possible we should try to bowl a 'dot' ball every time or get a wicket! To the batters we emphasized the need to hang in there, to take the blows to the body, to realize that there wouldn't be very much loose stuff to hit. It would be a war of attrition and they would be ruthless. We also underlined their knack of blasting a hole through the batting when you thought things were going pretty well; they have always taken wickets in bunches over the past few years and their fast bowlers are inspirational when they sense the hutch might be open. For both bowlers and batsmen, it was going to be a very stern test and these two meetings served to get them thinking in detail about what lay ahead and we all felt better for exchanging our thoughts around the dinner table.

The constructive feedback we got from those two meetings convinced me that we would surprise the West Indies and we certainly caught them cold in the early part of the Test series. By the time we got to Jamaica, we were slightly concerned about Angus Fraser; he looked a yard slower than usual and his rhythm and timing weren't right. The

'The huddle' in operation during the Jamaica Test of 1990. We tried it in India a few months earlier and it proved to be a good way of concentrating the team's mind just before play started

The Jamaica Test of 1990 and as the rest of the England team enjoy the fall of another West Indian wicket, David Capel and I are thinking about the strategy for the incoming batsman

One of the sixes in my innings of 333 against India at Lord's in 1990

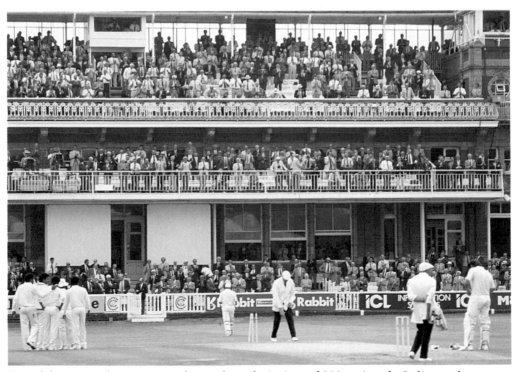

One of the outstanding memories for me from the innings of 333 against the Indians – the members at Lord's rise to greet me back to the pavilion when I was finally dismissed

There are times when the captain *has* to blow his top on the field. This was one of them for me – at Bowral on our disappointing England tour to Australia in 1990/91

Leading from the front in the run chase during the Adelaide Test of 1991

With Devon Malcolm in 1990. I'm a great believer in encouraging bowlers to let them know I'm on their wavelength

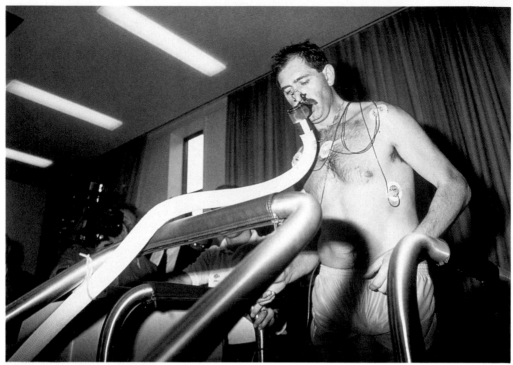

What the modern Test cricketer has to go through to get fit for a tour – Lilleshall in 1990, before we went to the West Indies. My lungpower passed the test!

Essex have won the 1991 county championship after two successive near-misses, and I'm relishing the moment that sets the seal on a memorable summer for me

Viv Richards and I were keen that the 1991 series should be a happy one as well as memorable. It was both and the public seemed to agree

At my age you should never lose a chance to stretch those hamstrings!

Four more runs for me during my most important innings for England – that 154 not out against the West Indies at Leeds in 1991

Christchurch, 1992, and Phil Tufnell has bowled us to a great Test win over New Zealand. I think you could say I was pleased with him!

game against Jamaica was grinding out to be a boring draw and we could have called the match off early, but I wanted Gus to have another gallop to get him right. He bowled fourteen overs, looked much better for the work-out in match conditions and a few days later, took 5 for 28 on the first day of the Jamaica Test to set up our win. Gus had slipped the hand-brake just in time.

Injuries of course are a problem and they never seem to strike when the team is doing well. At one stage in the Australian tour David Gower, Allan Lamb and myself – the three senior batsmen – were far from fully fit and there was talk of me going home to recuperate from my hand injury. Yet I felt I'd be able to do something for the side if I stayed on even though I faced four weeks without being able to play. For the first time in my seventeen years as a professional cricketer, I had started to pick up injuries in 1990 and it was very frustrating for me. It was a novel experience to take a back seat while Allan Lamb took over team meetings, but it had to be done that way. The captain – whether acting or not – must be the dominant character and Allan would have lost the respect of the players if I had kept chipping in. He had been an excellent vice-captain to me in the West Indies and he deserved my full support, even though it was hard for me to have the role of backing up the things he'd say after he'd finished.

I don't think Allan felt ill at ease by my presence during my month of inactivity because I was at great pains not to interfere or contradict him in any way. In a sense I was non-playing vice-captain. On tour the role of the vice-captain is very important; he's there to advise, to spot things, to channel suggestions from other players through to the captain, and to pass on any complaints. One of the main advantages in the role is that you can be close to the decision-making, but have no ultimate responsibility: the buck still stops with the captain. But the conscientious deputy also puts himself in the position of the skipper and thinks how he would have done the job that day. They should be like-minded and have no difficulty in agreeing an overall approach to the cricket and the team that's been selected. He's not there as a rubber stamp, but you have problems if your views become diametrically opposed.

One of the best vice-captains of my time has been Bob Willis – he was of the sergeant-major stamp, a great trier for England who set a tremendous example, and was totally loyal to the captain. He wasn't afraid to hand out rollickings when necessary and I remember one in particular in Colombo, when we looked as if we might throw away the Test against Sri Lanka. A few harsh words from Bob at the interval soon got us back on the right track and I know his captain, Keith Fletcher, appreciated his intervention.

When things go wrong on tour, it's so easy to get things out of proportion. In 1986, I wanted to go home from the Caribbean because I felt I was being used as a political football. Lester Bird, the Deputy Prime Minister of Antigua was making inflammatory comments about me going to South Africa, even though there'd been an agreement that none of us would raise that subject again. I had kept my side of the bargain and now demanded the right of reply. The then secretary of the Test and County Cricket Board, Donald Carr, flew out to persuade me to bite the bullet, but it was only out of loyalty to David Gower, my captain, that I agreed to stay on and play in the Antigua Test. The incident brought out the stubborn side of my nature and if I'm being honest, it must have had an adverse effect on the rest of the team, as they tried to avoid the ignominy of another 5–0 series defeat. It brought me a reputation in some quarters of being miserable on tour and I can understand why.

We were all pretty miserable on the Indian tour of 1981–82 and I'm sure that feeling had a bearing on the decision of some of us to go to South Africa afterwards – some thought, 'If this is Test cricket, is it worth the hassle?' India had gone one up in the series in the first Test at Bombay and we weren't getting a grip on things. In these situations, every touring party wonders at some stage about the umpiring. Added to the turgid nature of the cricket – with the Indian spinners barely managing ten overs an hour as they slowed the game right down – it was hardly the best recipe for Test cricket, that Indian tour. We allowed ourselves to get sucked into the negative atmosphere and Keith Fletcher also slowed the game down when it suited him and I suppose on that basis we were wrong, but we're all only human and it was a very tiresome series.

We were also wrong to become embroiled in spectacular disputes about the umpires on the 1987 tour to Pakistan. The siege mentality settled on us early and the result was the most remarkable day I've known in cricket, when we all stood around for a day at Faisalabad, waiting to play. In the first Test at Lahore, we felt the Pakistanis had enjoyed some luck with umpiring decisions in our first innings and it all blew up when Chris Broad was given out at the start of the second innings, caught at the wicket off Iqbal Qasim. I was at the other end and there was certainly a noise of some sort as the ball beat the bat. Chris stood there and said, 'I didn't hit it, I'm not going,' and he started to exchange heated words with the close fielders. I came down the wicket and told him he had to go – and he still refused. Eventually I got him to see sense and off he went. Perhaps I should have stayed down my end, leaning on the bat handle and then we might all have been able to go home early! I suppose Chris Broad's Test career might have ended there and then if he had refused to budge, but our tour management gave him only a stern reprimand. I attended the appropriate meeting and spoke against disciplining Chris, which in retrospect was wrong of me. I feel we should have fined him – not only for the gravity of the offence but also to alert the rest of our tour party that that kind of dissent is simply not allowed, whatever the provocation. I've come round to that way of thinking since becoming England captain, although I don't blame Mike Gatting for thinking that Chris had been subjected to enough censure.

Yet the pot was still simmering when we got to Faisalabad and the scenes when Gatt and Shakoor Rana shouted at each other were very disturbing if you have cricket's best interests at heart. Gatt has been an excellent sportsman and never caused other umpires a moment's bother but the whole thing just mushroomed at Faisalabad and he was eventually out of control. It looked awful on television and although we mentioned the incident when we got back to the dressing-room, we had no inkling that events would move so swiftly. Shakoor Rana was wound up about his honour being questioned, a matter that they are very hot on over there, and soon we had a major incident on our hands, with the umpire refusing to stand until the England captain apologized. We all supported Gatt at our meeting and many players felt we shouldn't take the field under any circumstances. In the end I said to the young players, 'Do you realize what it means if you do that? You'll be breaking your tour contract and you could never play for England again.' Some of them hadn't thought it through and I said we should go ahead and play, after issuing a statement that we deplored what had happened and that we fully supported our captain. Gatt was under immense pressure and I felt desperately sorry for him.

If something like that had happened in England, a high-ranking official from the TCCB would have been in our dressing-room, telling us to get out there immediately, or our Test careers were over and to worry about any statements later. That has to be right: you can't play cricket without the umpires, no matter how incompetent they are, and it's the captain's job to stamp out dissent. I was worried in Pakistan about the way that cricket was heading. We couldn't say it was all their fault, because our captain had been seen jabbing his finger at an umpire, and in the process undermining his authority. There are good umpires everywhere – including Pakistan – and if you don't accept the official's decision, then you have anarchy. I don't recall England complaining officially about bad umpiring on our tour to Australia in 1978–79, even though Geoffrey Boycott felt hard done by on occasions and so did I. The difference between that tour and Pakistan in 1987 was that we were winning in Australia and could therefore take the umpiring decisions in our stride. Players mustn't just complain when things are going badly for them and it's a misconception for England cricketers to say that standards of umpiring are poor abroad. I accept that umpires are honest and do their best and I don't believe that the introduction of 'neutral' umpires will necessarily improve things, because I don't believe that home bias is a problem.

Discipline off the field can suddenly go down the tube if the captain isn't careful. Players have to turn up on time because if one doesn't the malaise spreads and you're forever waiting for people. Mike Brearley told the coach driver to go without me at Perth in 1979 and although I was only two minutes late coming down to the hotel foyer, he was right and I had to make my own way to the ground. When David Gower and John Morris hired a Tiger Moth and buzzed the ground where we were playing Queensland, many thought it a good wheeze and suggested the tour management over-reacted in fining them both a thousand pounds. David said he did it to raise morale, but a better way of doing that would have been to give a better example in cricketing terms to the younger players. We weren't playing well, I was struggling to keep the lid on discipline in other areas and David knew very well that it's a convention that you don't leave the ground without permission of the captain. He didn't ask my permission because he knew he would have had a negative answer. I also don't think it was a very clever idea to go back to the airfield and pose for photographs for the media, that just appeared to be snubbing his nose at the management.

Peter Lush, the tour manager, took the affair a good deal more seriously than myself or Micky Stewart and although there was no question of David being dropped for the next Test at Adelaide, he had to be fined heavily. David's point that he had never misbehaved on the field was a fair one (he has been exemplary in his conduct on the field) but he was a former England captain, vastly experienced and he knew the score. So many people suggest that David didn't play for England again in 1991 because of the Tiger Moth incident, but that simply isn't so. I was disappointed in him, but didn't take it personally. His omission was for more important reasons than a joy-ride in a Tiger

Moth. I honestly considered that incident closed once he had been fined, even though it was one more element in the 'Gooch the Roundhead versus Gower the Cavalier' issues cooked up by the media. Just because David is temperamentally different from me doesn't mean we were at loggerheads on that Australian tour, or at other times when we played together. I bear no ill-will towards someone I have always liked and admired, both as a cricketer and human being. As captain, I just felt something had to be seen to be done over the Tiger Moth incident, otherwise I would have fallen down in disciplinary matters and that would not have been lost on the rest of the team. I have always liked David's dry, whimsical sense of humour, but I'm sure even he would agree now that perhaps he went too far over this one incident that – as far as I'm concerned – was quickly a thing of the past.

Allan Lamb was another senior player to get into hot water off the field on that disastrous Australian tour – and again it was his own doing. Lamby was not out on the Saturday night in the Brisbane Test and we certainly needed a major contribution from him the next day, with me still out injured and Gower already gone in the second innings. Instead Allan chose to go with his wife to a casino fifty miles down the coast and have dinner with Kerry Packer and Tony Greig. Nothing wrong with that except he was not out overnight and in your mid-thirties I would have thought that rest back at the hotel would have been preferable to standing in a casino. But Allan is a high-spirited, restless character who thrives on action and he is easily bored, so he has his own ways of relaxing. Fair enough, but he left himself open to media criticism when the news of his casino trip leaked out, and when he was out in the first over of the day on the following morning, the press had their story. That's the sort of thing which happens when the tour is going badly. The press demand a course of action, they are unable to understand that it may just be that the opposition are playing better. I know that Allan Lamb didn't stay out late that night, or do anything wrong – but the fact remains that he left himself open by going to the casino. Once the story was out, Allan was bound to be pilloried next day if he got out cheaply, but if he'd scored a century, there wouldn't have been a story.

We had the same problem of irrelevant press criticism on the 1986 tour of the West Indies when it was suggested that the reason for us losing so many Tests was because we weren't going to the nets often enough. This neatly ignored the fact that net facilities on that tour were awful; even dedicated practisers got very disillusioned. We would pitch up and find that the groundsman had watered the practice wicket and it was unusable. Bob Willis, our assistant manager, would sometimes spend ages loading balls into the bowling machine, designed to help us combat fast bowling, so that his specialist skills were not being used properly, and we remained very short of *quality* practice. Suspect net facilities can be very demoralizing to a touring party because you gear yourself up for some hard, concentrated work, only to find that you've been let down. In 1986, we went from ground to ground, having been assured that all would be well, only to find we couldn't net properly. It was very demoralizing and the press couldn't seem to understand that we were *desperate* to put in some quality time. I'm glad to say that things were greatly improved on the 1990 tour to the West Indies and the standard now is pretty good in all the Test-playing countries.

The captain of a touring party has to look out for signs of boredom and fatigue among his players. In many cases it's got to be a case of self-motivation for each individual but a word or two of sympathy doesn't go amiss. It's hard when you are out of the team and a long vista of dressing-room duties looms. Bob Taylor used to combat that when he understudied Alan Knott by telling himself he was one of the sixteen best English players in the country and that if he was at home, he'd have to look for a job outside cricket and probably be discontented. In the end Bob got what he deserved for all that unselfish teamwork on tour.

The players have to understand it's a job that's well paid and you have to put the time in. We all moan about the various itineraries as we zig-zag all over the place, but there's so much one-day cricket now (and therefore greater prize money) and the players can't have it all ways. They are the ones who want shorter tours. There are fewer official functions to attend on tour these days because of the concentrated amount of cricket we have to play but improved travel communications does mean a crowded itinerary. It was hard to fly from Barbados to Antigua and play two Tests in a row, with just a day off in between but that had to be done in 1990 because of costs and to get us back home in time for the start of the English domestic season. That is all understandable, but I do think that Test cricket was devalued by playing those two Tests so close to each other. Test cricket should be thought of as something *special*, with rarity value. I will be surprised if tour itineraries get less crowded because of financial considerations. Ideally it would benefit international players if they had one winter off out of four, to rediscover their zest for cricket, but I can't see that happening because the players want the money and will go on private tours if necessary. It's a vicious circle – the players want good money for a short career but they need proper rest. That's why the TCCB has put several England players on year-long contracts, so that they can monitor their movements and hope they don't get burned out like so many tennis stars. It's hard to give of your best when you're jaded.

It's also hard to do yourself justice on tour when you're homesick. I speak as someone who always misses my wife, three daughters and my home life whenever I'm away on tour, so any player who knocks on my door and tells me something similar gets all my sympathy. A player can easily lose his drive and enthusiasm if he's out of the team on tour and has had a painful call from back home. That is the time when you really have to show character, buckle down to the job and remember that you're out there for a specific purpose, that you've worked hard for the honour and would have been disappointed not to have been selected the previous September. One way of solving the problem of homesickness is to fly out your wife or girlfriend, but I have come to the conclusion that this isn't the best policy for the party as a whole. I used to think it was fine to have them around but since becoming captain I have to say that the atmosphere and the approach to the tour from many of the players change when their ladies arrive. There's a fragmentation, the players seem to be off out more and you lose your closeness as a playing unit. Allan Border suggested this to me – he feels the problem is that the ladies are there on holiday while the guys have to work at their profession. I'm not saying they shouldn't come – how could I with grown adults? – but team spirit is definitely diluted. Wives and girlfriends also constitute a problem for the tour management. They can't ignore them and treat them as a nuisance because then it's the player who suffers. They should be made welcome, but it's an extra task for the tour manager.

There are so many things to occupy the captain on tour. It can be very satisfying though to see the unit gel together, to overcome endless hassles of climate, food, illness, injury and contentious umpiring. Somehow the team spirit you forge on tour is more valuable than when you play a Test series in your own country, going back to your county regularly and only meeting up every fortnight or so for a few days. In retrospect all the bad times on tour can be seen in perspective and as part of life's experience. I still dine out on the time in India when Derek Underwood ordered tea for two at ten in his hotel room, only to be woken up at two in the morning with tea for ten!

7
Setting the right example

The man in charge has to set the right example on and off the field, he can't ask anyone to do what he's not prepared to do. Gaining the respect of the players is of paramount importance for a captain and I feel that if it means going out on a limb and risking unpopularity, so be it. It's more valuable for a captain to be respected and admired than liked.

As I've got older I've become a more determined cricketer: when I was younger, I relied a lot on natural ability, played a lot of shots and if I got myself out, didn't worry unduly because I tended to give the bowler a chance. By the late seventies, I realized I had to buckle down to the physical and mental demands of opening for my country if I wanted a meaningful Test career so I had to get fitter and develop greater concentration at the crease. I am pleased that I'm still competing at my age against younger players. I was happy to have done so well in the physical aptitude tests at Lilleshall before we went to the West Indies in 1990. I take the view that if someone wants my place in the England side they will have to work very hard. I definitely get a boost to the ego, seeing off younger challengers.

I'm not a naturally fit person, I don't have the lean body of a Gower or a DeFreitas that doesn't carry much excess weight. If I have a few drinks or a good meal, that means I have to work out to restore my weight to what it should be. I get a sense of achievement in doing that, I feel motivated to reach a particular target. A cricketer *has* to come to terms with the onset of middle age in playing terms, you can't just rely on preparing in the same way as ten years ago because your reactions and reflexes are not as good. I had this kind of conversation with Wayne Larkins in Australia and he felt that at his age (around the same as myself) it was better for him to hit a few balls, get the feel of things and then ease himself into his batting out in the middle, without too much exertion in the nets beforehand. I think Wayne felt that experienced players knew how to pace themselves but I had to disagree. You can't afford to let things drift, to delude yourself into thinking it'll be alright on the night.

A casual glance at the way Viv Richards, Desmond Haynes and Malcolm Marshall were still driving themselves on the outfield on Test Match mornings in 1991 would suggest that there are no easy ways to success when you reach your mid-thirties, no matter how outstanding the talents involved. Anyone watching the Australians work at their cricket can't fail to be impressed by them and they take that commitment out onto the pitch with them. They put so much effort into their preparations because they want to get it right at eleven o'clock every day when it's needed. They also have some excellent players and their professionalism means that their talents can flourish within the framework of discipline and dedication. England had a very good side under Mike Brearley but if you transported those players into today's cricket, they would have to work harder at their preparations to maintain the same standards. Mike expected his flair players – Ian Botham, David Gower, Bob Willis – to turn on the tap for him, no matter how they were performing in county cricket, and they invariably did. Yet the great deeds of Botham and Willis in 1981 only served to muddy the waters in the next few years of English cricket. The belief lingered that the top players could coast in the minor games and time their commitment to the appropriate moment in a Test series or tour. I believe that cricket is no different from other sports: the physical stresses and demands get greater every decade. Not in technical standards – I believe a great player would flourish in any era – but you have to keep running further to stand still in modern sport.

Why do players of any sport go out onto the field of play? Fundamentally I would say for *enjoyment*. If you don't like what you're doing out there – either in training or the actual playing – it must be very hard. I believe there are some cricketers who actually don't enjoy the game as much as they should. They do it because that's what they are best at, there are no other meaningful careers on offer and they may as well stick with what they know best. So they go through the motions in their preparations, without any inner enjoyment and relish for the task. Yet if you're motivated and keen, the improvement in your skills ought to come naturally.

When I trained with West Ham in the early eighties, I was interested to see the amount of extra training Tony Cottee used to put in most afternoons. A natural goalscorer, he would smash a football into the net like a rocket, over and over again. I could see how much he loved perfecting his best asset. Stuart Pearce rockets in goals from long free-kicks for a pastime with Nottingham Forest – do you honestly think he doesn't put in extra work on his great talent? Not every full-back can beat international goalkeepers from twenty-five yards with a dead ball kick. Paul Gascoigne didn't develop his wonderful ball skills sitting on a barstool, telling press photographers to leave him alone. The natural talent was there, but hard work as a lad brought it out of him.

I *love* to see great talent prosper in all sports and I like to see a bit of arrogance in a cricketer, a hint of a swagger that suggests that player knows his own worth, but there's no point in having that inner confidence unless you can be relied upon to come up with the necessary when it's crucial. To be reasonably optimistic that you can still do it at the highest level, you must work at your preparation. Dennis Lillee was still doing that in his mid-thirties and few cricketers have worked harder to underpin natural talent with steel and pride in performance. This is why David Gower frustrates me so much. He has always been one of my favourite batsmen to watch and I have never been too bothered by his instinctive approach to his batting while at the crease. If he wants to waft away outside the off-stump and drive the slips mad with anticipation, let him get on with it – his genius is the type that can turn sketchiness into brilliance within a couple of overs.

I was batting with David in the Adelaide Test of 1991 when he fell for the trap the Australians had posted for him – flicking a wide ball down the legside into the hands of deep backward square leg, a man there for a specific purpose. It was the over before lunch and David walked ruefully back to the pavilion as I followed, some way behind. Many thought I had deliberately left him to walk in as a form of chastisement, but that wasn't so. I was laying out my batting gloves and inners to dry in the sun and having a word with the groundsman. I didn't say a word to David at any stage about his disappointing dismissal because he had fallen that way before to the Australians and would no doubt be cursing himself. I took the view that a batsman who scores two such superb centuries as he did at Melbourne and Sydney can't be pilloried when he gets himself out at Adelaide. It's the way he plays and he has been a great player for England. Yet I feel that David is no longer a banker in his mid-thirties, his batting is a shade unpredictable, I think he ought to be working a little harder in his preparation to give himself a greater chance of consistency. I think David's defence mechanism is to appear nonchalant but deep down I'm sure he cares greatly about his career, much more than he lets on. I

don't expect or even want this particular leopard to change its spots –
not least of all because he has been a wonderful servant to English
cricket and its supporters – but I would like him to realise how much
he is respected by the other players for his wonderful, natural ability
and that he has it in him to be a great force for the good of top English
players of the future. Nobody could fail to be impressed to see a man of
his stature buckling down in his mid-thirties to the task of getting the
best out of his supreme talents.

I don't want to turn my players into robots. I want them to play in
the way that suits them. Yet there is a *bare minimum* I expect in terms
of preparation for a day's play. I like us to get out there on time for
practice, look keen and hope the opposition notice you mean business.
A decade ago, the England team used to come out for practice in dribs
and drabs and I never felt it was judged to be an important part of our
approach to a Test Match. Ian Botham often used to take to the
physiotherapist's couch with a slight groin strain, missing training, but
always ready to take the field on the first morning. Micky Stewart and I
have put a stop to that. It's disheartening if everyone isn't ready on
time to practise together. If you're conditioned to a disciplined
approach, it becomes more natural and – believe it or not – fun. I really
enjoy getting stuck into fielding practice, getting a sweat worked up,
encouraging the lads and pulling a guy's leg if he makes a fool of
himself with a daft dive. If you hear a lot of shouting, rude comments
and laughter from a team that is practising on the outfield, you can be
sure that they're enjoying working at one of the disciplines of cricket –
and that the team spirit is good. It is all done for a purpose, not just to
go through the motions and then have a rest in the dressing-room
before play begins. Some of our fielding in Australia was abysmal and
never improved because the basics weren't being observed. I was
taught early on that you must be expecting the ball to come to you each
time and that you move forward, alert. Getting the basics right as a
unit is the least the captain should expect – and the presence of
outstanding fielders in the side is the icing on the cake.

It's a matter of pride to me that I work hard at my fielding practice,
and show how much I enjoy it. I've always been an adequate fielder,
not particularly quick around the field but with a good pair of hands.
As I get older I know I have to work harder at my reactions and in 1991
I came out of the slips with England for a few sessions because I wasn't
too happy with my performance. There were better, younger catchers
than me in the side – Graeme Hick and Chris Lewis for example – but I
still felt a little tenderness in my hand after the operation in Australia

and I had lost confidence. Concentration was also a bit of a problem. I'd be thinking about a possible bowling change and just wouldn't be ready when the ball was on its way. In the slips, concentration is vital, you must be in the correct position to react to every ball. If your hands aren't exactly right, then the ball carries to you at the wrong height and doesn't hit you in the right area of the palm. It's a good idea for a captain to come out of the slips for an hour or so, because concentration can be impaired. Obviously it helps a captain's stature in the team if he isn't a sub-standard fielder and I was happy with my three catches in the Leeds Test of 1991 when we beat the West Indies. The catch at slip to take Gus Logie got most of the headlines but that was simply a reaction catch, they either stick or they don't. I was more pleased with the two skyers to take Courtney Walsh and Viv Richards because they were in the air a fair time, they were swirling around in a cloudy sky and they were pressure efforts – particularly the one to get Viv in the second innings. More importantly, those three catches represented the whole point of my insistence on working hard at fielding practice. Every morning we'd be put under pressure, expected to take swirling, high catches while hoping that we could carry that confidence with us onto the field when play started. I hope the overall standard of England's fielding in that Leeds Test made some of the detractors of the Stewart/Gooch regime more aware of the point of the 'sergeant-major' approach. If there were *still* reservations, they might ponder on the way Allan Border has improved as a fielder in his middle thirties, when many are slowing up. During his two seasons at Essex, Allan was a fair fielder, but not outstanding in any department. Through sheer determination, he has made himself into an excellent man to have in the short mid-wicket area, where he brings off many outstanding dives and stops and a lot of run-outs. When Border shies at the stumps he invariably hits them. Why? Because he has worked at it. The Australian captain sets a terrific example to his side in the field.

I believe Ian Botham's captaincy was undermined by his inability to set the right example on and off the field. He remained one of the lads, living life to the full. On the 1981 West Indies tour, Ian never quite got it right in terms of leading the players correctly. In Barbados, we played a practice match between ourselves and I scored a hundred. I was therefore on the field all day, in great heat and I felt a little tired as a result. I was also in the habit of taking a fifteen-minute run along the beach every morning with my wife, Brenda, just to get the body moving and blow away the cobwebs. After that practice match, we all gathered in a bar for a drink and some food and I felt drowsy. Anyone who knows me is well aware that a phone call to my home after nine in the evening isn't a great idea because I'm an early riser. The next day in Barbados the captain announces that he doesn't want to see any player running in the morning because they were falling asleep early in the evening. I lost my rag, told him I'd been in the field all day in the practice match and that the only reason why he knew about my early morning runs was because he'd looked out one morning and seen me on the beach! I wasn't prepared to take that from Ian. He also set a poor example to the tail-enders in the Barbados Test on that tour. We were really up against it after Michael Holding had bowled Geoffrey Boycott in his first over and the crowd were baying for more. Gradually the innings disintegrated and the captain stood as our only hope of respectability. Ian was put through the mincer by Holding. He bowled him some absolute snorters and when one of them reared up and hit him in the chest, he threw down his bat and gesticulated as if to say, 'How the hell can I play that?' That was a bad example to set to the bowlers, who were sitting there with pads on, hardly looking forward to *their* turn to bat in such a situation. I believe a captain must show self-discipline and resilience, otherwise he can't expect any of that from the rest of his players.

I admired Mike Gatting's 'up and at 'em' approach to the job as captain. I thought he was excellent on the field – sharp and positive. He was respected for his ability and his readiness to laugh at himself and yet he could keep his distance from the team when necessary. He led from the front – always first into the nets – and clearly cared for his players. He never looked for excuses if he fouled up and he was more conscious than anybody that one moment of ill-discipline from him probably cost us the World Cup in 1987. It was close to a routine run chase when Allan Border came on to bowl at Gatt and, considering he is such a terrific player of the spinners, Border represented little threat to him. Yet he played the reverse sweep to Border's first ball, got a glove on it and was easily caught by the wicket-keeper. Gatt was distraught, he knew he had let the team down in a pressure situation where he would be expected to lead us to victory. He was unlucky – you rarely get gloved on the reverse sweep, and he does play the shot very well – but in hindsight it was ill-advised and he was on a hiding to nothing if it didn't come off for him. He was bound to be pilloried and he took responsibility.

Unfortunately for Gatt, he fell foul of the authorities at Lord's and he was sacked for matters unconnected with cricket. My view is that if he was going to be sacked, it should have been for the events in

Faisalabad rather than some alleged high jinks with a barmaid during a Test Match, especially as Lord's said they believed Gatt's account of proceedings at the hotel in June, 1988. Judged on the highest code of conduct, Gatt was wrong to get involved in that slanging match with Shakoor Rana. He should have made his complaint in private, despite the great provocation. We all make mistakes and some pay for them more than others. Gatt's problem was that our cricket authorities rightly view seriously any confrontation on the field and after Faisalabad, he was on thin ice. I learned from Gatt's experience that the England captain is placed on a higher pedestal than any other skipper. He has to be seen to be doing the right thing at all times in public: the profile is high yet the material rewards are correspondingly larger. You can't expect the perks without taking on the extra responsibility.

The captain has to talk a good game to his players before they take the field, but he must also carry it through when the pressure is on out there. In my opinion, David Gower fell down in this respect in 1989 when we lost badly to the Australians. He was his usual fluent self at our team meetings, talking knowledgeably about what lay ahead, but when we got out onto the field, he didn't transfer those thoughts into deeds. Not everybody is a sergeant-major type of leader and none of us expected David to change his style, but he wasn't *seen* to be in charge. He looked detached from it all, standing at cover, and the players felt they didn't know where they stood with him. If the captain doesn't show enthusiasm, then there's little chance of the players doing so. John Emburey got very hot under the collar a couple of times because he could see the way the game was drifting away from us and I tried to talk to him, while being careful not to interfere too much. In the end I backed off unless David asked me specifically for my thoughts.

He obviously felt he couldn't change his captaincy style, which had served him well in India and against Australia in 1985, but he had to accept the consequences of his failure to get us motivated in 1989. The players let David down badly in 1989, but he seemed to let things drift too often and didn't set the right example. He was too remote and appeared to have his mind elsewhere too often. That is just David's style and I don't blame him for trying to be a different personality as captain. You are born with your own characteristics and David's was moulded in the days when he went to prep school, then public school and also lived in Africa for a time. I suppose you could call his upbringing an upper-middle class, colonial one – where you are encouraged early on not to show your true feelings, to be a little remote. Throughout his career, David has tended to bite the bullet and pretend he hasn't been hurt, to shelter behind that easy charm that makes him so deservedly popular. He is the least snobbish of blokes and excellent company but when he captained us in 1989 he struggled to get the best response from the players eventually. That's not a criticism of David as captain, more an awareness that we're all the products of our environment and that sometimes qualities which make you an attractive personality don't add to your ability to lead men. In another summer David's style would have been just the right mix of captaincy attributes, as he in fact had demonstrated before as England captain.

It's very satisfying when the captain manages to get a player motivated sufficiently to improve his standing in the game. I was delighted with the positive attitude Phillip DeFreitas showed when we omitted him from the tour party to Australia in 1990. Shortly afterwards he asked me point blank why he hadn't been picked: I told him his attitude wasn't quite right, he needed to work harder at his game to get consistency. When he flew out to replace Chris Lewis a few months later, he showed that he had taken the message to heart. He got stuck in, bowled tighter and didn't let us down. He was a revelation against the West Indies the following summer because he realized what's involved to compete at the highest level. DeFreitas has always been an accurate bowler – that's why he has been so valuable in one-day internationals for the past few years – but he found an extra yard of pace to go with it. In Test cricket, that makes a big difference. The purists have long had a down on him about his bowling action, but Bob Willis and Colin Croft weren't exactly technically perfect and they took a lot of Test wickets. He worked hard at moving the ball away from the right-hander and became a formidable bowler in 1991. Phillip's batting also developed that Test summer. I told him he should set himself a target of being Lancashire's regular number six and to start *thinking* like a batsman. I believe he has it in him to be a very good seven or eight for England, someone who can get you a few fifties with a degree of regularity. What he has to do is limit himself to what shots he needs to play. It can be done. Mike Watkinson has worked his way up the Lancashire batting order and when I first played against John Emburey in a second eleven match he batted at number eleven and didn't look all that special. But he has sorted out how to play and has been a very useful number eight for England.

I have nothing but praise for the way Phillip DeFreitas has reacted to being at a career crossroads, at the attitude he showed in outbowling every other England bowler in 1991. He knew he needed to work harder to lose that inconsistency and he kept coming back for hostile spells. He *wanted* it badly and as captain that gave me immense pleasure.

Robin Smith is also my kind of player. He's not only a crowdpleaser but he fights it out: you need to bowl him out, he won't give it away. I was enormously impressed by his attitude in Australia when he couldn't get a run all series. Nobody could have been more conscientious in practice, more keen to take advice, more concerned he was letting down the side. In the end he was out of luck. The sort of character you show in adversity is important when your side needs a major performance from you. I was proud to have led from the front at Leeds in 1991 with my unbeaten hundred to set up victory against the West Indies but in the next Test Robin surpassed my effort. We expected the West Indies to come back strongly at Lord's and they did. We haven't been used to going one up in a Test series against them and, judging by our experiences in the Caribbean the year before, we knew they would be formidable once stung. That third day at Lord's was probably the crucial one of the series because without Robin's unbeaten hundred we would have been bowled out cheaply and made to follow on. He had to shepherd the lower-order batsmen to a respectable total, impart his own confidence to them and make sure they hung around. Robin showed great responsibility and I would have been proud to have played an innings like that one.

I expected such dedication from Robin, but at last it seemed as if that sort of example was rubbing off on the rest of the players. We were beginning to turn up at each Test *expecting* to compete on level terms against opposition that had steamrollered us too often in the past. Beating them in Jamaica marked the watershed. They thought they were still invincible and after that defeat, they gave us more respect so that on every day in the 1991 series, we competed with them, gave them a good fight.

For me, setting the right example also involves getting on with the game and trying to avoid getting the umpires' backs up. There is a fair amount of dressing-room paranoia about umpiring these days and I don't like it. It needs to be nipped in the bud before it gets too contagious. When Robin Smith was given run out at Leeds by Dickie Bird in 1991, he appeared upset by the decision as he walked back. 'Was that out?', he asked as soon as he came in. We had gathered round the TV action replay and we all agreed it was a great decision by the umpire. Robin's mood changed straight away at this news but it underlines the fact that the batsman isn't always the best judge of the decision's merits. I believe that now and then some established batsmen can get the wrong end of a marginal lbw decision because the umpires know the way they play. Terry Alderman got me out a lot in 1989 when my footwork wasn't so good. I'm now a little saddled with that reputation and sometimes I wonder if that tells against me – but I wouldn't dream of showing dismay or dissent to the umpires. They have their own job to do and have to give it as they see it. At Old Trafford in 1990, I did slip from those standards though. I instinctively rubbed my upper arm as the Indians appealed for a catch behind, but umpire John Holder wasn't impressed and gave me my marching orders. He was quite right, even though I thought it was the wrong decision. Too many batsmen are trying to lead umpires away from giving them out by indicating it didn't touch their wrist or bat, or in the case of lbw appeals, that it *did* touch their bat. In an Essex match, I had to tell Salim Malik to apologize to David Constant after he pointed to his sleeve, having been given out, caught behind. The umpire said he'd be reporting Salim for dissent and although he did apologize, the player was still reported. In the West Indies in 1990, I had to take Nasser Hussain to one side in his first game for us after he made a song and dance about being given out. Nasser is a fiery sort of character but that's no excuse for that kind of dissent and he was told in no uncertain terms that he had to go when given out. I didn't see the incidents in the Sydney Test of 1991 when Eddie Hemmings and Alec Stewart got hot under the collar about the umpires, but after studying the video they clearly had to be fined because they were representing England and hadn't controlled their displeasure in public. Phil Tufnell behaved petulantly during the Melbourne Test and when the game was over I stayed out in the middle, trying to find out from the umpire Peter McConnell exactly what had gone on. Apparently Tufnell had shown his displeasure when a decision didn't go his way and reacted badly. The umpire quite rightly took exception to this, but made it worse by getting involved in a heated exchange. It was wrong for Tufnell to kick the ground and swear but I don't think the umpire helped matters. Sometimes the umpires might get more respect from the players if they later admitted they had simply got it wrong. I once asked David Lloyd if he thought he'd ever made a mistake when he'd been a first-class umpire and he said, 'No – every time I thought about it afterwards, I believed I was right.' Now I like and respect David Lloyd but I found that surprising. I know it's correct to start from the assumption that the umpire is right because you don't have a game otherwise – but I wonder if it would be wrong admitting privately to a captain that he'd made a mistake? Perhaps we players get too wrapped up in ourselves and forget the wider responsibilities umpires have to cricket. In my twenty years in the game, I have admired umpires around the world as they carried out a job I would find very difficult.

In general I see no point in making a song and dance if the decision doesn't go your way. The umpire isn't going to change his mind and when this happens in the field I call for the ball and get the game moving again. When Gladstone Small beat Allan Border first ball outside the off-stump at Adelaide in 1991, we were all convinced he'd been caught behind. Not out. Some of our lads stood there, disbelieving, and Gladstone was particularly upset. I was in the slips at the time, called for the ball and threw it up to mid-off to get the game moving again, otherwise it would have looked even worse. Later that year at the Oval, we were sure that Robin Smith had caught Malcolm Marshall at silly point on the fourth evening and Alec Stewart went on a victory tour from behind the stumps. He finished up at the umpire's end and made it quite clear what he thought about the decision. I wasn't happy about that – the whole thing lasted for almost a minute – and it could have boiled over. Alec got very excited but that would never change the umpire's mind. Without their involvement we can't play cricket, it's as simple as that. Brian Taylor, my first captain at Essex, drummed that point home to me and I recall the words that Doug Insole as chairman of the club used to let the Essex players know what was expected of them: 'The Essex way is to try to play hard but fair, and have fun if it's there as well. Don't go outside the boundaries of fair play in chasing a win. We'd rather lose by playing fair than doing anything underhand or cheating.' Nobby Philip once found out the hard way when he was playing for Essex that some umpires won't be intimidated. We were playing at Liverpool and Nobby thought he had picked up a wicket with a caught behind. In his excitement he ran all the way down to us in the slips but when he saw the appeal turned down, he sprinted all the way back to the umpire and appealed again. He'd chosen the wrong man to take on. The redoubtable Arthur Jepson stood his ground, stared back and growled: 'Still not out.'

Some players feel that if an umpire turns down an appeal, it's a good plan to look downcast so they can hope for success next time they look for a favourable decision. I think that's gamesmanship and it can work against the bowler if the umpire is feeling bloody-minded. Instead of getting a 'make-up' decision, the bowler might find he gets a lot of 'not outs' because the umpire was unimpressed by his behaviour. That would also be wrong – each decision should be judged on its merits – but in human terms one can sympathize with the umpire. Does the captain get favourable decisions from the umpire because he files reports on him and thereby has a say in his career prospects? When I first started I think the captain who was a front-line batsman got away with a few marginal decisions but I don't think it's so prevalent now. I certainly view the umpires dispassionately, as they do when making *their* decisions. I am totally honest when I write my reports on the umpires after each match and I don't get personally involved. It doesn't concern me that I might be determining his future employment because his competence can have a bearing on a player's career as well. If he keeps making bad decisions then he's not good enough for the job. Such matters should be dealt with privately, not on the field of play. One of the worst instances of dissent I have seen involved an lbw decision that went my way, at Northampton. Winston Davis just wouldn't accept the decision of Kevin Lyons and simply refused to bowl. It was a close call, but I couldn't believe it when he mouthed obscenities at the umpire. It went on for about four minutes before his captain, Allan Lamb, calmed him down and he was persuaded to bowl again. Davis was rightly fined for that, it must have looked terrible to the crowd and sponsors. Viv Richards took a lot of stick for his excited reaction that led to Rob Bailey's dismissal during the Barbados Test of 1990 but I didn't have any real complaints. The situation was very tense and Viv used to get very pumped up at slip in these situations, especially with England still one up in the series and looking to hold out for the draw at Barbados. The ball appeared to brush Bailey's thigh pad, the bowler offered a half-hearted, belated appeal while Viv did his war-dance of joy. Lloyd Barker, the umpire, finally gave out Rob and some sections of the media suggested he had been pressurized by the close fielders. Yet we've all been in this kind of situation where you appeal because you *think* the batter has hit it, the decision goes your way and when the bowler runs down your end, he says, 'I'm not sure he hit that – but I'll have it anyway.' The fielding captain makes no attempt to call back the unlucky batsman and we talk about 'the rub of the green'. None of us are whiter-than-white. Everyone close to the wicket goes up in a big appeal if you're sure it's plumb and if you only *think* it's out, everyone still goes up. I don't believe in appealing for everything but if you think it's close and it's worth a shout, then give it a *big* shout. I'm pretty sure that if the roles had been reversed in Barbados, we would have been looking for a favourable appeal as that ball brushed a West Indian batsman on its way through to the keeper.

The borderline between legitimate aggression and gamesmanship is very blurred now in cricket. I don't mind a bit of needle out in the middle and have had many battles with bowlers like Merv Hughes and Geoff Lawson of Australia. I was determined not to take much of it from them when we toured Australia in 1990–91. I've heard things shouted like, 'He can't play it with a surfboard' and that would amuse me but whenever Merv offered an opinion to me, I'd say 'Talk to someone who cares' or, 'What's your problem then?' What you come back with is meaningless but I wouldn't turn the other cheek. I didn't want to get involved in shouting matches but that helped to get me pumped up out there. I knew they were trying to unsettle me, to get me to play a rash shot and the adrenalin flowed enough but I still kept my self-control. Their bowlers are brought up to be aggressive, especially if they think you've been a bit lucky. I don't ever advise any of my batsmen to get involved with the verbals although some, like Alec Stewart, need no second bidding – Alec has played a lot of grade cricket out in Perth and he's never short of a reply if provoked. I don't condemn that at all, as long as it doesn't get out of hand. In the cut-and-thrust atmosphere of a Test Match these individual battles add to the tension and aren't dangerously provocative, as long as the spectators are unaware of what's going on out there. If it *looks* bad, then I don't condone it.

I know umpires and authorities are worried now about 'sledging' on the field but as long as it's kept private and doesn't spill over into something nasty and visible, it doesn't bother me too much. I don't believe everybody should walk onto a cricket field with a zipper on his mouth. There's certainly more comment out there now than when I first started but a lot of it is encouraging comment from fielders to bowler rather than offensive stuff directed at the batsmen. I don't like organized verbal aggression, the fielders must be quiet once the bowler is running in – but I like to hear my players geeing each other up. It's good to show the opposition you're keyed up and I fully understood why the Aussies got meaner towards us on and off the field after we had beaten them well in 1985. After that tour Allan Border was criticized by Ian Chappell for being too friendly with Ian Botham and David Gower and he was certainly a different character in 1989. We hardly saw the Aussies socially, nor did they pass the time of day with us on the field or in the nets. They distanced themselves from us and showed they really meant business. I've never been one to go into the opposition dressing-room for a drink at close of play and I don't blame the Aussies at all for toughening up.

I don't want to appear holier-than-thou about gamesmanship because every captain has condoned it over the years. When Allan Lamb contrived to get just twelve overs an hour out of our bowlers in the Barbados Test of 1990 he was only doing what I would have done if I hadn't been injured and unable to play. We were looking for a draw at Barbados to hang onto our 1–0 series lead and the fewer deliveries we gave the West Indies batsmen in their second innings, the longer it would take for Viv Richards to declare and set his bowlers at us. I think a minimum of fifteen overs an hour in Tests is the least any side should manage, but in the absence of strict rules on the matter, I would have been pretty ruthless at slowing the game down if it suited me. Any England player who went on that Indian tour of 1981–82 became an expert in the ruses adopted to avoid delivering many balls – and eventually we got dragged into it and played tit-for-tat. I decided not to 'walk' in Australia even if I knew I was out because it was clear none of the Aussie batsmen bothered with walking, they waited for the decision. So I followed suit, and I think the rest of my team did the same. Bowlers rough up the ball on occasions but we batters also run down the wicket to rough it up for our bowlers near the end of the innings. It's a case of swings and roundabouts. I have often put myself between the stumps and the ball when it is thrown at my end as I scamper a quick single. I hope the ball will hit my body and I'll avoid being run out and it sometimes does just that – for example at Trinidad in 1986 when we needed one to win off the last ball of a one-day international and I got there by running straight down the pitch, obscuring the stumps for the fielder. You can't regulate such things out of professional sport, we all know the little tricks of the trade.

Having said all that, I do feel that sportsmanship is declining in first-class cricket. That is due solely to money in my opinion. Too much acclaim and cash is bound up in victory and I'm sure the age we live in has much to do with that. I do think the umpires should have greater powers to deal with dissent on the field. The side that transgresses should be put at a disadvantage. The idea of the 'Sin Bin' ought to be looked at, where a bowler who abuses the umpire can't bowl for at least a session. There should be an instant deterrent, as opposed to frequent warnings, which are usually ignored. The spectators should be made aware of the sanction immediately, so they can be sure that the penalty is for bad sportsmanship. I hate the idea of cricket coming to this but it's part of our modern, high-powered society where only winners are appreciated. If you can't control the players, it'll just be a free-for-all and we've been rather too close to that at times recently.

Should a captain drop himself if his form isn't good enough for a place in the side? Some of Mike Brearley's critics suggested that when he was England captain, but it's a pretty drastic step. I never considered dropping myself during my poor run in 1987 although I did drop down to the middle order for a few games. It can be a psychological boost to the opposition, especially during a Test series. The side has got used to the captain's influence, his personality, his preferred style of play and it would unsettle the players if he stood down. Significantly, Lancashire's performances deteriorated after David Hughes dropped himself from the Benson and Hedges Cup Final team and for most of the remainder of the 1991 season. I would be tempted to leave well alone unless the situation had become critical. I hope I shall know when to stand down at Essex without being told to do so. If I am down by about fifteen per cent, it may be that I'll still be worth it as captain for my overall influence. That's what happened with Keith Fletcher during his last few years as he imparted his wisdom to me. I might end up down the batting order but as long as I can still make a useful contribution I'd like to stay on. I wouldn't like to stand in anyone's way, though; I think too much about Essex CCC for that to happen.

Setting the right example involves so many aspects of captaincy. I don't like to hear other captains whinge about bad luck or poor umpiring. Men like Gary Lineker, Bobby Charlton and Trevor Brooking are celebrated as much for their character as their playing prowess and they are the kind of sportsmen I admire. I like to treat my players as adults but it's important to let them know the groundrules, what constitutes reasonable behaviour. This is mapped out to them all the day before a Test starts. For me, the preparation for a Test begins when I arrive for our first practice. It continues after play and lasts till I've left the ground for the final time. If a player is out late during the Test or has too much to drink one night, then he is in trouble with me and it will also affect my judgement of him as a player in the future. He would be letting down himself, the team and his captain; there are plenty more who would love to play instead of him. It's great being an England player if it's going well for you, but even one slight transgression is a problem, because you are in the public eye. The press call this 'Gooch's work ethic captaincy', but I prefer to see it as giving yourself a chance to do well instead of turning up late for practice, knocking up a few catches, turning your arm over and expecting things to happen for you on the day. Do we want to be the best side in the world, or just mediocre? We have the talent in England to be among the best if we could only harness it. We have sat back and drifted for too many years, we have been the worst at motivating ourselves. I prefer the way of Liverpool Football Club – if you don't *want* to compete hard but fairly, then you'll win nothing. Liverpool keep winning, so why can't the English cricket team?

8
Man-management

To me captaincy isn't just about hitting a ball or who should field at slip. You should be prepared to nursemaid everyone in your team if that's what it takes to get them all working for you in the right direction. Everyone needs sharp reminders at some stage in a season or tour and if the players also know they can come to you to discuss a problem, then you're a long way towards getting the team spirit right. If you're remote and off-hand when a player is vulnerable, it takes a while to restore your status in his eyes. A cricket captain is like a soccer team's manager: slightly distant, trying to organize a style of play, hard on anyone who needs disciplinary action, but with an open door for private discussions. The rollickings have to be meaningful, because if they become monotonous the players just switch off. The captain must be a part of the team, but also *apart from the team*. This is where Mike Brearley was so outstanding. His training as a psychologist meant he could assess players' characters so well. He could communicate at all levels – intellectually, with gutter humour, with sound commonsense – and I never recall him making any of us who lacked his education feel inferior. He would never talk down to a player, he let him know what was expected and tried to help him attain that standard. He made you want to play for him. When I was dropped for the Perth Test in 1979, Mike handled it absolutely right. I knew it was a difficult decision for him and he knew how disappointed I would be but he came to me before the team meeting, explained the options frankly and left me in no doubt that he still rated me as a player. A player can't ask for more than that.

Brearley handled Geoffrey Boycott very well. Boycott was never slow in telling people he was a top player and he knew he was a superior batsman to Brearley, but the captain didn't ever let it rile him. I think he admired Boycott's professionalism and was interested in his quirky character. He would ask Geoffrey for his thoughts in team meetings and out on the field and Mike was sensitive enough to keep the lines of communication open between the two of them. I'm sure that Geoffrey felt he deserved to be the England captain ahead of the inferior player but he knew in his heart of hearts that Brearley was an excellent leader of men, something that Geoffrey admired. It was interesting that the only cricketer that Brearley couldn't get on with was his Middlesex colleague, Phil Edmonds. Perhaps it needed someone of Edmonds' intellectual and personal self-confidence to stand up to Brearley, but they certainly got under each other's skin. I remember a major bust-up between the two of them in the dressing-room during the Perth Test of 1978 when Brearley felt Edmonds hadn't been attending to his twelfth man duties. It almost ended in blows and it was strange to see the captain nearly losing the self-control that helped make him such an impressive person. Perhaps the fact that Edmonds felt he was the right man to captain Middlesex didn't help to ease the tension that must have simmered for several seasons.

I've only disliked one person in any team I've played for in first-class cricket, so that's a pretty satisfactory record. We all have little spats with team-mates at some stage or other but I have learned from Mike Brearley and Keith Fletcher that the best thing to do is get it out in the open and then forget about it once the row has exhausted itself. The captain must ignore personalities when looking at someone's fitness for the job. The question to be asked is: can he play? If he makes the team better, he has to be in at the expense of the nice, popular guy who isn't as good a cricketer. In professional sport you can't pick someone because you happen to like him. I admit I can be a little biased against someone I suspect could be a better player if he put more effort into his game. The standards I set for myself are very high and I can be intolerant of those who aren't doing themselves justice. I don't brood overmuch if someone gets it wrong as long as he has tried his best and hasn't neglected his game.

My black-and-white attitude to my profession was at the heart of my disaffection with several of the players who toured Australia with me in 1990–91. Yet there were faults on both sides and I accept my man-management should have been more subtle and more flexible. Despite endless team meetings and frank discussions, I failed to get through to many of the players and didn't carry them with me. My frustration at the inability to master the basic disciplines of playing cricket led me to order extra work as the remedy but perhaps I was too dogmatic and didn't spot the resentment earlier. There was a communications gap. Perhaps I ought to have spent more time with some of them in the evenings, trying to win them over in a more relaxed atmosphere. It was different in the West Indies, with less social distractions. I mixed with different groups of players each evening, getting to know their feelings about the tour and cricket in general. It was important to me to be accessible so that they wouldn't bottle things inside and they could relate to me. I told them, 'You might not like what I say to you about your prospects, but I'll say it straight to your face. At least we'll be talking.'

In Australia everyone was pulled in too many directions for us to have that intimacy as a tour party. As captain it was my responsibility to bridge the gap between me and some of the players and I failed. Some of them saw me as morose and grumpy and I couldn't get them to realize that I was just so disappointed with our efforts.

David Gower represents my biggest failure of man-management since I've been England captain. I struggle to get through to him. I must bear a lot of responsibility for that, because I have always wanted us to be on the same wavelength ever since I became England captain. We are, after all, in the entertainment business and David Gower has been a fabulous entertainer since he first played for England. When you consider the free way he bats, his record at Test level is marvellous – all those beautiful centuries, more runs than any other Englishman except Geoffrey Boycott, an average way over forty (and a good deal better than mine). Who wouldn't want a guy like that in the side? Yet on that Australian tour, I had more meetings with the management about David than anyone else and I'm sad to say that I felt more at ease with him out of the England team in 1991. I was very keen to have him in Australia because of his class and experience and no one was happier than I when his big hundred at the Oval against the Indians justified his inclusion. He scored three hundreds in four Tests over the next five months and I still have *total* respect for him as a player. Yet we don't see eye-to-eye on what I expect from a senior player. I need a lot more from him than just seeing his immense talent flower on occasions in a Test Match; if he was more enthusiastic about his cricket between nine-thirty in the morning and six o'clock at night, he could please himself what he does the rest of the time. To me his lethargic attitude can rub off on some of the others, those who admired and respected him.

I really wanted to get the best out of David and towards the end of the tour, I had a private dinner with him in New Zealand when I spoke

114

very frankly. As usual, he was very eloquent, confirmed he still had England ambitions and would be trying hard to get in the side for the West Indies series. I was exasperated and told him that it was no longer enough to offer smooth words and that he had to show me he meant business. I was particularly concerned that David didn't appear all that interested in his profession anymore, that he only seemed to want to play Test cricket. Not even the one-day internationals appeal that greatly to him, because he sees them as a distortion of the real thing. He doesn't care for the Sunday League and the Championship matches seem a grind to him as well. So David has to change his attitude, he must clock up big scores and show consistency to get back into the England team under my captaincy – and then set a good example in various ways as a valued, senior player. I fear he is too set in his ways to alter – as I am – so we can't get on the same wavelength. We've never fallen out, I like him a lot but he frustrates me.

I think my failures as captain and opening batsman in 1987 have helped my man-management technique. I'm sure there were times when one of my Essex team-mates would have wanted to talk to me about a personal problem but backed off because I appeared preoccupied with my own troubles. That saddened me and since then I have tried to be more understanding. I could relate to the batting worries experienced by Graeme Hick and Robin Smith in 1991 because I knew what it feels like to think you've lost the key to that particular door that's marked 'England batsman'. I told Robin just to keep working away at his game, that the luck would turn his way, that he had no major technical defects and that the memory of scoring runs for England would stand him in good stead. I really believe you don't become a bad player overnight and Robin proved me right later in 1991.

Graeme Hick was different because he couldn't rely on the knowledge and experience of having done well in Tests. The West Indies series marked the first time in a glittering career that he'd had a bad run and it was hard for him to come to terms with the fact that a chink in his armour had been highlighted by the West Indies' fast bowlers. I wanted him to stay at number three during his bad trot because that's where he has made his runs and where he feels comfortable and he knew he would be exposed wherever he batted. Graeme knows he was found wanting in 1991, that he never really looked like making runs but I have faith in him. I like his attitude, the fact that he is a brilliant fieldsman anywhere and a useful off-spinner is in his favour and I think he has the class and courage to bounce back.

During the four Tests he played in the summer of 1991, I let him know I was ready to talk to him whenever he wanted, but I couldn't tell him how to bat. Detailed technical advice would probably have to wait until the end of a busy season and then it would need to come from someone he trusted.

Mark Ramprakash had different problems in the West Indies series – getting out so often in the twenties after doing all the hard work. Each time he had looked composed and impressive but then a rash shot or a good ball would see him off. By the end of the series he was a disappointed young man with a psychological hang-up about beating that twenties barrier. I'd say to him, 'Don't worry, Ramps, this will stand you in good stead when you go on to make a big score for England.' There was no better example to point to than his county captain, Mike Gatting, who took a long time to score a Test hundred and then they came in a bunch. I told him that when you go up a grade and get into the international arena so the need for extra concentration becomes more important and that it's hard for a young player to master those mental demands overnight. Young Mark needed sympathetic handling because he cared so much about his standing in the side so I just kept trying to reassure him and hoping that the luck would flow his way. If a top cricketer goes through an entire career without any technical problems or a crisis of confidence, then he's a freak. Even Don Bradman was dropped after his first Test appearance.

Since I became England captain I've felt it's important to help the young players understand the special pressures of Test cricket. It's hard initially to cope with all the hype and the microscopic interest in your successes or failures. The opposition bowlers and batters may be familiar to you from county cricket but it's a good deal removed from that type of game when they're wearing their country's sweater. Bobby Charlton once said that it took him twenty internationals before he felt he had arrived as an England footballer and I know what he meant by that. After I had failed in my first two Tests in 1975 I was rightly dropped and my form for Essex deteriorated because I had lost a great deal of confidence. Exactly the same thing happened to Hick and Ramprakash in 1991, as their levels of concentration dipped when they returned to their counties. It's all to do with getting used to playing at the top level and getting accustomed to that much-touted word 'pressure': better than being an also-ran, though.

Senior players also have technical problems at times and the captain must be able to talk about them to the player. After the 1991 season ended I had a quiet word with Jack Russell about his batting. I felt he had got confused about the way he should bat. His glovework as a keeper speaks for itself but Jack knows that he must get runs to retain his value to the side. He had batted brilliantly against the Australians at Lord's in 1989, made a gutsy hundred against them at Old Trafford and resisted stoutly in the Caribbean for long periods. Yet I felt that Jack's sheer determination to sell his wicket dearly meant his strokeplay had become stifled. I told him he was just as good a batsman as the likes of Greg Matthews and that if he could just relax a little and work out what shots he would play, then he would become a banker to make useful runs for us at number seven or eight. Jack knows that I am looking to him for regular fifties and the occasional hundred for England and that if he can manage that, he'll be difficult to dislodge from the Test side.

There are times when the captain has to dish out some harsh words as soon as his team gets off the field. This is something I'm reluctant to do all that often – it smacks of the headmaster's study and six of the best – but now and then it has to be done. I did it twice on my last Australian tour, at Adelaide and Bowral, after two particularly inept performances. There had been little pride in performance, no sign of our superior ability and in short we were a shambles. I locked the dressing-room door and said so. We had played dimly in one-day cricket, the form of the game that we play such a lot around the world. There was no intelligence, no spark and they had to be told so. Yet those two earbashings didn't do much good, because we continued to lurch from disaster to mediocrity.

By the end of the last Test, at Perth, I knew that the press would be asking me to summarize our tour and I was determined to speak my mind. My loyalty to the players had been stretched to breaking point and although I had mumbled the usual platitudes to the media throughout the tour I was going to speak frankly this time. I'd thought long and hard about breaking cover but felt that it would have impact because it was something I rarely do. I told the assembled media at Perth that I wasn't happy about the attitude of some of my players and that they would have to examine their performances closely in the light of their future. I also took full responsibility for our poor tour, as the man who got the squad he wanted and then failed to get the right response from some of them. Despite clever and persistent prompting, I refused to name the players that had disappointed me; anyone who had followed the tour could fill in the blank spaces. That press conference upset some of my players; they felt I hadn't been fair to them and said so to me. I *wanted* them to be upset, to show me that they cared about their England careers and it was time to be straight and open about my misgivings. Sometimes tempers need to be lost to clear the air and it helps the captain if a senior player loads the bullets to be fired.

At Sydney in January 1979, we came off the field at the close of the first day, well aware that we might have lost the Test already. We had been bowled out for 152 and they were just fifty-odd behind with nine wickets in hand. England's all-round cricket that day had been poor and our work in the field lethargic. As we plodded off, Mike Hendrick said to no one in particular, 'We need a right bollocking – now.' Mike Brearley chose the perfect time and tore into us when we walked through the dressing-room door. He was so good at things like that. Harsh, angry words from someone usually so calm and collected had an extra significance and they certainly cleared the air. The next day we bowled and fielded with greater purpose, then Derek Randall batted for ages in great heat to score 150 and our spinners bowled Australia to defeat. I'm certain Brearley's words on that first night galvanized us but it took a good pro like Hendrick to light the blue touchpaper for him. Our team spirit was so good that Hendrick had the confidence to go to the captain and suggest he handed out the rollicking.

Dropping a player from the England team is never an easy decision and it's even harder to pass on the news first-hand. The captain must take that responsibility, otherwise he loses the respect of his players. I had early experience of this in September 1988 when I had to ring Gladstone Small to tell him he had just missed out on the India tour. His wife, Lois answered the call, and I could tell by her tone that hopes were pretty high in the Small household. When Gladstone came on the line, I had to give it to him straight even though I knew he expected to be on that trip. I also had to tell Gladstone he'd been dropped for the First Test against India in 1990 and this time it was slightly easier because he knew that he had lost his zip and was just bowling medium pace, but it's still hard when a guy has done such a lot for you in previous England appearances. I told him what I tell all the disappointed players – keep working hard, you're still in our plans.

Ninety per cent of the time it's not possible to tell a player to his face that he's been left out, so you have to rely on the phone. For the one-day internationals in May 1991, I rang all those players who had been with me in Australia who hadn't made this latest squad. It was a courtesy call because they had been in the last England squad and although I didn't go into great detail on the phone, I felt every player deserved an explanation and I hoped he'd try to prove me wrong. I normally leave the phone calls until the morning that the squad is to be announced because the news can leak out early and the unlucky player might hear about his omission from a reporter before I can get to him. This lack of available time can lead to logistical problems, not least because I am a county captain with the appropriate responsibilities and I do occasionally spend a bit of time in the middle as an opening batsman. Sometimes Micky Stewart has to make the initial call and I follow it up later. I had difficulty getting through to Neil Fairbrother when he was left out of the first Test at Leeds in 1991, despite doing so well in the last one-day international a few days earlier at Lord's. For some reason, I didn't have the ex-directory phone number of Lancashire's secretary, nor that of the payphone just outside the home dressing-room at Old Trafford. It was a nightmare and eventually I had to hand responsibility over to Micky Stewart. Later that summer I was sorry not to be able to contact Devon Malcolm with the news that he was being left out. I tried hard to contact him but when I rang the ground at Cheltenham where he was due to play on the Sunday, I was told he wasn't playing and they also gave me the wrong hotel number where the team was supposed to be staying. So I suppose Devon heard the news first on the radio or punched it up on CEEFAX, which displeased me. One of these days, the system will be fool-proof but I believe the captain gets more respect from the players if he gives them unpalatable news straight from the shoulder.

I wish I had been more honest and open to Allan Lamb when the decision was taken to relieve him of the England vice-captaincy in May 1991. I think I could have handled the situation better. On the Tuesday before the first one-day international at Edgbaston I should have taken Allan to one side when the England squad had gathered for training and told him what we had decided. Instead I shelved it because too many other things were going on and we needed time to discuss it on our own. The England committee had decided a few days earlier that it might be wrong to have the captain and his deputy of the same mature age and that we should start looking for someone younger to be the vice-captain. The decision had nothing to do with Allan's misdemeanour at the casino during the Brisbane Test, there was no sinister motive behind the thinking. On the Thursday night in Birmingham – with the game going into a second day – Allan and I had dinner and he told me that the press were asking him about the vice-captaincy. Was he still the number two? I apologized to him that he hadn't been told officially, but I still told him what the committee had decided. As a friend and a captain who had been perfectly happy with his work on three tours under me, I felt I owed him that. Allan said he was disappointed not to have been told earlier and I agreed it was wrong, it had been a cock-up. The following Monday, Allan and I were spotted having an animated conversation on the players' balcony at Lord's. The gist of Allan's complaint was that Ted Dexter had told him no official decision had been made, it was a fluid situation and that he might be called on again to do the job of vice-captain. So there were divergent versions from captain and chairman and I could see why Allan was a bit fed up. So he issued a statement to the effect that he no longer wanted to be considered for the post. I think we had made a rod for our own backs with talk of a vice-captain for home Tests because in all my time with England, there had rarely been a publicly nominated number two so why not just leave it at that? It's not as if we have been flush recently with many candidates of sufficient seniority to do the job. Perhaps we should have left well alone. More importantly I don't think I handled the situation as well as I might and I think it altered my relationship for a short time with Allan Lamb, which was sad.

It can be difficult for an England captain to keep tabs on his county's fortunes when he's away at a Test Match, especially when he's the captain of that club as well. I don't like to be seen to interfere in things at Essex while I'm away yet I want the players also to know that I'm still concerned about their welfare. I'll make one or two calls while at a Test to Keith Fletcher or my deputy to see if they want to discuss team selection for the game I'll be in charge of when the Test Match ends. I'll enquire about the score, who's doing well, but wouldn't go further than that and certainly wouldn't talk tactics or make suggestions. I heard that Mike Gatting tried that once during a Test and John Emburey his vice-captain gave him an earful down the phone from the Middlesex dressing-room!

There is a massive number of responsibilities for a county captain that don't actually involve work on the field of play. He has to negotiate the salary structure with the club at the end of the season, attend numerous meetings, try to keep the main sponsors happy, and take painful decisions about players' careers. I find that particularly hard, especially when you've grown up with somebody – like Alan Lilley who was released by Essex at the end of the 1990 season. Alan and I had been good friends for years but the club had to take a dispassionate decision about his future and I'm glad to say he was given an important post in charge of our younger players when he retired.

Despite all the extra work, I am very glad that I have at last been able to manage captaining both England and Essex. If I thought my frequent absences were harming the interests of Essex CCC then I would resign but they are a very efficient club. It's as important for me to do well for Essex as for England. It can be very hard to gauge what's going on from a distance when I'm away on England duty for a third of the season, so I rely on input from people at the club whose opinions I respect. It's not vital for a successful side to get on well off the field but it does help. In any walk of life, it's harder to enjoy your work if you don't like one of your workmates. At Essex Brian Taylor and then Keith Fletcher instilled the philosophy of enjoying your cricket and being successful at it and we have had a very harmonious dressing-room in my time. We have turned down at least one world-class cricketer who wanted to sign for us because we didn't think he would fit in to our particular atmosphere. Neither Doug Insole, Keith Fletcher or myself will tolerate backbiting among players at our club and if it isn't sorted out swiftly, their futures at Essex are bleak. It's not all sweetness and light at Essex, though. There have been a number of minor skirmishes in the dressing-room and during the 1991 season, two players almost came to blows over a practical joke that went wrong. I was away with England at the time but when I came back I made it quite clear to both players that I wasn't taking sides but there must be no repetition of the incident. Things like that have to be cracked down on hard and fast – and impartially. I didn't want to know who was largely to blame. I've seen players with other sides getting punchy with each other, picking up bats and threatening all sorts of mayhem, bickering about the batting order and why a certain bowler always gets to operate from the best end. It can be hard living in each other's pockets for so many days on the trot, month after month, and outbursts of temper are only to be expected occasionally. These minor disputes must be handled calmly and quickly to avoid escalation. Every player has his own idiosyncrasies and the secret of a happy dressing-room is to accommodate them as long as the rest of the guys can see the point of such tolerance. When Don Topley first came into the Essex first team, his clumsiness used to annoy some of the side; he was forever falling over someone or spilling something. I could see he was troubled by the irritation of the players so I called them together one day and said, 'Look, you're getting onto Toppers too much – leave him alone and let him get on with his cricket.' When I came back into the dressing-room later, the lads had written all round the wall the message, 'We love you Toppers'! Soon afterwards I was standing on the balcony watching the play in my bare feet when Toppers contrived to stand on my feet while wearing his spikes. After I had sworn at him, I was directed towards the message on the dressing-room wall: I believe the phrase is 'touché'! Sometimes people can be harsh in a team atmosphere. The trick is to take all the stick, give some of it back but don't bite too readily because you'll get even more. David East made the mistake of letting us know he didn't like his nickname of 'Ethel'. A very popular guy, David, but some of the lads reckoned he could be a bit of an old woman. Hence the nickname. Now David would take that from senior players but not from the young lads. He made the great mistake of saying to the second eleven players, 'Don't call me Ethel', and that stuck with him even more after that!

Neil Foster constitutes an interesting challenge of man-management. He can be awkward at times but that mental hardness does help him as a cricketer. He was more difficult in his early days under Keith Fletcher because he was very ambitious about playing for England and holding onto his place. Now he's more mature, with a greater awareness of his worth and his long-term injury has made him more philosophical. Although still inclined to be abrasive, Neil handles team-mates well when he stands in for me as captain and his influence in that department, as well as his bowling, had a lot to do with Essex winning the Championship in 1991. He has the odd moan now and then about his sore knee and I do try to keep him fresh for the relevant parts of a match but there are times when I have to be selectively deaf – when I've thrown him the ball, told him to get on with it and walked away as he's still having a go at me. I'll think to myself, 'That's a bit strong, Fozzie', but it's best not to make an issue out of it because he does give me everything once he's had a whinge. Some players feel better after a little moan and it's best not to take it too personally. My great mate, John Emburey, speaks his mind and is very honest and open but no captain should take his slight moans too seriously because he cares a great deal about the team and is a very popular, respected cricketer who would never try to lower team spirit. Derek Pringle likes to be different, he takes an alternative view just for the hell of it and plays Devil's Advocate in discussions. That can disconcert cricketers who aren't as intelligent as he is and he has to be careful to avoid talking down to team-mates. Derek still lives in Cambridge, where he went to university a decade ago and there's something of the eternal student in him, he is an anti-Establishment figure who perhaps doesn't really mean all that he says. When he has captained Essex he has been very good tactically, reading the game well, but he falls down on man-management because of the way he is perceived. When players eventually graduate to the captaincy, they are invariably categorized in the way they behaved when they were just one of the boys and Derek is now lumbered with the image of the over-keen debater. That is why he struggled to get all the players behind him when he captained the side.

Another difficult area for the county captain is selecting the right overseas player and making sure he fits in. The rest of the squad know he will be well paid for his talents and they will be looking for commitment and results from him. At Essex we also look for character and a willingness to join in the banter and contribute to a happy team spirit. We have been very lucky with our overseas players in the past twenty years and that has been due to successive captains and committees ensuring the new man fits in. We had a new challenge in 1991 – the first overseas player for Essex from the Indian sub-continent, and many were wondering if he would give us the expected commitment. I was certain Salim Malik was a top batsman and from what I had seen of him when he played for Pakistan, he was a nice guy. I did most of the negotiations with Salim, because it's important that the captain establishes a rapport with his overseas player as a lot is expected of him. Some of my negotiations were conducted from Perth during the Final Test in February and I can confirm it's not easy getting calls from Western Australia through to Pakistan! When Salim finally came to Essex he proved himself to be out of the top drawer in every way. Yet I soon discovered he was rather different from the rest of us. Just before the season started in earnest he rang me up and said, 'I can't come to practice today, captain – I've got to pray, it's the Muslim Christmas.' Well, there's not a lot you can say to that, is there? Midway through the season I took a major chance and allowed him to go home to Pakistan for a week. It was against my better judgement but his new wife was missing him, he was obviously homesick and she couldn't get over because she was doing exams at university. I consulted officers at the club, the fact that he had done so well for us counted in his favour and in the end I said, 'OK, Sal, you're on but don't let me down.' We had just one Sunday League match at Essex during that period and I was sweating about Salim getting back for the start of our next Championship match at Horsham. The day before there was no sign of him, so the club checked his flight from Pakistan – and he wasn't on it. My head was on the block and I was kicking myself for being soft in the head. At 9.30 on the morning of the match at Horsham, Salim was there. I had no idea how he got back from Pakistan, but he hadn't sold me short. I was pleased about that, because it suggested that he and I had built up a good relationship. That is the essence of the man-management task facing any captain.

9
The individualist

A thorny problem for a captain, this one. Especially this captain if you believe only *some* of the things that are written and said about me and my style of leadership. Gooch the dour, unimaginative man who spouts clichés about working hard and wants all his players to be of the same stamp as him. No room for flair in a Gooch side, what's the game coming to? Soon they'll all be drinking Perrier water, eating quiche and going up the stairs to bed by ten o'clock. A hundred laps of the boundary by nine in the morning, followed by half an hour of press-ups and straight back to the nets whenever you're dismissed. Is there no place for individualism and flair in Gooch's team anymore?

It all makes for good newspaper headlines on a dull day and I'm well aware that underneath a cliché there often lurks the germ of truth. I do believe in hard work, particularly as it applies to me; that hasn't always been the case though and I was in my late twenties before I started sorting out my approach to consolidating my place at Test Match level. I was just as keen on seeing flair rewarded at the expense of plodding mediocrity – as you'd expect from someone who played alongside, and greatly admired, the likes of Kenny McEwan, Ian Botham, David Gower and Derek Randall. It eventually dawned on me that the truly great players are the ones with immense flair and skill who also manage to stay at the top for a little longer than a couple of years. Players like Richard Hadlee, Dennis Lillee, Greg Chappell, Viv Richards, Imran Khan and Malcolm Marshall. Great talent brought those players their international chance but buckets of dedication, physical courage and commonsense kept them performing to such a high standard. All I really ask of my players is *to do themselves justice*. Not everyone has outstanding flair, but if someone is lucky enough in that direction, he'll have a more meaningful career if the flair can flourish within a framework of controlled discipline. That isn't a contradiction in terms. When Viv Richards chose to defend he batted with textbook authority, despite the matchless ability to play astonishing strokes. In my time, nobody has improved on the technical excellence of Gordon Greenidge's game, yet he regularly pulled good bowling attacks apart. Richard Hadlee was often too good for top batsmen, pitching the ball on middle and leg and hitting off-stump, but unplayable deliveries like that were also backed up by a stock ball that gave a batter no chance of easy runs. Malcolm Marshall never stopped probing, using his brains to get you playing differently, in a way that made you feel uncomfortable and therefore vulnerable. He didn't just run up and bowl and rely on flair alone, or his ability to swing the ball both ways from an unusually whippy, open-chested action. These were all great players who knew it wasn't enough to trust in feeling inspired on the big day. As someone once wrote, 'Genius is the infinite capacity for taking pains.'

I know I'm labelled as the captain with a soccer mentality, banging on about 'doing the business, getting stuck in, giving everything' and all those other platitudes but that label doesn't bother me. Everybody has an opinion of the England cricket captain and such perceived wisdom tends to stick despite the absence of hard facts. David Gower has always been labelled as 'laid back' yet anyone who has seen him lose his temper might revise their opinion. Mike Brearley the egg-head enjoyed a crude joke as much as anyone, Ian Botham the great inspiration has a very sharp cricket brain, but the character generalizations are never altered in the eyes of the general public. I fully admit that I'm a football fan but my team is West Ham – the apostles of flair football over the years – and my favourite players are Trevor Brooking and Bobby Charlton. If I was only interested in hard work and physical stamina in sport, then I would prefer teams and players that ran all day and stopped the opposition from playing.

I don't want to run a Gestapo-style régime as England captain. I just want us to do better in the international game. We have to acknowledge that we have been far too inconsistent over the last decade and that we haven't made enough of the talent at our disposal. A run of eighteen Test matches without a win suggests very clearly to me that we were under-performing. We should not have lost 5–0 in two successive series against the West Indies, despite the gulf in fast bowling expertise, and a 4–0 defeat in 1988 was just as depressing. So we had to look closely and critically at ourselves and ask about the priorities for the England players. Is it to have a nice lifestyle, a bottle of champagne before going out to play for your country the next day, to shrug the shoulders at another defeat and expect to be picked again soon? Or to take steps to win something and still have the enviable lifestyle? If you're successful at cricket these days, you can earn enough to keep the wine cellar well-stocked and run a smart car but it's only right that the extra material rewards demand greater commitment to the job. I like a few drinks as much as anybody (honestly!) but won't go over the top if I know there's a hard day ahead of me. I admit I wasn't always so professional but for years now, I've firmly believed that you get from this game what you put into it. One of the main attractions of being England captain is the opportunity to reverse our decline in Test cricket – when even newcomers like Sri Lanka gave us a good game in the eighties and all the other Test-playing countries won a series over here. I don't recall the media and the public saying, 'Don't worry, selectors – keep trusting in flair, it'll be alright.' What they said was, 'Why are we so awful? Why is everybody beating us?' The captain of England owes it to the domestic game to knit our talents into a pattern that will thrive in Test cricket and if we start winning consistently, the crowds will flock to the Test matches. That in turn will financially benefit all facets of English cricket and we might be able to keep soccer off the back pages for a little longer. The terrific public reaction to our improved performances against the West Indies in 1991 confirmed how much the supporter wants us to do well, to play with pride. I shall never forget the emotional scenes at the Oval when a packed crowd saw us win on the final afternoon and I felt very proud of the manner in which we had competed on equal levels with the opposition all summer. That England squad had been fashioned on my terms after the disappointments of Australia. Decisions had been made that may have appeared unpalatable but the reasons for drastic action were valid. It had to be done my way.

Ian Botham has been the biggest individualist I have encountered in my cricket career and one of his great strengths has been his powerful ego, his conviction that he was the greatest of the all-rounders of his time. Throughout his career, he has marched to a different drum to the rest of us and in general terms, that hasn't perturbed me too much because whenever he got on the field, he was a hundred per cent trier and a very supportive team-mate. Because of his charisma he *can* be a handful and some younger, sensitive players have been at times disorientated by the usual Botham paraphernalia when a story broke – the phone in the dressing-room ringing constantly, the TV cameras whirring, flashlights popping, the press sniffing around for some meat on half a story. Ian's immense mental resilience and self-confidence would allow him to shrug all that off but it must have been hard for some of those young Somerset players trying to learn their trade in the glare of the Botham circus.

For the rest of his life Ian Botham will be news and it was only to be expected that he would have provided the media with a great story before we left to compete for the 1992 World Cup in Australia. We had the usual half-truths: Botham would rather appear in pantomime and a television quiz game than play for England. He was holding the England selectors over a barrel and demanding terms for the tour that suited him. Cricket writers who are normally fairly sensible were frothing at the mouth at Gooch reneging on his principles and Botham dipping out of the New Zealand Test part of the tour because he just didn't fancy it. Who does Botham think he is? Has Gooch taken leave of his senses? The answer to the last question is 'No' and the truth behind the negotiations in September 1991 indicates that I *can* bend from my alleged dogmatic stance and that I *do* feel there is scope for the individualist in a team game.

I was very happy with Ian's return to Test cricket for the last two Tests of the summer. He had been very good news at the Edgbaston one-day international in May, until injury put him out for a time and then it was a case of him having to work his way back by county performances. He did exactly that and his presence as the all-rounder gave us balance. He batted responsibly against the West Indies, caught well and bowled intelligently. The Golden Arm was still there: if I had caught Desmond Haynes off a straightforward chance at slip, he would have had a wicket in his comeback over in Test cricket after an absence of two years. Even more impressively, he showed how much Test cricket still meant to him. Apart from a stomach upset that genuinely laid him low on the first morning at the Oval, he practised conscientiously with us and clearly enjoyed it. He was full of positive ideas out on the field and I gave him the freedom to pass any thoughts on to the bowler at the time. He would run all the way up from slip, have a word with the bowler as he walked back, then sprint back to his place in the slips. The younger players thought he was terrific, he made them feel they'd known him for years and he *communicated* a relish for the job. I am convinced that Ian's presence in the side at the Oval gave us an extra dimension of big-match flair and in the process gave us a better chance of beating them. His belief rubbed off on the younger players and they looked up to him.

After the Oval, I would have been mad not to want Ian Botham with us during the World Cup the following February and March. I knew there would be complications and Micky Stewart and I started trying to resolve them amicably and to everyone's satisfaction. Ian had already signed to appear in pantomime either side of Christmas so obviously he would not be able to fly out with us to the New Zealand leg of the tour on December 27. Nor would he be fit enough, having not been involved in our training schedules. Resisting the temptation to tell Botham that his life had been one long pantomime, I was aware that he had done the same thing last year, that the money was excellent and that he had had to make a decision about it before we brought him back into the England side in August. He hadn't been selected for the last two England tours, he wasn't one of those placed on a year's contract to secure his exclusive playing services and there had been no concrete commitment by the England selectors that Ian would be recalled. Who could blame him for tying up a good deal for himself and his family, rather than waiting until September to see if he had been picked for the winter tour? He felt a loyalty to the producer of the 'Question of Sport' television programme that had given him a good public profile over the past three winters and they had already scheduled in the recording dates for the next run – and they clashed with the World Cup. It seemed as if he was boxed in and wouldn't make it.

BBC Television agreed to reschedule recording dates for 'A Question of Sport' which would allow Ian to make it out for the World Cup. I found out about this from Ian a week before the touring party was to be named and I told him that I would want him out in New Zealand as soon as possible in January. He would be no use to me turning up just a fortnight before the World Cup started because I needed to be happy with his fitness. Ideally he ought to be in New Zealand for the last two Tests so that if necessary he could get in some match practice and – if sharp enough – compete for a Test place. He agreed that at his age he couldn't just expect to turn it on after being away from cricket for so long: this from Ian Botham, it must have got through to him at last! I was convinced that he really wanted one final crack at the World Cup and that he knew he had to give himself the best chance of doing well by getting to New Zealand, in time to acclimatize himself and do some hard work. In the end the difference between us was three weeks and I could live with that.

At no time did he hold a gun to our heads, it was never a case of 'take it or leave it'. We reached a satisfactory compromise which was necessitated by Ian seeking winter employment before he knew that the England selectors still wanted him. All he ever did was tell us of his commitments and then we sat down and tried to resolve the problem. I would do that for any player provided I thought he was worth the compromise. The initiative to work something out was a joint effort, prompted by our satisfaction with his efforts at the Oval and Ian's conviction that he wanted to make a big impression towards the end of his international career. I was sure he wanted to be the star again and his ego wouldn't permit him the luxury of turning down the opportunity to prove so many people wrong yet again. That has always been a very powerful motivation to Ian Botham. He knew that the media would crucify him if he looked unfit when he got out there, that if he screwed up it would reflect badly on him and me. I wasn't concerned what the other England players might feel because I knew that a rejuvenated Botham would simply improve our chances. If he had let us down it would be the familiar story of the media turning a medium-sized molehill into Mount Everest. That has happened on other tours when Botham has slipped. Everything was spelt out clearly to Ian before we left at the end of December and I was confident that his renewed hunger for the big time would be decisive.

Ian and I both know he is not the force that he was. In his younger days, he was a genuine, high-class swing bowler with pace and a top-drawer number six batsman. He still bats well and is capable of taking apart any attack but his bowling now relies on crafty variations unless the wicket is green and suits him. He might struggle to live up to his past Test performances, the sort that can give you a century or five wickets in an innings regularly. He is more suited now to the role of fourth seamer because he's not as penetrative as he was. Yet he still gets wickets through his reputation and he puts the ball in the right spot: there were more 'gimees' from Ian when he was a front-line bowler but now he is ideally suited to one-day cricket because the batsman has to take risks against him to get him away. He hits the seam, still swings the ball and I was pleasantly surprised during the Oval Test to see that his quicker ball still had a bit of zip in it. Ian is a very knowledgeable cricketer and I enjoyed seeing him share his thoughts with others in the side. Encouraging words on bowling are ten times more valuable coming from him rather than me because he has been a great performer.

Ian's genius papered over the cracks in my early years in the England team and fostered the belief that you could get by if the ceiling of talent was high enough. We got out of jail twice in 1981 because of his massive ability and sense of occasion but results like Headingley and Edgbaston only come along once in a lifetime and you need more than a re-run of those videos to prepare for a Test series against Australia. Both Bob Willis and David Gower struggled to stop Ian bowling when they were captain, because he loved to bowl and there was undeniably a chance of something happening when he was on. A young Botham today might have to be more restricted in his social excesses if he were to have a long career and end up with the same amount of runs and wickets for England, because more is needed now than when he first played Tests in 1977. I would hope that he would have been just as charismatic a player, just as influential on the opposition by the force of his personality. I can't think of too many other batsmen that all the England players would go out onto the balcony to watch. There was always something happening when Botham was at the crease and he has been tremendous value for English cricket and the spectator. Above all he still *loves* the game and proves that there's still room for the individualist in cricket.

David Gower is a player I admire as much as Ian Botham but I question if he has ever had Botham's desire to win, to get enjoyment out of his chosen career. Botham has been sidetracked now and then into daft activities but fundamentally he still looks forward to playing cricket, to having a laugh with the guys but giving everything on the field.

More and more, David appears to enjoy a high profile personality, and I have to question the way he maintains his standards. Since Botham and Gower returned to the England side under my captaincy, I have said the same thing to them about preparation: 'Do the minumum that's necessary to maintain your standards as you get older. I don't expect you to run around like a twenty-year-old but don't make it difficult for me. I believe the older players have to set an example. If the younger ones see us fooling around in the nets, they'll think it's okay to do the same.' It was out of respect for what they had achieved as players and an awareness that neither of them had ever appeared to relish practice that I asked them to set the right example. They wouldn't be trained into the ground. Botham threw himself into it with gusto and laughed and joshed a lot. He knew that attitudes had changed since he was last an England player and was sensible enough to go along with what was needed. On the other hand I think that in Australia David could have given more to the team in terms of advice, encouragement or example in practice. I felt that all he gave me was his great talent when he walked out onto the field to bat. I was prepared to accept the distinctive way he bats but not the way he prepares for a game. If someone had said, 'David, you don't have to go to the nets today,' he might find that very acceptable. I get the feeling that David feels the hard work is just done for the sake of appearances but that's nonsense. You don't go through the motions for two hours just to impress the media but to improve your own standards. In Australia David didn't seem to notice that his fielding had deteriorated. He was a brilliant fielder in his youth and although he can't help the fact that his chronic shoulder injury means he can't throw very well anymore, his general approach was lackadaisical and he misfielded too often for a natural mover of his class. With so many average or poor fielders in our squad it would have been heartening to see someone of David's experience put in some hard fielding practice in the hope that he would have set a good example, but it was not to be. Maybe David's routines and methods that served him well a few years back don't work so satisfactorily now. Do you prepare in an enthusiastic manner or do you just hope to get by on minimum output? Although still a brilliant player on his day, David now tends to get himself out in daft ways. He's careless with a talent that comes so easy to him. I believe that when you get to your middle thirties the eyes and reflexes aren't so sharp, that you have to accommodate the passage of time and adjust your technique. I wouldn't dream of wanting David Gower to alter his instinctive style that has made him such an exciting batsman but I think if he worked a little harder in practice at the shots he plays so well and sorted out which balls he should leave alone, then he would still be an instinctive player – but a better one. I want to see him bat gloriously more often and I feel he'd have a better chance if he did more than just hit a few balls, assume the touch was there and it would all come good when he wandered out to bat. I believe those days become scarcer as you get older.

Of course David has a tremendous record to back up his claims that he knows the best way to approach his batting in a Test match. Forget for the moment that he has scored so many runs with such class and elegance over the years: what about the bravery he has shown against fast bowlers all over the world? It takes a very special batsman to maintain Gower's type of consistency over more than a decade, and not experience the horrors or the twitches against top-class fast bowling. Of course, he has had a mediocre series now and then but no one can ever question his guts when it has been really tough. The West Indies fast bowlers would be the first to agree; some of the half-centuries David made on the Caribbean tour of 1986 were, in the circumstances, worth their weight in gold. I remember how shell-shocked many of us were at times in that series against formidable fast bowling on wickets that occasionally were very difficult, but David's understated bravery never left him. He has been a great player in a long and very distinguished career. I'd just love to see concrete evidence from him that he wants even more success badly enough to adapt to the passage of time.

It would be wrong for me to be too sweeping about David's batting because in Australia he showed what a superb batsman he still is. He didn't miss out after that tour because of my reservations over his erratic tendencies on the field. His attitude was much more relevant. I consider myself still to be a friend of David and we have never actually fallen out. It's just that I've decided to go about the job in a different way. He has had an uneasy relationship with Micky Stewart over the years; his concept of what's needed to do well at international level doesn't seem very close to that of Micky and I can only speculate what David felt when he found out during the summer of 1989 that Micky really wanted Mike Gatting reinstated as England captain the previous spring only to have the decision vetoed in favour of David. I wasn't involved in any of that but when the captaincy came to me that September, I just got on with the job in the way I saw fit. Perhaps David grew to dislike our approach to preparation because it symbolized an ethos that didn't agree with him. The fact is he was happy to be picked for the Australian tour and an intelligent man like him must have known what was in store for all the players – especially as he had seen our work at close hand in the Caribbean when he covered the Test series as a journalist. Now and again in Australia David would stop and have a word with the press when we were trying to get the practice organized. So we couldn't get started until he was finished with his chat. I couldn't care less who David talked to among the press contingent (even though some of them had cheerfully shafted him in 1989) but I failed to see what was wrong with doing the work first and then talking to them all day if necessary. I am well aware that if one player dawdles and holds up the practice, some of the others will do it as well and you're getting nowhere. For me the object of the practice was to do it professionally, to enjoy it, get it over with and then relax whichever way you wanted. David didn't seem to enjoy that part of the England set-up. At Christchurch towards the end of the tour, David deliberately held up our slip catching practice because he was talking to a chap. Allan Lamb, Mike Atherton, Robin Smith and I stood there, waiting for the fifth member to join us but he carried on chatting. 'No, we'll wait for David,' I said loudly and thirty seconds later, I said it again. 'Okay, okay' David replied irritably as the bloke handed over his card. When David finally joined us, we exchanged sharp words.

Later, when we had our heart-to-heart over dinner in Wellington I brought up that incident as an example of my irritation with him. David told me the bloke was also called David Gower and that's why they were chatting; he seemed genuinely more interested in that piece of information than in joining us for catching practice. I think it's safe to say that the other David Gower would have waited for the more famous version to finish his practice before chatting if he hadn't been encouraged.

In my own mind I gave David a fifty-fifty chance of getting in the England side for the West Indies series. I needed to be convinced that his desire to beat Geoffrey Boycott's record of England Test runs wasn't just something he now fancied because the media kept harping on about it. In the end he never got enough runs to warrant selection and I'm still sceptical if he will fit into the present set-up. It's hard to say if he'll get back in again under my captaincy: certainly the door is not closed but I just wonder if he is now too set in his ways to change. I would ask the question: does he enjoy his cricket? You have to question the motivation of a player of David's class who didn't get a first-class hundred in the whole of the 1991 season. He must have known that the best method of getting back in the England side was by sheer force of runs, to *make* us pick him. I got more letters about David in 1991 than about anything else: I was accused of being jealous of him, because he has a better Test record than me and that I was hopeless at fitting an individualist into the team plan. Everyone's entitled to their opinion and I shall have to live with the allegation that I truncated David Gower's Test career. When I'm gone as England captain it may be that he'll again be an automatic choice. It's my personal preference to do what I believe is right; there is more to Test cricket than just how you play out in the middle. David says he doesn't believe in cloning. Neither do I. Yet he failed to give me what I asked from practice – the bare minimum for a couple of hours. I thought it was vital for the inexperienced players to be able to say 'Look at Gower – he's got 7,000 Test runs and yet he's still putting in.' That enthusiasm would have rubbed off on the others and helped us knit closer together. There was no question of expecting David to battle away at practice and enjoy it. I was surprised he didn't notice how his great mate, Allan Lamb saw the importance of working hard at his game. And it's not as if I've ever suggested to Lamby that he should stop enjoying himself.

It may seem that I'm being over-critical of David but I really feel he has so much still to offer England. I just wish that somehow he could be sparked into the kind of positive action that would win him back his place in the England side. Maybe this criticism from me might sting him, because cajoling doesn't seem to have worked. David is still young enough to make a major contribution at Test level but for his sake and that of English cricket, he needs to approach things in a different way. He remains a magnificent batsman but his approach to the task isn't right in my opinion. A player has to put in more as he gets older, no matter his talent. David and I have never really had angry words or a serious disagreement about anything; we are simply different types when it comes to how we approach our cricket and I don't blame him for that. I certainly don't blame him for our failure in Australia – how could I after those two superb Test hundreds? I take ultimate responsibility for that disappointing tour because I was the captain and in the end it was my fault that I didn't get all that I wanted from David. Having liked and admired him for many years, I would be very sorry if Test cricket had seen the last of David Gower. But so much depends on him.

The return of Phil Tufnell to the England team at the Oval in 1991 proved very successful. He is nothing if not a character. Tufnell is a media man's dream because not only is he a highly skilful spin bowler but he is so expressive. He's readily identifiable, everyone jeers at him because of his fielding and they like to see someone playing for England who's about as bad as a club cricketer in that department. Phil is certainly a specialist, although I'd like to see him working at his batting like an Emburey or an Illingworth and making himself a safe fielder like a Boycott. His problem is that he gives the impression of being scared of the hard ball in the field and that affects his confidence as he hears the whistles and the cat-calls. Yet he's quite quick to the ball and doesn't have a bad throw. His fielding was much better when he came back into the England side against the West Indies and Sri Lanka and the direct link was that he knew he had to pull his finger out. The penny dropped.

Tufnell's attitude in Australia wasn't good enough. His fielding and general cricket awareness were poor even though he showed rich promise in his bowling. He had to be made aware that there is more to top-class cricket than concentrating only when the ball is in your bowling hand. I told Mike Gatting out there that Tufnell was in grave danger of squandering his career if he didn't stir himself and I know Gatt and John Emburey were both concerned that their Middlesex team-mate had too many rough edges and was building himself a bad reputation. If I had been Tufnell I would have been mortified at the jibes hurled at me from the Aussie spectators, at all those 'Phil Tufnell Fielding Academy' banners but he seemed to shrug it off. He mistook notoriety for celebrity status out there. A very short fuse when decisions didn't go his way hardly endeared him to the umpires either and he just got too het up about things. When I ran over to congratulate him on his first Test wicket in Sydney, he turned his back on me and that can't have looked too clever to the spectators. I wasn't bothered whether he liked me or not, it was more important to me to get the best out of a player I thought had genuine natural talent.

We sat Phil down several times in Australia and told him his attitude and concentration on the field had to improve. He also had to learn to curb his temper. I was at pains to tell him how much I rated his bowling but I needed more than just that from him. So he was sent back to Middlesex to clean up his act and Emburey and Gatting kept me informed of his progress towards some sort of maturity. I saw an interesting quote from him in a newspaper in midsummer: he said he kept hearing people say 'Phil Tufnell – good bowler, but. . . .' He said he was determined to get rid of the 'But'. I liked that, it showed the proper amount of self-criticism. So he came back for the Oval Test on merit, having taken a lot of county wickets and was an instant hero in the first innings when he bowled the West Indies out as they batted like amateurs against the turning ball. The short fuse was still there, though, and the umpires reported him for having a go at Carl Hooper when I caught him at short extra cover in the second innings. I was throwing the ball up in delight so I didn't see Tufnell snarling at the batsman. On one level I can understand Tufnell's aggressive pleasure, having been hit all over the place by Hooper, but he let himself down because the television cameras picked it up and showed the incident time and again. Added to his reputation, incidents like that must mean large headlines that *don't* focus on his fine bowling. It may be that Phil saw the light after the Oval because a week later, he phoned me up to say that the papers had made too much out of a spat between him and Norman Cowans on the field at Trent Bridge, when Cowans had dropped a catch off his bowling. Mike Gatting was forced to intervene and gave Tufnell an earful. Understandably the papers picked up on a fiery reputation that Tufnell had deserved and they made something out of it. The fact that Tufnell phoned me to talk about the Trent Bridge incident made me realize that he was at last coming to terms with the need for acceptable standards of behaviour and knew that I would be concerned when I read about his latest outburst. I like aggression in my bowlers – I think it helps them – but not snarling and swearing that is obvious beyond the boundary. Phil has to be careful about how he expresses himself on the field because it can get the umpires' backs up. He can't complain about his media label because he *has* been a bad boy and he's got to work three times as hard to rid himself of it. I can't comment on his early cricket career but there are clearly some rough edges that need smoothing out. His chainsmoking doesn't bother me and I think that characters like Phil Tufnell are good for the game. It wouldn't even bother me if he still wore his hair in a ponytail, as he did when he first came into the Middlesex side. But what I *do* know is that he is a high-quality spinner, with twenty years at the top in front of him as long as he matures quickly. Individualists like Tufnell are worth a captain's trouble as long as he can see progress.

10
Dealing with the media

I'm not what you would call media-friendly for a number of reasons: a shyness that's obvious when I'm with strangers, a long memory of suffering occasionally at the hands of some pressmen and my desire not to fire up the opposition by being trapped into making provocative statements. The game is hard enough without some out-of-context quote being stuck up on the opposition dressing-room's notice board, as Tony ('I intend to make them grovel') Greig discovered in 1976 at the hands of the West Indies. I *do* think good relations with the cricket media are preferable to a stand-off because you can use them as a mouthpiece for your actions and that of the team. I also acknowledge that the amount of coverage the media provides boosts the game of cricket and helps line the players' pockets via sponsorship and general raising of our profiles. Yet there is only so much of an England captain to go round and my primary job is to lead and nurture the team, not to sit giving press conferences every day. I'm judged on what my side does out on the field, not on how many good quotes I can offer the men with the notebooks and the microphones. I believe the captain shouldn't be at the beck and call of them when *they* wish, because they are insatiable and want new angles all the time. When I became England captain I quickly put a stop to the Saturday night press conference – designed to give a few leads to the Monday papers after the usual rest day on the Sunday. I wasn't being unsympathetic but I felt that a captain's press conference before and immediately after the Test is fair enough for both sides. During the game I felt I was entitled to concentrate on the strategy, to spend a lot of time with my team and also play to my own expectations. Micky Stewart took charge of the press conferences during the Test, unless I had done something outstanding as an individual and I can't see how the media can say that's being uncooperative. It's not as if I ever wow them with any

138

stunning insights into the workings of the dressing-room. I keep telling them, 'I don't know why you bother with all this because I'm only going to trot out the same old stuff – about the need to keep working and if we play well we've got a chance of winning.' The media get disappointed when I don't give them any extravagant comments but that's the kind of person I am. I like to keep things on an even keel, whether or not I'm doing well as captain or batsman and I don't care if that's boring. When you captain a cricket team, you have to be natural in all areas. I've never claimed to be scintillating in my repartee or ad-libs.

This will surprise my critics in the media but I am much better at this sort of thing than I used to be. I'm not saying I'm all that good at it now, but I'm less confrontational, more inclined to peaceful co-existence even though I do bore some of them. I've mellowed a lot, I don't hold grudges like I used to. Maybe that's something to do with being more relaxed in the job. I've learned from watching politicians being interviewed so that if I don't want to answer a pointed question, I'll give another reply that's not strictly relevant. Sometimes I'm asked who'll be twelfth man and it may be that I haven't made up my mind and the player concerned will have to be told before anyone else knows – so it's a case of skirting round issues like that at a press conference. If I really want to nail my colours to the mast, then I know the platform is there for me, as in Perth in 1991 when I climbed into the shortcomings of some of my players on the Australian tour. My advice to my players about the media is to remember that they're always working. Cornhill Insurance, English Test cricket's main sponsor, has a hospitality tent where players, guests and the media find themselves at close of play and although the game is over for the day, some of the press guys are still looking for a story. The players must be on their guard in such circumstances because a rash word over a drink can still find itself in the papers next day – whether or not it's supposed to be 'off the record'. It's part of the job, to glean useful information and get one up on the opposition. That's the nature of the circulation war. I'm particularly concerned about this on behalf of new players coming into the England team. Graeme Hick will have learned a lot about media relations from the summer of 1991 as he changed from being the new great hope to that of a chump in a space of a few weeks in the media's eyes. We took a conscious decision to shield Mark Ramprakash from media exposure during that West Indies summer because the management felt that it was going to be hard enough coming to terms with the greater demands of Test cricket without being hassled for a quote that could easily be turned against him. The media thought it a sinister decision and that we were being a bit precious about a young man who could probably look after himself but he was happy to be left to concentrate on his cricket. It was done for his own good.

When Ian Botham was England captain I saw at first-hand how a quote can be turned into a major story. On the rest day of the Trinidad Test in 1981, Ian Botham acknowledged to the press that we were up against it, but everyone still left to bat would be selling their souls dearly. Otherwise, he warned, 'heads will roll'. That was putting it on the line in a big way and when play resumed, the captain threw his wicket away, trying to hit his great mate Viv Richards out of the ground to be caught at deep mid-off. We lost by an innings and Botham hadn't led by example. The press were then perfectly entitled to ask – whose heads will now roll, skipper, how about yours? That served him right, it was a silly thing to say. Dealing with the media is a bit like fast bowling. Some do it better than others and the trick is not to appear ruffled: I'm afraid Ian has had a lot of run-ins with the media. I learned from his experiences that a quote can come back and haunt you, that something said in an earlier context can be dusted off to give a different slant a week or so later. At Lord's in 1991, I gave an interview to BBC Television during one of the many interruptions for rain and Tony Lewis understandably quizzed me on Devon Malcolm's disappointing form so far in the series. I said all the proper things and underlined we weren't about to discard Devon, because I rated him and he had done well for me. As soon as I said that it dawned on me how it would be interpreted as 'Gooch Stands By Malcolm' which was true up to a point but nobody has a divine right to stay in the side, especially if they are under-achieving. Come the next Test at Trent Bridge we had a difficult decision: do we play Devon or David Lawrence? It just came down on the side of David so then my quotes from Lord's about Devon were thrown back at me. I never said that Devon would play at Trent Bridge; perhaps I ought to have been even blander in that Lord's interview. I managed to get it right over one controversial matter during that summer, though. One of the tabloid cricket correspondents had developed a bee in his bonnet about the merits of four-day cricket and he kept trying to trap me into saying something provocative about it. He knew that my county club, Essex, have been broadly against the idea, yet the England committee favour the longer game. I can see merits in both arguments but I didn't see why I should be isolated and drawn into a discussion about it in my role as England captain. It would lead to something like 'Gooch Slams His County Over Four-Day Game' and I wasn't having that. Time and again, I'd be sat there, discussing the forthcoming Test Match, and this particular reporter would lob in a question about four-day cricket. Irrelevant to the task in hand but possibly under orders from the sports desk?

The writers at the tabloid end of the market are under enormous pressure to sell papers so they're looking for something controversial to stoke up sales. That's why Ian Botham has been a godsend and Phil Tufnell should keep them entertained for a few years to come. The circulation war is the writers' problem, not mine. One of the cricket reporters from a tabloid justified his paper's attitude to me along the lines of, 'We give players stick if things go wrong but if they do well we go over the top the other way. So Captain Cock-up then becomes Captain Courageous.' Now I agree that a sportsman has to be thick-skinned about media criticism and shouldn't be upset when he is justifiably slated for mistakes in the field but there are limits. I don't think it was very fair that former players were called in by the tabloids and in exchange for money, proceeded to dissect Graeme Hick's technique and conclude he just wasn't worth an England place. It wasn't all that pleasant to be called 'Gower's Goons' in 1989 and if I had been Mike Gatting, I would have been talking to my lawyers about that 'Gatt the Prat' headline in one of the tabloids. I had no qualms about suing the Sun in 1983 when they alleged that I wasn't at all fussed about England's efforts in Test matches anymore. The article (headlined 'I Couldn't Care Less About England') coincided with England's poor showing in Australia and my ban for going to South Africa in 1982. I believe the Sun had lifted a couple of quotes from a South African cricket newspaper, made a few up and the tone of the article incensed me. It made it look as if I was happy to sun myself on a South African beach, shrugging my shoulders at some good friends of mine being hammered by the Aussies while I picked up some easy money. I wasn't going to be fobbed off by an apology tucked away somewhere so I took the paper to court and won.

In 1986, when I made myself unavailable for England's winter tour of Australia, I was upset at the tone of an article written by an experienced cricket correspondent in a national newspaper. The gist of the piece was that I was letting England down, that as well as missing the Ashes battle, I would have the added perk of lying on an Aussie beach with a cold beer in my hand, without needing to worry about what was going on back home in the depths of an English winter. Yet that was precisely the point – I would have been worried about my family if I had gone to Australia that time. My twin daughters had been born in June, 1986 and with my other daughter, Hannah just a toddler, the three daughters were a handful for two parents, never mind my wife on her own. Any father would surely understand my dilemma and that is why I felt I owed it to my family to stay at home that winter. Yet that nasty, vitriolic article ignored the fact that England cricketers are also human beings.

I was even more astonished at a work of fiction in the Daily Mirror in February 1989 that led to an out-of-court settlement and an apology to me. It was stated as a fact that I had signed to go to South Africa, in the knowledge that I would be banned from Test cricket again. I took it up with their sports editor, got little satisfaction and took the paper to court. It was an amazing story; other names were bandied around but I was already signed and sealed, according to the Mirror. At no stage during 1989 was I ever asked to go on the tour that was eventually captained by Mike Gatting. I had dined with Ali Bacher and Joe Pamensky of the South African Cricket Union in February 1989 and someone must have tipped off the Mirror that I had been seen with them, no doubt talking terms. That conveniently ignored the truth, which was that I had been friends with Ali and Joe for years and that we always met up when they were in England. Joe and Ali wrote letters testifying that I hadn't been signed up and the Mirror's defence collapsed. That article did me no favours at all when you consider that I was still nominally England captain and wanted to carry on. It was untrue and offensive and I was worried that, whatever appeared by way of an apology, some of the mud would stick. Someone writes a tale, knowing it's not true and they're prepared to take the consequences, while the innocent victim wonders if the public believe the allegation, whatever's sorted out afterwards.

Soon after that Mirror fabrication I was turned over again by one section of the media. A local journalist who I know and trust rang me up to ask for my reaction to the possibility of losing the England captaincy to David Gower. I said I would be disappointed but that Ted Dexter was perfectly entitled to his opinion and I would continue to give everything to the team and to whoever was the new skipper, if it weren't me. An hour or so later, I punched up the news on my teletext and saw the headline: 'Gooch Says He Wants To Step Down As England Captain', with a single quote from me about Ted Dexter being entitled to his own opinion. I was very angry at the suggestion that I was happy to give the job away. I was sure the local journalist hadn't distorted my views but a couple of phone calls made sure the headline was corrected.

I get amused when some of the cricket media go all moralistic even though they have no idea of the tensions going on out in the middle. At Hyderabad in 1989, during the Nehru Cup, I had a few words with some of the Australians when they thought I had hit a ball from Geoff Lawson and I didn't walk. That was rich coming from the Aussies and their double standards annoyed me. Allan Border had a go at me in the field and I responded heatedly but it was all over in a moment. Afterwards Border apologized to me and we remained the best of friends. At the press conference one of the English tabloid writers wanted to know about the incident and I said it was none of his business, that it was a private matter and had been amicably sorted out. The journalist was really sniffy at me and said, 'It *is* my business, the public has a right to know.' I thought that was ridiculous, to me the folks back home would have been more keen on Wayne Larkins' excellent hundred and a win at last over Australia. The tabloids also did Chris Broad no favours at all during the Lord's Test in 1988 when he was seen swearing as he walked back to the pavilion after he had been given out. Now Chris had brought a lot of this on himself in recent months after serious instances of dissent on the field at Lahore and Sydney, but this one at Lord's was different. He was only doing what every batsman does at some stage – wondering *how* that could be out – and no other player, or either of the umpires was anywhere near to him at the time. The television cameras picked up Chris's displeasure and no one else in the ground would have known about it otherwise. The tabloid boys spotted the anger, wrote up the incident into one of major proportions, with his other offences being taken into consideration. So they demanded a course of action from a pedestal and Chris Broad was left out of the next Test. I don't know if form was the only reason but the England management had been put into a corner by the tub-thumping of the tabloids. It was Chris's own fault that he had built a reputation, but he was unlucky to have been sucked into a storm in a tea-cup at Lord's. The power of the media is very strong and cruelly distorting. The fact that we were again second-best in that 1988 series counted against Broad because if England are winning, minor incidents like that one tend to get passed over. Otherwise the story keeps running with some skilful follow-up material. There is always one ex-player happy to say anything for a few quid.

In the end, the players can't win. It's a short career and the tabloid job will still be there, long after the reporter and the aggrieved cricketer have gone from the scene. Sometimes it pays to be a little 'economical with the truth' when the media ask you something that you'd like to keep quiet. When I broke my hand in the Trinidad Test of 1991 I kept it from the media when they asked about my injury because I didn't want my own players to know about the extent of my injury nor did I want the West Indies to get a boost, because we were still batting and it was a very tense situation. I also try not to put too much pressure on myself when asked for personal goals. In 1990, I was just over 200 runs short of 3,000 first-class runs in a season and, with four innings maximum left to me, I admit I fancied it – especially when I heard the feat hadn't been achieved since 1961. I kept quiet about that target when asked because it's simply not my style to beat the drum about my own game. So many factors can go wrong and I've learned to be cautious. When you get a 'pair' in your first game for Essex seconds and another 'pair' in your First Test, you tend to take things as they come. Sorry if that's boring but I'm made that way. I *do* have a sense of humour, though, and I don't think the media realized I was winding them up when I described my 333 against India as 'Okay'. I came into the interview room at Lord's sipping from a can of Diet Coke and I knew they were hoping for some uncharacteristic reactions from me, possibly even an expression of excitement. I was absolutely thrilled at scoring 333 in a Test Match but didn't want to kill the myth of me being a miserable, downbeat bloke so I played it low-key. The odd sardonic remark and the trace of a smile might have let the media know I was pulling their legs and trying to preserve my dour reputation but they were too busy trying to find me a moon to jump over. It doesn't bother me if they find me hard going; I'll be honest and straight with them most of the time but my priority is to get the team right in all areas. I'm just an ordinary bloke, with no pretensions, and I get the feeling from the general public that they prefer me to be myself, rather than talk a good game with the media and run the risk of relying on their support. In 1989 David Gower experienced how that backing can quickly slip away when you start losing. In March and April that year, he had massive support in the media for a return to the England captaincy, while I had no backers from that quarter. I could handle that but it must have come as a shock a few months later when those same correspondents sat in press conferences and asked David for detailed reasons about bowling changes earlier that day. No wonder he lost his cool at times, the captain shouldn't be subjected to such intense cross-examination.

Soon the skids were under David and I was back, without any acclaim from the media, but that didn't concern me in the slightest. I wasn't going to captain the side with their opinions concerning me. Some of them write witty and distinctive reports of a day's play but there are some poor judges of a player sitting in front of typewriters and microphones. Too often a performance in a county game assumes far too much relevance to them and they talk up a player when they haven't a clue how he would cope with the special pressures of a Test Match.

In case I sound too dismissive about the cricket media, I must point out that I have good relationships with a few that I can call friends. I'll talk to them privately on certain matters but don't expect to be quoted and they rarely let me down. It's human nature but I am more amenable when someone takes the trouble to get to know me, so that I can start to trust him. Some reporters can be very rude, ringing me up without even the courtesy of asking for a spare minute, trying to interview me even though we are complete strangers. I take exception to that, it is bad manners and certainly not the way to get information from me. I got very stroppy in Australia in 1990 when I played my first game at Bowral after my hand injury and a TV crew thought they could just walk up and interview me without first asking. I had been dismissed, I was sitting on the balcony watching the match when a microphone was stuck in my face and questions were fired at me. I would have been perfectly happy about talking if they had only asked me first but their brusque manner forced me to tell them to clear off. That kind of bad manners isn't exclusive to Australian television crews. When I lost the England captaincy to David Gower I was playing in a benefit golf match and an ITN crew tracked me down to the course. When I walked off the eighteenth green they ran the camera and asked the questions. They didn't get much from me because I was annoyed that one of them hadn't taken the trouble to walk up to me on the fairway and just ask if it was alright to do an interview with me once I had finished. That would have been not only the courteous thing to do but the professional thing because you surely get a better interview if the interviewee isn't resentful. Just because politicians and film stars don't mind being door-stepped for a quick quote doesn't mean that deposed England captains have to wear it. I had already experienced the special media demands on the England captain the previous August when I led England for the first time at the Oval against the West Indies. When the game ended, I spent more than an hour going up and down the stairs in the pavilion, giving interviews to

BBC TV, ITV, TV-AM, Breakfast TV, BBC Radio and Independent Radio, as well as a long press conference. I said I wouldn't do that again, there had to be some form of sharing the interviews because by the time I had satisfied everyone, I got back to the dressing-room and almost all the players had gone. I wanted to thank all the lads for giving me such a lot on the previous four days, for helping me to enjoy my first game as captain but I felt flat. The same feeling of anti-climax hit me at the Oval after we had beaten the West Indies on the last day, amid unforgettable scenes. I wanted to savour the excitement and join in the celebrations with my team-mates but by the time I had attended to my media duties the fun had died down. It's not as if I had given them any extraordinary quotes, we all know I'm no Mike Brearley in that department.

Somehow I can't ever see me getting as riled by the media as Viv Richards in the Antigua Test against us in 1990. It was astonishing that he chose to go up to the press box in search of an English reporter at the same time as he was supposed to be leading out his side. That played straight into the journalists' hands, they had a great story without leaving their box (difficult to claim expenses, though!). I have to admit that I once 'did a Viv', although not to the same extent. We were playing at Chelmsford against Warwickshire and I was very upset by Doug Ibbotson's report in the Daily Telegraph about an incident when I'd been batting. Gladstone Small bowled one to me that I missed and the Warwickshire keeper dived forward and didn't hold it. The Telegraph report said I was lucky not to be caught – but I hadn't hit it and everybody in the middle knew that. If the keeper had caught it, I'm sure there wouldn't have been an appeal. I read the account of the day's play in our dressing-room next morning and our lads wound me up because they saw I was annoyed. 'Why don't you go to the press-box and sort him out?' it was suggested and impulsively I did so. I didn't know Doug Ibbotson at all, asked who he was when I got to the press-box and then tore into him in front of his colleagues. I shouldn't have done that, I ought to have had a quiet word with him in private. I felt bad about it in the end because Doug Ibbotson wrote to me expressing disappointment at being treated that way in front of all the occupants of the press-box and that he had also written many glowing things about me over my career. Fair enough but it's a poor view from the Chelmsford press-box so why not ask me afterwards if I had nicked it, or the bowler or even the umpire? Just a simple factual point that any cricketer would clear up for a reputable journalist. At least my discussion in the press-box came before play started, though. Not for the first time, Viv went one better than me!

We players shouldn't bleat when we are fairly criticized by the media as long as it's not libellous or untrue. We're there to be shot at and we enjoy the perks when they come along. Perhaps the Curtley Ambrose way of dealing with the media is the best of all. Midway through the 1991 series in England, David Norrie of the News of the World wanted to do a feature on the strong, silent but deadly Curtley. They were discussing the possibility with Viv Richards when the big man loped past. 'If you want to know about Curtley', he said, 'You ask Curtley and no one else.' David said, 'Even better, Curtley — it's you I wanted to talk to in the first place.' Yet Curtley had the last word: 'Curtley speaks to no one.' Somehow I don't think the England captain would get away with that!

11
Some captains of my time

KEITH FLETCHER

I first met Keith when I was a shy teenager, playing for Essex's Club and Ground side. I turned up on my scooter with my cricket gear strapped to the back and didn't say a word to any of the seniors, I just played and went home. Keith broke the ice: 'Who is he then? Does he speak?' and after that I started to learn such a lot from him. His biggest asset was the way he'd carry a push for victory to the very end after manipulating the opposition to his will. He brilliantly assessed the defects and the pluses of players, how to bowl at them, where to place fielders to frustrate them. His memory for tactical weaknesses was as extraordinary as his lapses on names: for at least a season he kept calling Derek Pringle 'Hignell'!

One of his faults was that he sometimes failed to communicate to players why they'd been left out. On the morning of a match a captain has lots to do, with discussions about the wicket, the shape of the side, the likely weather, what to do if he wins the toss. Amid all this, there could be confusion about who was to miss out and at times Keith had to repair the damage later in the day. As I know from my unhappy time as Essex captain in 1987 the job can be very time-consuming and frustrating. Keith was instrumental in encouraging me to take up the reins again in 1989 and he was enormously helpful in taking a lot of the organizational pressure off my shoulders.

I think it's a great pity that he never got to captain England for any length of time because he was still a fine player and the best captain around when he was sacked in 1982. Even when Mike Brearley led us so successfully, it was generally accepted that Fletcher was the better

148

batsman. When it came to it, Fletcher's face didn't fit under the new chairman of the selectors, Peter May. Flicking off a bail when given out in the Bangalore Test of 1982 did Keith's cause no good, nor did getting involved in the stalemate over slowing the game down in the same series. You had to play in that series to understand just how monotonously the Indians played it and eventually it was the old story of England playing the opposition at their own game. For most of the series, Fletcher made the running but he was hampered by the need to pack the side with batting, because of his fears that we would lose at least a couple of wickets each innings with questionable umpiring. As a result we didn't have enough bowling to force many breakthroughs on dead wickets.

I've often wondered what would have happened had we taken Keith into our confidence in India and told him of our plans to go to South Africa soon after the tour ended. We felt that he ought to be protected from it and it was best he knew nothing because that would have compromised him as England captain. Of all those involved, he ended up losing more than anyone. When we got to South Africa, I rang him up and asked if he would come out and captain us. He asked for twenty-four hours to think it over and finally decided to stay with England out of loyalty. It was a major shock to him when he lost the England captaincy a few weeks later so he missed out on the money and the continuation of his England career when he was the best man for the job. I think he was at his most impressive after that shattering blow. A lesser man would have faded quietly away but he didn't sulk, he got stuck in and inspired Essex to a lot of trophies in the next year or so. He talked me out of dropping myself from the Essex team in 1982, when I couldn't get a run and was feeling sorry for myself and he remained an inspiration. His reflex catching at silly point was also marvellous for someone of his mature years.

I fell out with Keith once. It was over money and the dispute simmered for a few months. At the end of the 1977 season I was disappointed to learn that under a new salary arrangement I was lagging behind the other capped players and I wasn't happy about that. My nose was put out of joint and – even though I had played for England – I was feeling a little insecure because things hadn't gone all that well for me since my England appearances two years earlier. I was looking over my shoulder and the new pay offer didn't exactly make me feel more confident. Despite going to see the club chairman, I got nowhere. Keith and I weren't exactly bosom buddies over that but it was never mentioned again. He shared with Mike Brearley the attitude that a row helps to clear the air but once it's done and dusted it shouldn't be aired again. Both believed in a clean slate and I hope I've inherited that characteristic.

More than anything else, Keith Fletcher instilled in me the desire to win, to compete all the time, to communicate that enthusiasm to my players. As he used to say, 'You don't win points sitting in the pavilion.'

MIKE BREARLEY

Mike had an inner toughness that sometimes revealed itself on the field if things didn't go the way he wanted and his outbursts of temper could be hot. After he had bawled out a player that was it – finished – and he'd revert to his usual calm authority. You knew where you stood with Mike Brearley, he had this great ability of making his men play for him. Unlike Fletcher, he was occasionally tough on matters like discipline off the field and punctuality and he preferred team meetings to Keith's quiet word with an individual. Both men were lucky with the quality of players at their disposal but no one could match Brearley's knack of getting the best out of Ian Botham. If he thought there was more in the Botham tank he'd wind him up on the field with a few tart comments and he would deflate him in the dressing-room if Ian started horsing around at the wrong time. In the verbal battle between those two, there would only ever be one winner.

Ian respected him and I think the age difference helped because anyone could see what a well-travelled, competent person Mike was. He also had a brilliant cricket brain, the ability to sum up a situation correctly and quickly. The difference in Botham's performance when Brearley returned as captain in 1981 was too great to be circum-stantial. He liberated Ian again, restored his self-confidence and allowed free rein to his marvellous talents. It's been said that Brearley overbowled him in his great years between 1977 and 1981 and the legacy of that may well have shortened Ian's career as a quickish swing bowler, but if I had been captain at the time, I would also have trusted a great deal in a bowler who thrived on hard work, loved to bowl and who had the talent to dismiss any batsman in the world with the perfect, unplayable delivery.

It was fascinating to observe the relationship between Brearley and Geoffrey Boycott. On the one hand, the cultivated master tactician with interests far beyond just cricket and, on the other, the prickly, proud Yorkshireman, obsessed with the game, not a favourite of the Establishment, certain that Brearley wasn't in his class as a batsman but grudgingly aware of his excellence as a leader of men. They rubbed along satisfactorily enough but that was largely due to Brearley's tact and sensitivity. When necessary he could be very firm with Boycott. Before the Sydney Test on the 1979–80 tour, Boycott was complaining of a stiff neck and the rest of the players came down to the team meeting with scarves around their necks to jolt Boycott out of his self-pity. When he started to suggest he was doubtful for the next day, Brearley cut him short – 'You're playing and that's it.' Everyone knew it would be a wet wicket after days of rain, and that Dennis Lillee would be a formidable test. Our captain knew that Boycott, with his masterful defensive technique, was our best-equipped player and he made it clear that he *had* to play.

I don't think Mike was at his best in Australia, where brashness sometimes spills over into insensitive rudeness. That 1979–80 tour was unhappy for him, not only because they beat us 3–0 with a side strengthened by the return of the Packer players but because the crowds gave him some terrible stick. They didn't like his beard, thought he was some posh descendant of Douglas Jardine and at times they succeeded in rattling him on the field. Ian Chappell insulted him during the match against South Australia when he put *all* his fielders on the legside for one over before lunch. Chappell bowled seamers at Mike and he blocked every ball. I thought Chappell's action was unnecessary and underlined that those two excellent captains would never be on the same wavelength. Somehow I could never envisage those two sitting down to a cosy dinner. Every England player captained by Mike Brearley would join him at the dinner table though. Mike's views on anything were always worth hearing. I have fond memories of a very nice man and an outstanding captain.

IAN BOTHAM

You can be the best player in the team but that doesn't mean you'll be the best captain. That is the main conclusion to be drawn from Ian Botham's unhappy time in charge of England. He was unlucky to face the West Indies in two series within a year and then Australia. It was also his bad luck that David Gower dropped Andy Roberts towards the end of the Trent Bridge Test of 1980, otherwise we would have beaten the West Indies in Ian's first Test as captain. Yet Ian never showed that he appreciated the importance of fine tuning in a side, to understand the needs of each player to get them playing for him. There is no justification for thinking that a genius or a maverick should be in charge, even though he is a star at playing that particular game: otherwise George Best, Bobby Charlton, Denis Law and Jimmy Greaves would have been successful football managers.

On the field, Ian was fine as captain. Positive, full of good ideas and intent on leading from the front. Even after he lost the captaincy he never gave up thinking aggressively. On the 1981–82 tour of India, we had our usual team meeting before the Madras Test and we went through the opposition. As we assessed each batsman, Botham had one stock response – 'He can't play the short ball, I'll bounce him out.' We're talking here about batsmen of the calibre of Gavaskar, Viswanath, Shastri, Vengsarkar and Kapil Dev. When we came to a player we didn't know much about Botham was true to form. 'Yashpal Sharma? No problem, he's dead. The bouncer!' Two days later, the Indians declared at 481 for 4 and on the way Yashpal Sharma had made 140 before being caught off a skyer from Botham's bowling. Our hero had the typical response to hand – 'Told you he couldn't hook!' Life has never been dull with Botham around.

I'm sure it still rankles that he had to hand over the England captaincy before he was sacked and that it took Mike Brearley to unpick the lock for him again as a player. He was wrong if he thought that it was only a matter of time before he recaptured his form while staying on as captain. By the time he resigned at Lord's, he was withdrawn. Ian didn't always set the right example in training, application and preparation. I don't think he was too young for the job, because he has remained essentially the same character, trusting to his instinctive talent as a cricketer rather than working at his game. Brilliant natural cricketers like Ian Botham don't always make outstanding captains. Such players are too vital to the side to be saddled with extra responsibility.

DAVID GOWER

There has been so much speculation about my relationship with David Gower in recent years that it's important to underline how much I admire and like the man. He has been a great sportsman, both in terms of actual achievement and also in the way he has conducted himself on the field of play. I've never heard one word of complaint about David

The hand injury which ruled me out of the last two Tests on the 1990 tour to the Caribbean. What a time to pick up my first serious injury in seventeen years of first-class cricket

Trinidad, 1990 – listening to some words of wisdom from Geoffrey Boycott. My former opening partner has been very helpful to me since I became England captain

No, I'm not rehearsing for a part in Godfather IV, I'm recovering with Micky Stewart after a run in Guyana on the 1990 tour

Ian Botham's first Test wicket for two years – and it's a popular wicket with his team-mates.
The Oval 1991, and Botham's self-belief is rubbing off on the others

Reaching my hundred in the Leeds Test of 1991 against the West Indies. There was still much to do . . .

One of the great moments of my England captaincy – victory at Leeds against the West Indies in 1991, the first against them in this country since 1969

It looks spectacular when they stick. Gus Logie gets that sinking feeling as I hang on to an instinctive catch at Leeds in 1991. It was our day . . .

The World Cup Final of 1992 and the two captains have different aims: I am hoping we can maintain our concentration in the field, while Pakistan's Imran Khan wants to push the score along with his partner, Inzamam-ul-Haq. In the end, Imran proved the successful captain from any umpire and despite the inevitable pressures at the highest level, he set a terrific example as captain in the principles of the way the game should be played. No wonder the guy is admired all over the world. He has been an adornment to the game at a time when the authorities have been rightly concerned at the decline in standards of sportsmanship. If every international cricketer behaved like David Gower when the spotlight is on him, there would never be any need for codes of conduct and referees. Others with less intelligence and sensitivity than David have tended to think themselves above the necessary standards that cricket demands but not David Gower, despite his stature. His popularity with all the players is also a tribute to his genial nature and lack of affectation; David isn't the kind of person who needs to draw attention to his achievements, his record speaks for itself.

I believe there is still a strong mutual respect between David and I. The fundamental difference between us is that I captain the side in a different way. I've noted how the other teams in Test cricket now approach the task and I think England needed to follow them and acquire greater professionalism and dedication. That suits my concept of how cricket should be approached when you're playing for your country. I appreciate others have a different vision, but as long as I have the honour of being England captain, I wanted things to run in the fashion that suited my beliefs. David differs from me in this respect and sadly we don't seem to be able to reach common ground.

I don't know David any better now than when we first played together for England in 1978. I like him, we are still good friends and I respect the dignified way he has restricted his public comments when he's been out of the England side. Other disappointed players with an excellent Test record like his would have taken a few swipes at me through the media but David has resisted. That essential remoteness of character in David must have been a factor in losing the England captaincy twice. When it came to the need to take the side by the scruff of the neck, to wring better performances from the players – David couldn't do it. At Lord's in 1986 David was sacked after losing the First Test to India, hard on the heels of a disastrous thrashing in the Caribbean. The chairman of selectors, Peter May, had already gone public about the need for David to be more assertive on the field, to crack the whip at times, instead of adopting his usual relaxed manner of dealing with his players. Now I had some sympathy with David's opinion that Test cricketers shouldn't need extra motivation from the captain but they do when they're up against it. In the Lord's Test against India he didn't show any signs of taking Peter May's message to heart, he was his usual self on and off the field. I'm not sure how close the relationship was between captain and chairman and David was clearly going to run things his way. His most pointed response to the ultimatum was to get some tee-shirts printed for the team. Ten of them had the words 'I'm *not*' and the other one, '*I'M* in charge'. I thought that was an amusing way of easing the tension we were all feeling and when David threw his tee-shirt to the new captain, Mike Gatting, the photographers got a great picture. That flippancy was probably a front for David's sadness but it's also been a characteristic that dogs him: how much does he really care about cricket? David has never been unaware of his commercial attraction and the possibilities open to him if he did well for a long time as skipper, but I was never sure if he wanted to explore the nitty-gritty of the job. It sometimes appeared like that when he captained Leicestershire: it wasn't the same style as when Ray Illingworth led them. I'm not sure how much the daily grind of county cricket appealed to David. If it rained, he appeared perfectly happy when it was called off, unless he lost the chance of a win.

There was a marked difference in David when he led us against Australia in 1989 from how he had been in 1985 when we played well to take the series 3–1. In 1985, after a bad start, he scored a lot of runs in his usual fluent style and the batters did very well for England that series. We also scored quickly, which gave us more time to bowl the opposition out twice. Our bowling wasn't all that special, but David handled our spinners (John Emburey and Phil Edmonds) well, he got some good performances out of Ian Botham, and Richard Ellison got Allan Border out a few times with late swing. The key to David's captaincy that summer was his own confidence with the bat and his ability to pressurize the Aussies in the field, with runs to spare. The boot was on the other foot four years later. We bowled badly in 1989, they clocked up large totals and then we batted poorly under pressure. It wasn't David's fault that our seam and swing bowlers let him down at Leeds, when he put the Australians in, with conditions favouring the bowlers. The captain can't bowl it for them, they have to show their international worth and they didn't at Leeds. After that defeat – losing eight wickets between lunch and tea on the last day – we were really up against it. In my opinion David became more and more withdrawn on the field, letting the game meander along as he stood at cover. He'd put a bowler on and leave him instead of changing things around more often, whipping him off after three overs if he wasn't bowling well and switching ends, just to try something different. The players became disillusioned as David seemed reluctant to talk to any of the senior ones about tactics. Our team meetings were always constructive and positive but when it came to the crunch, David didn't carry into action his impressive words. It's so much easier when your team is playing well but at other times, some of them have to be led very firmly and encouraged at length. That has never been David's style and I suppose it's to his credit that he wouldn't go for cosmetic gimmicks, like running around the pitch, smacking his players on the backside and geeing them up. If he had, we would have thought he had taken leave of his senses – but I believe we needed more from him as our captain in '89.

My critics will say that I didn't help him by asking to be left out of the Trent Bridge Test that summer. David and Micky Stewart both asked me to reconsider my decision, but I felt it was best for both parties that I stood down. I hadn't been playing well, we were already 3–0 down in the series with two to go and it gave them an ideal opportunity to have a look at a younger opener, to look to the future. At the time I acted in good faith, because I wasn't worth my place in the team. In hindsight, I was wrong to stand my ground and I should have agreed to play.

It wasn't the first time that I had asked to be left out of an England team. In 1986 I was also unhappy with my form and felt I didn't deserve selection but Mike Gatting wouldn't hear of it. I played in the next Test and scored 183, so Gatt was vindicated. In '89 I imagine I would have played if really pressed and now Micky says he would have forced me to play, but I was only trying to help the side. I suppose my threat to go home from the 1986 tour to the Caribbean can be construed as being less than helpful to David Gower but I stayed on eventually out of loyalty to him. I had played poorly most of the series and I was conscious that a major contribution hadn't come from me in difficult circumstances – but even though I felt upset at being used politically, I still gave my all to the team. There were important principles at stake and David was very sympathetic. I don't feel I let him down.

Despite his excellent effort in winning a Test series in India (and that after being one down early on), and even though he led England well against Australia a few months later, David's record as England captain will be questioned. He had two stabs at it but in the end people will say he simply lost too many Tests. Fourteen out of fifteen in three series is a lot; with more determination and motivation from David, who knows what would have happened in those fourteen Tests against West Indies and Australia?

MIKE GATTING

In 1984 I told a television interviewer that England ought to take Mike Gatting to India as vice-captain, even though his England career was on the line at the age of twenty-seven. He had been in and out of the team since 1977 and never settled or scored a Test hundred. Yet I thought he was a good enough batsman to score a lot of Test runs once he felt sure of his place and his breezy attitude to the game would be an ideal foil to David Gower's measured, relaxed style of captaincy. By all accounts the partnership worked excellently out in India and Gatt was a permanent fixture in the side for the next four years – clocking up the centuries and captaining the side for two incident-packed years. I have long felt that Mike was an excellent captain, my type of leader. He cared about his players, got them working for him, set a fine example at practice and preparation and led from the front out on the pitch. One of those English bulldog-type figures, Gatt epitomized that never-say-die spirit which sports followers admire. He had been brought up in a hard Middlesex school under Mike Brearley and Don Bennett and he would risk losing games if he had a chance of winning. He knows the game inside out now, he's used to the pressures of winning and he's one England captain whose form wasn't affected by the strains of the job – in fact his batting seemed to thrive on the extra responsibility. In time Gatt came to appear supremely confident in his own abilities and position as England captain and his downfall is a good example of the Banana Skin Syndrome. First the Shakoor Rana incident, then his dispute with the TCCB over what he wished to record in a book detailing his account of the events in Pakistan, then his sacking for being in the company of a barmaid late at night during a Test Match, and finally his last-minute decision to go to South Africa, incurring a Test ban. All in the space of twenty-one months. I felt very sorry for Gatt in all these situations but if he was going to be sacked as England captain it ought to have been for the spat with Shakoor Rana. That would have been something directly referable to his conduct on the pitch and, added to Chris Broad's tantrum at Lahore, it could be construed that the captain had lost control of discipline and flipped under pressure. An example could have been made of Gatt for the good of the game. Instead we all got a £1,000 bonus in Pakistan for hanging on in trying circumstances, which was curious, as we were contracted to see the tour through. It seemed strange that Mike was sacked for the incident with the barmaid, a non-cricketing reason for losing the job. It smacked of Trial by Tabloid.

I was very surprised that Mike decided to go to South Africa in 1989. He was obviously disillusioned about being passed over for the England captaincy in favour of David Gower, even though Micky Stewart and Ted Dexter wanted him. Mike had never struck me as someone who was all that concerned about matters in South Africa and he had pulled out of negotiations for the previous tour early on. He has always been a Union Jack person, to whom playing for England was very important. Micky Stewart tried hard to stop him signing up to the last minute and I think if he had stayed out of it, he would have been England captain again. Turning down a lucrative offer to go to South Africa would have won him back a few spurs at Lord's, I imagine.

I wish Mike Gatting had been in the England team under my captaincy in the last couple of years because he is my type of cricketer and bloke. He still has ambitions to lead England again. When we met up in Australia on the 1990–91 tour he told me, 'You'll probably carry on for a year or two. There don't seem to be too many contenders for the job, I'm four years younger than you and I hope my ban will be lifted soon.' He had it all worked out and certainly he would be my choice for the job. It all depends on how many black marks he still has at Lord's. I know I speak on behalf of other England cricketers when I say there's a sense of waste that Mike Gatting isn't playing for us.

ALLAN BORDER

Definitely a cricketer's cricketer, this man. One that the players look up to – for his achievements, the way he was worked at his game and his leadership by example. His excellence at short mid-wicket demonstrates that he has enough professionalism to work at his fielding and improve it, in his mid-thirties. That is the kind of attitude which earns a captain respect from his team. Allan Border is not the kind of leader who wouldn't do himself what he expected from the other ten players. A tough, nuggety character, he has no qualms about bawling out someone in the side and he can get grumpy if things don't go his way. I put that down to caring deeply about his cricket, rather than any lack of sportsmanship. I consider Allan a friend but you would never think so from the hard, unrelenting way he approaches the game on the field. That's fine by me, I've never been all that keen on fraternizing with the opposition during Tests.

Initially he was a reluctant leader of Australia after Kim Hughes had left the job tearfully. He tended to get very impatient with the side's shortcomings and, more than once, he was tempted to quit. On the 1985 tour to England, he carried the team's batting fortunes on his shoulders and when he failed in the last two Tests, nobody was prepared to fight it out like their captain. The tour party had been weakened by defections to South Africa and one or two who actually came to England had been paid to get out of their South African contracts, so morale wasn't the highest in that squad. Border soon sorted out the kind of players he wanted for Australia's future and winning the World Cup in 1987 was a great shot in the arm for him. He also completed two seasons at Essex where he impressed everyone with his supportiveness and professionalism. It was all part of his gradual learning process as a cricketer and he must have picked up a great deal from Keith Fletcher. He certainly noticed where I like to make my runs and when he led Australia over here in 1989 they were a much more disciplined outfit than in '85. Terry Alderman knew that I tended to hit the straight ball through mid-on and even through mid-wicket if I felt in good nick, so the presence of fielders close in on the legside to me made tactical sense. Border and Alderman managed to get me thinking about the way I was playing, sowing a little seed or two of doubt in my mind and I had a poor series. Geoff Lawson and Alderman bowled sensibly and accurately to their fields, Merv Hughes was the wild card – occasionally weighing in with an unplayable delivery – and their game plan was too efficient for us. It was clear who was in charge out there and Border got everybody working together with a common purpose. They used just twelve players in the series, while we played twenty-nine. They were confident, aggressive and fit, with just two serious injuries on the tour. Their approach to training was very impressive and in every way, the tour was a triumph for the captain. He had no intention of leaving anything to chance and we were out-thought and out-performed all that summer.

He remains a top batsman as he approaches an age that is very un-Australian for a current player. I'm sure that he would dearly like to start scoring Test hundreds again but he can console himself with the thought that he used to get them when his country really needed them. It's hard to think of a player more respected in world cricket.

CLIVE LLOYD

One of the more creative Test captains but only in that he devised a strategy to bowl out sides. It was ruthless, based on fast bowling from either end for hour after hour, short of a length with not much that was ill-directed. So there weren't many runs to be had as they dripped away at you like water on a stone, operating at a slow over rate. That meant the West Indies have been difficult to beat since 1976 one of the reasons being that the game is played at a slow tempo. The only weakness they had under Lloyd was against spin, but it isn't easy to produce a turning wicket which doesn't also help the faster bowlers, so he didn't lose many games.

Several straws in the wind combined to make the West Indies the best team in the world under Clive Lloyd's leadership. The amount of money to be earned by playing for Kerry Packer made them realize how important it was to get fit and remain so. In the Caribbean it has long been a social leg-up to be a Test player and the financial incentives were there for the dedicated. So their players stayed longer at the top than previously. Some great fast bowlers emerged under Lloyd's merciless direction and the West Indies could also call on Viv Richards, one of the greatest batsmen of all time. By the late seventies they were carrying all before them and Clive Lloyd was their guru. Their bowlers were capable of bowling anyone out on any type of wicket. There was no point in expecting to neutralize them on slow, low English pitches because they were fast and accurate enough to be effective, while our fast-medium bowlers would get carted all over the place by their class batsmen. If you prepared quicker wickets, their bowlers would be even deadlier. The likes of Holding, Roberts, Croft, Garner, Marshall, Walsh and Daniel had pace, variety, control and stamina. How good a captain do you need to be in perming four from that lot? Perhaps Lloyd's greatest achievement was getting them out on the park and ensuring they had the right commitment. He had great stature, he was a bit of a Godfather to them and he certainly welded them into an imposing unit, perhaps one of the greatest. He was also still a fine batsman and could hold his own in the field, despite knee problems. One of the great imponderables is: how would Lloyd have fared as captain of a lesser side? You can't argue with his record, though.

VIV RICHARDS

You have to have a good team to be a winning captain and with so much talent at his disposal, Viv Richards *ought* to have won a few series. That he ended up undefeated in any series he captained is a fine effort, even if Viv sometimes appeared to think no further than swapping one fast bowler for another every hour, on the hour. In the 1990 series out there, he was accused of allowing his team to approach the first Test in Jamaica in complacent mood. By the middle of the series his pride had been stung and they were looking more like their old selves. Give them credit for forcing a win in Barbados when we almost held out for a draw until the new ball and Curtley Ambrose did for us. Then they outplayed us in Antigua when we bowled badly in their first innings. Viv had been angry at his players and whipped them into shape at the right time.

He was very hard on the field and he set a terrific example in standards of fitness and fielding. I personally feel he was a lot more insecure than he appeared from the outward swagger. He had been kept waiting a long time for the captaincy as Clive Lloyd kept coming up for one more series and it seemed he had to prove himself too often in the eyes of many in the Caribbean. His inability to shrug off criticism in the media indicated the pressure he felt, and cracks did appear in his temperament when things weren't going well. At times his batting had a hint of the January Sales about it – everything had to go – but that stemmed from his supreme self-confidence at the crease. His commitment and pride were still high, though, and on his last tour to England, he played superbly to win the Edgbaston Test when they looked rocky. That innings was a real captain's effort – watchful at first, coaxing his partner Carl Hooper to be careful and then running away with it in a barrage of great strokes. When Viv Richards put his mind to it, he could be awesome.

Perhaps Viv didn't make bricks out of straw, holding out for a draw, in the way that Brearley, Ian Chappell or Border could. That first innings collapse at the Oval at the hands of Phil Tufnell was typical of them when they lost concentration against the turning ball, and Viv set no sort of example with his shot that led to his dismissal, caught behind going for the slog. He made sure they batted responsibly in the second innings though, and he looked ominously good until he holed out to mid-on. In defeat at the Oval he was as gracious to me as he was at Leeds and Jamaica and I respect that side of his captaincy.

Viv's retirement from Test cricket has left the West Indies in a state of transition and it will be very interesting to see how they cope with the loss of Greenidge, Haynes, Richards, Dujon and Marshall in a short space of time. It could be their biggest challenge for two decades – but don't expect them to go back to bowlers like Ramadhin and Valentine!

12
World Cup '92: third time unlucky

It would have been the greatest moment of my career if England had managed to beat Pakistan in the World Cup Final, bringing home the trophy for the first time in five attempts. It was not to be and instead I achieved a record I could have done without – the only man so far to appear in the losing side in three World Cup Finals.

As I sat in the dressing-room at the Melbourne Cricket Ground, coming to terms with defeat, I wasn't sorry for myself. I looked at Ian Botham: he seemed more upset than any of us, looking close to tears, the very picture of dejection. Ian had given me everything in the World Cup campaign and the same went for every one of my players. That knowledge helped sustain me in the aftermath of Pakistan's famous victory. No matter how long I analysed that game, pondered over the various turning points, the fact remained that Imran Khan had got a great performance out of his team on the day. They came good when it was most needed, in the semi-final against New Zealand and on the big day. We were perhaps twenty per cent down on our performance when it really mattered, but as captain I couldn't fault a single player for attitude or dedication to the job in hand. At the death we had failed, but sport is like that. A team is not going to play well every day it is tested out in the middle and that is the eternal fascination.

I was very proud to have been associated with all the England players on the three-month tour of New Zealand and Australia and the contrast with our trip a year earlier to the same places couldn't have been greater. This time we gave everything we had and fell at the final hurdle. Is that really a major failure, the cause for prolonged gloom? I shall take into eventual retirement my three losing appearances in the World Cup Final and that will stay in my memory along with the good times like the 333 against India and the achievements against the West Indies – but at least I got there on three separate occasions and the fact that thirteen years straddled those Finals must indicate that I've been fairly consistent as a player for a period of time. I told myself afterwards in Melbourne, 'There are a lot of people worse off than me.'

I really enjoyed all of the tour and respected the drive and determination of the boys involved. They showed what I had been looking for under my captaincy – a pride in performance for our country and a professional attitude to the job in hand. We proved that we can compete with the best in the world, that there is nothing wrong with the ability of our players or the system that produces them. It was a great achievement to be the first to win a Test series in New Zealand since 1979, to get to the World Cup Final and hang together throughout a long, arduous tour. I agree we lost at the wrong time but our record of being undefeated in any game until the World Cup match against New Zealand shouldn't be underestimated. Some say we peaked too soon and that we ran out of steam in the closing stages but that ignores the fact that we batted and fielded very well in the semi-final against South Africa. And we simply had to play well early in the competition because the draw had set us against the stronger sides in the opening games. It was just as well we were all fired up right from the start and our consistency showed when we completed a record of eleven straight wins in one-day internationals. Any captain would be delighted with a run like that (especially in the fluctuating type of cricket that is the one-day game), but when it came to the crunch, we just couldn't do ourselves justice in the Final. No mystique about it.

Our excellent performances in New Zealand in the first two months of the tour were exactly what I wanted. We swiftly disposed of the media's line that that part of the trip was just a warm-up for the World Cup. I had always said that any team I captain wants to win every game and New Zealand was the very best type of preparation, because we took our great confidence with us into the World Cup and several of our guys did themselves a power of good in the Test arena. Alec Stewart, Derek Pringle and Chris Lewis all benefited from playing well in New Zealand and they did very well for us in the World Cup. By February, September's issue in the media about warming up in New Zealand and viewing the World Cup as the paramount objective was no longer being discussed. It seemed to get home that confidence breeds success – and the knock is to hang onto that confidence for as long as possible. Whatever happened in the World Cup, the tour that started at the end of December was a huge success. I don't think I captained the side any differently from before, but our lads were highly motivated right from the start of the tour and my main task was to keep encouraging them. As vice-captain, Alec Stewart was very supportive of me and the degree of self-motivation and character shown by my players was a great credit to all of them. Compared to a year earlier in the Antipodes, I was delighted with the response I got from each individual.

Winning the First Test in Christchurch was a huge boost to our confidence, especially the way in which we made the New Zealanders buckle under pressure. I can't recall playing in a Test where the game has been won in the last over: usually the issue is cut-and-dried long before that. By the time we got to the tea interval on the last day, I thought they would block it out for a draw, especially with John Wright still there. We went for one last shot after tea and Phil Tufnell found the inspiration. He nagged Wright into his dismissal for 99 and that turned the game, because we got another couple of wickets quickly and began to exert pressure on them. Yet at the start of the final over, you still wouldn't have expected anything but a draw, especially with Martin Crowe at the crease. The runs-to-time equation was then very important and before that final over started, Alec Stewart and Robin Smith said to Martin, 'You know you only need a four to make it safe – that way there won't be enough time to get us in to bat.' To my amazement. Crowe went for the big hit to ensure we wouldn't have enough time to go in again and he holed out. Death or glory – and he failed.

That moment shows the fine line between glory or failure because Martin Crowe faced a tough time after that. By the end of that series, I knew that he had been asked to resign as New Zealand captain by some of their selectors. When I came off the field for treatment on the final day of the Test series, I saw John Wright having a meeting with their selectors and it didn't take a genius to work out what they were discussing. I felt for Martin: I knew from personal experience that when a side is struggling the captain takes the flak. He managed to survive and once he started to bat well in the World Cup they were transformed. They decided on the right tactics in the field, they supported each other superbly and Crowe's personal confidence with the bat helped him captain the team with more flair. They were positive and pulled together very impressively. Many have suggested to me that if they had beaten Pakistan in the semi-final, we would have coasted home against New Zealand, but I am not so sure. They kept bubbling along, playing to their strengths and underlining the value of teamwork. Beating Australia at the start of the World Cup gave them great confidence as a unit and I wasn't at all surprised that they went so far. Martin Crowe's contrasting fortunes as captain simply confirmed how difficult it is to be too dogmatic about someone's credentials to lead a side. Once he started to show his world-class skills as a batsman, you could see the confidence soar in the Kiwi camp.

I think the revival of the New Zealanders demonstrates just how well we played to beat them in our one-day series and 2–0 in the Tests before the World Cup started. Winning the Second Test was a fine performance because we showed the traditional English virtues of grit and determination. We toughened it out on the first day when we could have been bowled out for very little on a green, dampish pitch and then we bowled superbly to give us a precious lead in a low-scoring game. We outbowled them over the second innings and ran out comfortable winners on a pitch that was rather like the Headingley one in Tests throughout the 1980s – a result wicket, in other words.

That win at Auckland was the kind which pleases a captain – it was a solid, professional display after being 91 for 6 on the first day. We stuck at it and fought it out. I was very pleased for Phil Tufnell. He took a few cheap wickets and following his match-winning effort at Christchurch it was clear he was our trump card. The New Zealanders didn't seem to have too much of an idea how to play him and his soaring confidence was reflected in the way he fielded in New Zealand. You wouldn't have believed it was the same guy from a year previously as he attacked the ball in the outfield and got his throw in quickly. He did all I wanted in the field and there was a maturity in Tufnell that was very encouraging. He came to the World Cup as our first choice as slow left-arm spinner but unfortunately he seemed to lose a bit of confidence when he took some stick. Eventually the specialist one-day spinner – Richard Illingworth – took over the spot and didn't let us down, but I'm sure Tufnell learned from the experience. His main consolation from the tour must be the decisive part he played in helping England win the first two Tests against New Zealand. When the keepers of relevant statistics told me after Auckland that this was the first time in thirteen years we had won four Tests in a row (home to West Indies and Sri Lanka, then these two in New Zealand), I was happy with that fact. Consistency is what every captain aims for.

Before we left New Zealand for the World Cup, we had to make a very tough decision – to leave Jack Russell out of the campaign. We could only take fourteen and it was very hard on Jack that he had to miss out. Mark Ramprakash was unfortunate – he hardly got a bat and then when he did, he was usually unluckily dismissed – but Jack had played a vital part in our Test Match successes in New Zealand. He had kept wicket superbly – enjoying standing up to Tufnell for long periods –his batting was positive and useful and at all times he was a great source of information and encouragement to me and the bowlers. Yet we had to make harsh decisions, based on a particular strategy, and we favoured having a few all-rounders who were worthy of the name in the context of a limited overs game. That meant Dermot Reeve, Ian Botham, Chris Lewis, Phil DeFreitas, Derek Pringle and, to a certain extent, Graeme Hick. It had worked for the Australians in the recent past and we thought it was the right policy for fifty-overs-a-side games.

With Alec Stewart impressing in New Zealand as a front-line batsman and taking into account his competent work as a keeper, we had no option. Alec's hundred on the first day of the New Zealand series was out of the top drawer. He set out to bat all day, and was only dismissed in the final over by a great delivery that came from nowhere. By the time that Test series was over, Alec had impressed me as the kind of batter who was coming to terms with the demands of the big occasion. He no longer looked 'iffy' – likely to play a cameo innings, then get out after an hour. He had put together three hundreds in his last four Tests and his adequate keeping meant that poor Jack had to miss out. It was very hard to break the news to Jack but he took it like a great pro. Moments like that aren't particularly pleasant for a captain but I had to go with the strategy that we thought was preferable to win the World Cup. I don't think Alec Stewart's positive approach deserted him in the World Cup and several times he set a terrific example with the bat.

Our policy of favouring all-rounders gave us elbow room as well, particularly when the injuries started to stack up. When we played South Africa in the qualifying round, the absence of myself and Allan Lamb still meant we had a powerful batting line-up and in the Final, the presence of Derek Pringle at number nine wasn't a bad insurance policy. We may have been chasing the game at Melbourne by the time Derek came in, but he had already helped us win a one-day international at Dunedin earlier in the tour. I don't advocate picking all-rounders ahead of specialists but if the all-rounders are good enough, you should stick with them in one-day cricket. I was pleased with the bowling options we had for our World Cup squad. Apart from Gladstone Small's experience which we eventually called on, we had bowlers who could also bat. Dermot Reeve also gave us variety and grit, and massive enthusiasm – qualities that proved invaluable at times. Graeme Hick's off-spin was again an important extra ingredient. The options at my disposal meant that at least one of our front-line bowlers missed out each game but that is the nature of cricket. The captain has to do what he thinks is right at the appropriate time and the variety of all-rounders I had in the World Cup was a pleasant problem to have.

Talking of all-rounders, Ian Botham had his usual share of banner headlines and hyped-up reactions but I knew that would be the case when we went for him the previous September. We were prepared for the snide comments that he would be overweight after his panto season in Bournemouth and I admit he did look a bit big when he turned up. But it was clear he had been training and he immediately put his heart and soul into the team effort. You only had to see his pride, pleasure and excitement at winning his hundredth Test cap in New Zealand to realise how much this tour meant to him. His motivation and effort were things the team could draw on and he was excellent in meetings when we discussed the next day and the strategy. The younger players got a lot from him and he was positive and supportive to all of us. At the start it was a case of 'Overweight Botham', then once he started performing well the press changed to 'How Does He Do It?' but that didn't surprise me at all. He hadn't lost the appetite for the big time or the fire in his belly and the way he beat Australia was straight out of his Golden Days scrapbook. There is no doubt he still possesses the knack of turning it on (like the superb delivery that dismissed Sachin Tendulkar when he could have won the game for India) but he seems to reserve the best performances for Australia. He gave us a massive boost when we thrashed the reigning World champions and I'm convinced it was the right decision to reach a compromise and get him over once the panto season had finished. Ian paced himself and conserved his energies for the big games and as someone of a similar age I could relate to that, so there were no complaints from me when he missed nets at given times. He was at all times a credit to his reputation and a fierce, patriotic competitor for us. And he doesn't think he's finished as an England player. His dejection at missing out in the World Cup Final stemmed from an awareness that those days have gone, but within a day he was hinting heavily to me that he'd love to open the batting against the Pakistanis in the Test series in the forthcoming English summer. You can't fault the man for self-belief and competitiveness.

In the end, a series of injuries took their toll of our squad and that must have reduced our effectiveness, even subconsciously. Yet far too many judges have said that we concentrated too much on physical fitness to the detriment of basic cricket skills, particularly before the tour started. The curse of Lilleshall, in other words. I just can't accept that and I believe people are looking too deeply for reasons why we lost a cricket match to a collection of highly talented individuals who happened to gel on the day. Up to the start of the World Cup, we had got by on injuries, apart from strains to Derek Pringle and Phil DeFreitas and the horrendous knee-cap injury to David Lawrence, which was the worst I have ever seen in any sport that I have experienced at first hand. Then we had a spate of muscle injuries that can happen at any time – just look at Liverpool in the 1991/2 season. Does anyone seriously think their incredible injury problems have been down to anything other than back luck, or do they believe that the training methods that have served them so well in the last quarter of a century are now totally discredited?

Pringle and DeFreitas picked up injuries that can always happen to bowlers, I tore a hamstring for the first time in my career, Robin Smith put his back out while practising before the semi-final and Allan Lamb continued his history of leg injuries. Yet none of those was directly due to the amount of hard work we did before the tour started. In fact the stamina we built up in the autumn and early winter helped us greatly as we endured nineteen different flights and endless waiting for our travel connections. The Lilleshall Factor gave us an extra competitive edge which was obvious in our fielding. In the early matches of the World Cup, the likes of Lewis, Smith, Hick, DeFreitas and Fairbrother were inspirational and the example they set dragged better fielding performances from the rest of us. You only had to compare us in the field a year earlier Down Under to see that. Without that splendid fielding early on, we might not have got through those testing games against strong opposition. Instead we could enjoy the discomfiture of Australia and the West Indies as we kept winning, in the process justifying our hard work before the tour started.

I admit I was surprised that Australia didn't qualify for the semi-finals. Defeat in the first match to New Zealand was a major blow to them and they suddenly changed their system, chopping and changing their side. Perhaps they over-reacted too early and should have stayed with the same unit for the first four games or so. By then they had lost confidence and individuals who were crucial to their cause were no longer playing well. Not that I complained; they were the team we all feared and elimination for Australia was more than I had expected. I also admit that halfway through the competition. Pakistan didn't look a threat at all, especially when we bowled them out for 74 at Adelaide. I was aware that when they're bad they're awful and when good, they are excellent but I would have needed a lot of persuading that they could pull themselves together in time to string some consistent performances into a winning run. That semi-final win, chasing a large total to best New Zealand, was a tremendous performance. As I knew to my cost from the Nehru Cup in 1989, Pakistan can be very dangerous chasing a total and I thought Javed Miandad's leadership with the bat in the New Zealand game was outstanding. He held the side together, scoring at a run a ball. Rock solid. He had the bit between his teeth and I knew Javed would be a fierce opponent in the Final. So it proved.

Compared to our semi-final, Pakistan's performance was almost routine. The strange regulations that governed the World Cup if rain stopped play meant we were portrayed as the villains when the game against South Africa was finely balanced. I got some flak for taking my side off when it was raining but I wonder who would have behaved differently in the same situation? As the rain poured down, Brian Aldridge, one of the umpires said to me, 'The batsmen are happy to continue. Are you?' I said, 'Brian, I want to protect 22 runs in 13 balls and the conditions are vital. Do you believe the conditions are fit to play?' He said 'No,' and that's when I elected to come off. I admit I did think about staying on but the overriding factor was the equation of runs needed to balls to be bowled – and they were suddenly on a high. Chris Lewis had just had a bad over and it was far from certain that we could defend 22 off 13 balls. Since then, I have had a lot of letters blaming Kepler Wessels for slowing down the game, to ensure that South Africa didn't bowl their full fifty overs but I don't think that was deliberate. Having said that we could easily have got forty runs off those five overs that were denied us, Kepler made the right decision in pure cricket terms to bowl first; it was damp and overcast, and a good time to bowl. But he took the chance on rain and when it did come, he had gambled and failed. In a normal cricket match, I would have done the same as Kepler but not in this World Cup, where the odds are so stacked against the team batting second.

Television were so keen on having a whole game each day – rather than one that can be continued the second, or even the third day – that things became rather too artificial for my liking. These anomalies only dawn on you when reality stares you straight in the face, and it's fair to say that none of the captains in the 1992 World Cup really sussed out the small print of rain-interrupted matches until the events took their turn. Under the regulations, it meant that if Derek Pringle had bowled ten maidens in his allotted spell, and it then rained – we would have to chase the same total minus those ten overs. So our bowler's excellence would have told against us. That cannot be right. Under the old rule of superior run rate, we would have beaten Pakistan in Adelaide, having bowled them out for 74 and started our reply. After rain, our revised total after sixteen overs would have been enough to give us the game and rob Pakistan of a precious point. That single point they got from being outplayed by us at Adelaide kept them in the tournament, helped to eliminate Australia and eventually stored up a defeat in the Final by a rejuvenated Pakistan.

The rain rules affected most teams. Australia benefited against India, South Africa had the advantage over Pakistan who in turn were lucky against us, and we had the benefit over South Africa. The generous, sporting reaction towards us by the South African players emphasised to me that the players all felt trapped in a rather artificial framework and that a fairer system was urgently needed for the next World Cup. I believe that some form of standardisation is vital. The world cricket authorities must get together and work out a fairer system in the event of a rain-ruined match. It would be preferable if the game could be carried over into the next day as it is in England, but clearly television has a decisive word on such matters these days. Fundamentally, it is wrong that you should be penalised for bowling well so that the opposition batting side's least productive overs are taken from your eventual target if it rains. No reward for skill there, I think.

As for the Final itself, it was a mirror image of 1987, when we were below par on the day and Australia got home in Calcutta. One-day cricket is like that. There were several turning points and I suppose one of them came when I dropped Imran Khan after we had tied him down with some excellent bowling. He skied one to the mid-wicket area and as soon as Neil Fairbrother slipped, coming round from square leg, I called for it. I took responsibility for a catch that swirled around and it was a difficult one, but I dropped it under pressure and who else can be blamed for that? In the end, it was a typical Imran innings – sketchy at the start, but blossoming towards the end as he played some fine shots. If I had caught that skier, the rest of their batters might have panicked – and certainly I was surprised that Salim Malik had had a bad tournament by his standards – but equally a new batter could have walked in and picked up the pace straight away. Crucially they had wickets in hand when they stepped up the pace and if we had kept them to 230 I would have been delighted. Yet they got away from us in the last twenty overs, as they capitalised on the excellent foundations laid down by Imran and Javed Miandad. In such circumstances, experience is very important. They just kept playing and playing, biding their time. If I had won the toss I would have done exactly the same as Imran and batted first. It looked an excellent batting wicket – it proved to be so – and we thought that if there was to be anything in the pitch it would be early on and then it would roll out flat. On our two previous World Cup games in Melbourne, we had batted very well in a run chase but it would have been right to bat first on the day of the Final.

Before Ian Botham and I went out to bat, I thought that a target of 250 in fifty overs was perfectly possible, so long as we batted really well. We had done so in similar circumstances in the qualifying game against South Africa – when rain again altered the asking rate – and a similar performance this time would get us mighty close. In the end, we were always just chasing our tails. We lost a couple of wickets early on – but so did they, thanks to Derek Pringle's excellent opening spell – but they continued to bowl very well indeed. We all knew about the danger exerted by Wasim Akram, but Aquib Javed was a revelation. He swung the ball a lot – and late. Again the hand of Imran was evident in his development. After that, the legspinner Mushtaq Ali was very impressive. Having played several times against Abdul Qadir, I can confirm that the control of Mushtaq in the Final was just as good as anything I'd seen from his famous mentor. With that white ball, it was very hard to see which way it was spinning and he trapped Graeme Hick with an excellent googly. Then he got me caught in the deep as I top-edged a sweep, playing what I thought was a 'business' stroke in the circumstances – trying to work him away for ones and twos, just to keep the score ticking over. Yet even with four wickets gone, I still felt we had an excellent chance. The asking rate at the time was never more than seven an over and, with Allan Lamb and Neil Fairbrother building a good partnership, it was still on. The two wickets in two balls by Wasim Akram proved absolutely crucial. He bowled Allan Lamb off-stump with an absolute beauty, then beat Chris Lewis with a quick one that came in on him. That left us with just four wickets and yet again I was reminded of Geoffrey Boycott's view that if you think you're going well as a batting unit, just add two wickets in the space of a few overs and see how that affects the game. That over from Wasim Akram was the decisive period in our innings.

Even though Allan Lamb had been chosen ahead of Robin Smith, no blame could be attached to him because he was building his innings in his usual calm way when Wasim came up and plucked out his off-stump from around the wicket, bowling left-arm fast. That is top-class bowling. If Lamby had survived those few overs from Wasim, he was perfectly capable of winning the game but that is simply something to natter about with a drink in your hand. Look in the scorebook. Fair play to Wasim, a world-class performer, a guy whose style of bowling is very unfamiliar to us in England, now that John Lever has retired. The same goes for Mushtaq Ali; his type of bowling has to be good for the game because it is different, it is attacking and it makes for exciting watching. The presence of Wasim and Mushtaq alone will guarantee that this summer's Test series against Pakistan will be great entertainment.

I suppose the decision to omit Robin Smith in favour of Allan Lamb for the Final must be the hardest I've ever had to make. Robin's fitness wasn't a factor – he had recovered from his back problem – and yet I couldn't tell him until the morning of the Final before Derek Pringle had proved his fitness and I was sure about the balance of the side. I wanted the extra insurance provided by Dermot Reeve's all-round abilities and it was hard for me to tell Gladstone Small he hadn't made it. Gladstone had tears in his eyes when I told him, and I was conscious of how well he had bowled in his second spell in the semi-final when the pressure was really on him. I wanted to keep Pringle as opening bowler, because he had swung the ball successfully throughout (those white balls really did swing!) and it was imperative to me that Lewis and DeFreitas should be given enough elbow room to be able to bowl in the middle of the innings.

DeFreitas bowled well in that part of the innings throughout the tournament but the key was Pringle. At the start he gave us control. His temperament never let him down. As for Lamb, I came down eventually on his ability to snatch a game out of the fire. It was hellishly difficult, because Robin had played very well in New Zealand and even though he had gone off the boil a little as the World Cup progressed, he was still a top performer and feared by every team. Whoever got the nod would have to bat at six because I didn't want to disrupt the successful grouping of Stewart, Hick and Fairbrother and, although I knew we would miss Robin's excellent fielding, Lamby shaded it for his experience. It was the classic case of selecting a side for a given situation and I have to be assessed on that basis. I can be judged to have got it wrong because Wasim Akram fired out Lamby with a great piece of bowling, but on another day – who knows? At times like that, a captain can feel rather lonely!

So England failed in one particular match because we under-performed and the Pakistanis played exceptionally well. Their top players – apart from Salim Malik – did them proud just when they needed it and anyone who loves sport and all its complexities will understand how fragile a thing is confidence and luck. I shall continue to draw massive consolation from that tour, despite the ultimate disappointment. So many players advanced their cause. Chris Lewis convinced me that he has the natural talent to be a Test-class performer with bat and ball. He has the same amount of ability that Ian Botham had at a similar stage of his development, although I admit that Botham eventually proved a marvel because of his great character and supreme self-confidence. Whether Lewis ever approaches Botham's marvellous record is another matter, but he is brimful of quality. He bats straight, plays some wonderful shots and has the talent to score a Test hundred and take five wickets in an innings as an opening bowler. I told him on the tour that he ought to aim to be a number six or seven for England, capable of scoring a hundred while at the same time being one of our opening bowlers. He can do that. As for him fielding, he is as good an all-round fielder as I've ever seen, the complete performer anywhere.

Alec Stewart came on by leaps and bounds on the tour. I have no idea whether he will be England's next captain – it is too early to say – but he did himself no harm at all as my vice-captain. He is now established as a Test player and he gives us an option because he seems to be happy both as an opener and as a number three. As for Graeme Hick, I still believe he can make it at Test level, even though he hasn't yet scored a Test fifty. He was an excellent tourist, a lovely guy with a terrific attitude to his profession, yet he knows he hasn't yet established himself. He murdered the bowlers in games other than the Tests in New Zealand and, even though he was extremely valuable in the World Cup, I'm sure he will be disappointed overall with his contribution. I see him as another Mike Gatting from the early 1980s – full of runs and class at county level, just waiting for one innings to break through for England. Don't forget it took me twenty Tests before I scored a Test hundred. I honestly feel that once Graeme sorts himself out, he will blossom and prosper for many years to come.

With the likes of Phil Tufnell, Jack Russell, Mark Ramprakash and Nasser Hussain in contention, with the prospect of a fit Angus Fraser and Mike Atherton – who wouldn't be optimistic for the future of

England? I honestly believe we are firmly on the right lines towards getting things right at international level and I am very excited about our prospects, so long as we continue to approach our task professionally. As for me, I was a little disappointed with my batting on the tour. I battled well to get a hundred in the Auckland Test but after that I was a little ordinary, judged by the standards I set myself. I lost a bit of confidence in New Zealand and apart from a good innings against the West Indies, I wasn't happy with my efforts in the World Cup. Having been in for so long in the Final, I would have liked to have built on the foundations instead of getting out for 29 when set, but there you go. Thankfully, the game of cricket will never be an exact science and after a couple of very satisfying years, perhaps I was due a nudge in the other direction from the gods.

As for my future, I would love to play for England against Pakistan – and as captain. It would be a great pleasure to go some way towards easing my personal disappointment of the World Cup Final if we could beat them in both the Test and the one-dayers. I will be very surprised if it's not another terrific summer of international cricket and that is something which all of us who love the game will want. After this summer, who knows? One thing I will say: after missing out at Melbourne, the only realistic international ambition left to me is to regain the Ashes as captain from the Australians. They are due in England in the summer of 1993 for the resumption of a battle that never ceases to excite any player from either country. After great disappointment as player in 1989 and as captain against them in the 1990/91 tour, it would be an immense pleasure to see them off in 1993. Even though the game has taught me to be cautious when judging the future, I must admit that one final series victory against the Aussies is an attractive prospect for me.

CAREER RECORD

Compiled by Robert Brooke

GRAHAM ALAN GOOCH

Born Leytonstone, London 23 July 1953
RHB RM
Essex CCC 1973–92
94 Test matches 1975 to 1991/2

Test records:
Highest score – 333 *v* India at Lord's 1990.
Highest match aggregate in any Test match – 456 *v* India at Lord's 1990.
Highest aggregate of runs in 3 match series – 752 *v* India 1990.

G.A. GOOCH'S POSITION FOR RUNS SCORED FOR ENGLAND

RUNS & AV'GE		PLAYER
8114	(47.72)	G. Boycott
8081	(44.15)	D.I. Gower
7624	(44.10)	M.C. Cowdrey
7249	(58.45)	W.R. Hammond
7189	(43.56)	G.A. Gooch

GRAHAM GOOCH TEST-BY-TEST

1. ENGLAND *v* AUSTRALIA (Edgbaston) 10–14 July 1975
   Australia won by an innings & 85 runs.
   Gooch (5) c Marsh b Walker 0
         (5) c Marsh b Thomson 0

2. ENGLAND *v* AUSTRALIA (Lord's) 31 July–5 August 1975
   Match drawn.
   Gooch (5) c Marsh b Lillee 6
         (5) b Mallett 31

3. ENGLAND *v* PAKISTAN (Lord's) 16–19 June 1978
   England won by an innings & 120 runs.

175

Gooch (2) lbw b Wasim Raja 54
Gooch & D.I. Gower (56) added 101 for 3rd wicket

4. ENGLAND *v* PAKISTAN (Headingley) 29 June–4 July 1978
Match drawn.
Gooch (2) lbw b Sarfraz Nawaz 20

5. ENGLAND *v* NEW ZEALAND (The Oval) 27 July–1 August 1978
England won by 7 wickets.
Gooch (2) lbw b Bracewell 0
     (2) not out 91

6. ENGLAND *v* NEW ZEALAND (Trent Bridge) 10–14 August 1978
England won by an innings & 119 runs.
Gooch (1) c Burgess b Bracewell 55
Gooch & G. Boycott (131) added 111 for 1st wicket

7. ENGLAND *v* NEW ZEALAND (Lord's) 24–28 August 1978
England won by 7 wickets.
Gooch (1) c Boock b Hadlee 2
     (1) not out 42

8. AUSTRALIA *v* ENGLAND (Brisbane) 1–6 December 1978
England won by 7 wickets.
Gooch (2) c Laughlin b Hogg 2
     (2) c Yardley b Hogg 2

9. AUSTRALIA *v* ENGLAND (Perth) 15–20 December 1978
England won by 166 runs.
Gooch (2) c Maclean b Hogg 1
     (2) lbw b Hogg 43

10. AUSTRALIA *v* ENGLAND (Melbourne) 29 December–3 January
1978–79
Australia won by 103 runs.
Gooch (4) c Border b Dymock 25
     (4) lbw b Hogg 40

11. AUSTRALIA *v* ENGLAND (Sydney) 6–11 January 1979
England won by 93 runs.
Gooch (4) c Toohey b Higgs 18
     (4) c Wood b Higgs 22

12. AUSTRALIA *v* ENGLAND (Adelaide) 27 January–1 February 1979
England won by 205 runs.

Gooch (4) c Hughes b Hogg 1
    (4) b Carlson 18

13. AUSTRALIA *v* ENGLAND (Sydney) 10–14 February 1979
England won by 9 wickets.
Gooch (4) st Wright b Higgs 74

14. ENGLAND *v* INDIA (Edgbaston) 12–16 July 1979
England won by an innings & 83 runs.
Gooch (4) c Reddy b Kapil Dev 83
Gooch & G. Boycott (155) added 145 for 3rd wicket, Gooch and
D.I. Gower (200*) added 191 for 4th wicket

15. ENGLAND *v* INDIA (Lord's) 2–7 August 1979
Match drawn.
Gooch (3) b Kapil Dev 10

16. ENGLAND *v* INDIA (Headingley) 16–21 August 1979
Match drawn.
Gooch (3) c Vengsarkar b Kapil Dev 4

17. ENGLAND *v* INDIA (The Oval) 30 August–4 September 1979
Match drawn.
Gooch (3) c Viswanath b Ghavri 79
    (3) lbw b Kapil Dev 31

18. AUSTRALIA *v* ENGLAND (Sydney) 4–9 January 1980
Australia won by 6 wickets.
Gooch (1) b Lillee 18
    (1) c G.S. Chappell b Dymock 4

19. AUSTRALIA *v* ENGLAND (Melbourne) 1–6 February 1980
Australia won by 8 wickets.
Gooch (1) run out 99
Gooch & G. Boycott (44) added 116 for 1st wicket
    (1) b Mallett 51

20. INDIA *v* ENGLAND (Bombay) 15–19 February 1980
England won by 10 wickets.
Gooch (1) c Kirmani b Ghavri 8
    (1) not out 49

21. ENGLAND *v* WEST INDIES (Trent Bridge) 5–10 June 1980
West Indies won by 2 wickets.
Gooch (1) c Murray b Roberts 17
    (1) run out 27

22. ENGLAND *v* WEST INDIES (Lord's) 19–24 June 1980
Match drawn.
Gooch (1) lbw b Holding 123
Gooch & C.J. Tavare (42) added 145 for 2nd wicket
     (1) b Garner 47

23. ENGLAND *v* WEST INDIES (Old Trafford) 10–15 July 1980
Match drawn.
Gooch (1) lbw b Roberts 2
     (2) c Murray b Marshall 26

24. ENGLAND *v* WEST INDIES (The Oval) 24–29 July 1980
Match drawn.
Gooch (1) lbw b Holding 83
Gooch and B.C. Rose (50) added 146 for 1st wicket, after G. Boycott
retired hurt at 9–0
     (1) lbw b Holding 0

25. ENGLAND *v* WEST INDIES (Headingley) 8–12 August 1980
Match drawn.
Gooch (1) c Marshall b Garner 14
     (1) lbw b Marshall 55

26. ENGLAND *v* AUSTRALIA (Lord's) 28 August–2 September 1980
Match drawn.
Gooch (1) c Bright b Lillee 8
     (1) lbw b Lillee 16

27. WEST INDIES *v* ENGLAND (Port-of-Spain) 13–18 February 1981
West Indies won by an innings & 79 runs.
Gooch (1) b Roberts 41
     (1) lbw b Holding 5

28. WEST INDIES *v* ENGLAND (Bridgetown) 13–18 March 1981
West Indies won by 298 runs.
Gooch (1) b Garner 26
     (1) c Garner b Croft 116
Gooch & D.I. Gower (54) added 120 for 3rd wicket

29. WEST INDIES *v* ENGLAND (St John's) 27 March–1 April 1981
Match drawn.
Gooch (1) run out 33
     (1) c Greenidge b Richards 83
Gooch & G. Boycott (104*) added 144 for 1st wicket

30. WEST INDIES *v* ENGLAND (Kingston) 10–15 April 1981
    Match drawn.
    Gooch (1) c Murray b Holding 153
        (1) c Lloyd b Marshall 3

31. ENGLAND *v* AUSTRALIA (Trent Bridge) 18–21 June 1981
    Australia won by 4 wickets.
    Gooch (1) c Wood b Lillee 10
        (1) c Yallop b Lillee 6

32. ENGLAND *v* AUSTRALIA (Lord's) 2–7 July 1981
    Match drawn.
    Gooch (1) c Yallop b Lawson 44
        (1) lbw b Lawson 20

33. ENGLAND *v* AUSTRALIA (Headingley) 16–21 July 1981
    England won by 18 runs.
    Gooch (1) lbw b Alderman 2
        (1) c Alderman b Lillee 0

34. ENGLAND *v* AUSTRALIA (Edgbaston) 30 July–2 August 1981
    England won by 29 runs.
    Gooch (4) c Marsh b Bright 21
        (4) b Bright 21

35. ENGLAND *v* AUSTRALIA (Old Trafford) 13–17 August 1981
    England won by 103 runs.
    Gooch (1) lbw b Lillee 10
        (1) b Alderman 5

36. INDIA *v* ENGLAND (Bombay) 27 November–1 December 1981
    India won by 138 runs.
    Gooch (1) b Madan Lal 2
        (1) c Kirmani b Kapil Dev 1

37. INDIA *v* ENGLAND (Bangalore) 9–14 December 1981
    Match drawn.
    Gooch (1) c Gavaskar b Shastri 58
        (1) lbw b Kapil Dev 40

38. INDIA *v* ENGLAND (Delhi) 23–28 December 1981
    Match drawn.
    Gooch (1) c Kapil Dev b Doshi 71
    Gooch & G. Boycott (105) added 132 for 1st wicket
    (1) not out 20

39. INDIA *v* ENGLAND (Calcutta) 1–6 January 1982
    Match drawn.
    Gooch (1) c Viswanath b Doshi 47
         (1) b Doshi 63

40. INDIA *v* ENGLAND (Madras) 13–18 January 1982
    Match drawn.
    Gooch (1) c & b Shastri 127
    Gooch & C.J. Tavare (35) added 155 for 1st wicket

41. INDIA *v* ENGLAND (Kanpur) 30 January–4 February 1982
    Match drawn.
    Gooch (1) b Doshi 58

42. SRI LANKA *v* ENGLAND (Colombo) 17–21 February 1982
    England won by 7 wickets.
    Gooch (1) lbw b De Mel 22
         (1) b G.R.A. De Silva 31

43. ENGLAND *v* AUSTRALIA (Headingley) 13–18 June 1985
    England won by 5 wickets.
    Gooch (1) lbw b McDermott 5
         (1) lbw b O'Donnell 28

44. ENGLAND *v* AUSTRALIA (Lord's) 27 June–2 July 1985
    Australia won by 4 wickets.
    Gooch (1) lbw b McDermott 30
         (1) c Phillips b McDermott 17

45. ENGLAND *v* AUSTRALIA (Trent Bridge) 11–16 July 1985
    Match drawn.
    Gooch (1) c Wessels b Lawson 70
    Gooch & D.I. Gower (166) added 116 for 2nd wicket
         (1) c Ritchie b McDermott 48

46. ENGLAND *v* AUSTRALIA (Old Trafford) 1–6 August 1985
    Match drawn.
    Gooch (1) lbw b McDermott 74
    Gooch & D.I. Gower (47) added 121 for 2nd wicket

47. ENGLAND *v* AUSTRALIA (Edgbaston) 15–20 August 1985
    England won by an innings & 118 runs.
    Gooch (1) c Phillips b Thomson 19

48. ENGLAND *v* AUSTRALIA (The Oval) 29 August–3 September 1985
    England won by an innings & 94 runs.

Gooch (1) c & b McDermott 196
Gooch & D.I. Gower (157) added 351 for 2nd wicket

49. WEST INDIES *v* ENGLAND (Kingston) 21–23 February 1986
West Indies won by 10 wickets.
Gooch (1) c Garner b Marshall 51
     (1) b Marshall 0

50. WEST INDIES *v* ENGLAND (Port-of-Spain) 7–12 March 1986
West Indies won by 7 wickets.
Gooch (1) c Best b Marshall 2
     (1) lbw b Walsh 43

51. WEST INDIES *v* ENGLAND (Bridgetown) 21–25 March 1986
West Indies won by an innings & 30 runs.
Gooch (1) c Dujon b Garner 53
Gooch & D.I. Gower (66) added 120 for 2nd wicket
     (1) b Patterson 11

52. WEST INDIES *v* ENGLAND (Port-of-Spain) 3–5 April 1986
West Indies won by 10 wickets.
Gooch (1) c Richards b Garner 14
     (1) c Dujon b Marshall 0

53. WEST INDIES *v* ENGLAND (St John's) 11–16 April 1986
West Indies won by 240 runs.
Gooch (1) lbw b Holding 51
Gooch & W.N. Slack (52) added 127 for 1st wicket
     (1) lbw b Holding 51

54. ENGLAND *v* INDIA (Lord's) 5–10 June 1986
Gooch (1) b Sharma 114
Gooch & D.R. Pringle (63) added 147 for 5th wicket
     (1) lbw b Kapil Dev 8

55. ENGLAND *v* INDIA (Headingley) 19–23 June 1986
India won by 279 runs.
Gooch (1) c Binny b Kapil Dev 8
     (1) c Srikkanth b Kapil Dev 5

56. ENGLAND *v* INDIA (Edgbaston) 3–8 July 1986
Match drawn.
Gooch (1) c More b Kapil Dev 0
     (1) lbw b Sharma 40

57. ENGLAND *v* NEW ZEALAND (Lord's) 24–29 July 1986
    Match drawn.
    Gooch (1) c Smith b Hadlee 18
          (1) c Watson b Bracewell 183
    Gooch & P. Willey (42) added 126 for 5th wicket

58. ENGLAND *v* NEW ZEALAND (Trent Bridge) 7–12 August 1986
    New Zealand won by 8 wickets.
    Gooch (1) lbw b Hadlee 18
          (1) c Coney b Bracewell 17

59. ENGLAND *v* NEW ZEALAND (The Oval) 21–26 August 1986
    Match drawn.
    Gooch (1) c Stirling b Hadlee 32

60. PAKISTAN *v* ENGLAND (Lahore) 25–28 November 1987
    Pakistan won by an innings & 87 runs.
    Gooch (1) b Abdul Qadir 12
          (1) c Ashraf Ali b Abdul Qadir 15

61. PAKISTAN *v* ENGLAND (Faisalabad) 7–12 December 1987
    Match drawn.
    Gooch (1) c Aamer Malik b Iqbal Qasim 28
          (1) lbw b Abdul Qadir 65

62. PAKISTAN *v* ENGLAND (Karachi) 16–21 December 1987
    Match drawn.
    Gooch (1) c Ashraf Ali b Wasim Akram 12
          (1) b Mudassar Nazar 93

63. ENGLAND *v* WEST INDIES (Trent Bridge) 2–7 June 1988
    Match drawn.
    Gooch (1) b Marshall 73
    Gooch & B.C. Broad (54) added 125 for 1st wicket
          (1) c Dujon b Patterson 146
    Gooch & D.I. Gower (88*) added 161 for 3rd wicket

64. ENGLAND *v* WEST INDIES (Lord's) 16–21 June 1988
    West Indies won by 134 runs.
    Gooch (1) b Marshall 44
    Gooch (1) lbw b Marshall 16

65. ENGLAND *v* WEST INDIES (Old Trafford) 30 June–5 July 1988
    West Indies won by an innings and 156 runs.
    Gooch (1) c Dujon b Benjamin 27
          (1) lbw Marshall 1

66. ENGLAND *v* WEST INDIES (Headingley) 21–26 July 1988
    West Indies won by 10 wickets.
    Gooch (1) c Dujon b Marshall 9
           (1) c Hooper b Walsh 50

67. ENGLAND *v* WEST INDIES (The Oval) 4–8 August 1988
    G.A. Gooch – Captain.
    West Indies won by 8 wickets.
    Gooch (1) c Logie b Ambrose 9
           (1) c Greenidge b Ambrose 84

68. ENGLAND *v* SRI LANKA (Lord's) 25–30 August 1988
    G.A. Gooch – captain.
    England won by 7 wickets.
    Gooch (1) lbw b Ratnayeke 75
    Gooch & R.C. Russell (94) added 131 for 2nd wicket
           (1) c Silva b Samarasekera 36

69. ENGLAND *v* AUSTRALIA (Headingley) 8–13 June 1989
    Australia won by 210 runs.
    Gooch (1) lbw b Alderman 13
           (1) lbw b Hughes 68

70. ENGLAND *v* AUSTRALIA (Lord's) 22–27 June 1989
    Australia won by 6 wickets.
    Gooch (1) c Healy b Waugh 60
           (1) lbw b Alderman 0

71. ENGLAND *v* AUSTRALIA (Edgbaston) 6–11 July 1989
    Match drawn.
    Gooch (1) lbw b Lawson 8

72. ENGLAND *v* AUSTRALIA (Old Trafford) 27 July–1 August 1989
    Australia won by 9 wickets.
    Gooch (1) b Lawson 11
           (1) c Alderman b Lawson 13

73. ENGLAND *v* AUSTRALIA (The Oval) 24–29 August 1989
    Match drawn.
    Gooch (1) lbw Alderman 0
           (1) c & b Alderman 10

74. WEST INDIES *v* ENGLAND (Kingston) 24 February–1 March 1990
    G.A. Gooch – captain.
    England won by 9 wickets.

Gooch (1) c Dujon b Patterson 18
    (2) c Greenidge b Bishop 8

75. WEST INDIES *v* ENGLAND (Port-of-Spain) 23–28 March 1990
G.A. Gooch – captain.
Match drawn.
Gooch (1) c Dujon b Bishop 84
Gooch & W. Larkins (54) added 112 for 1st wicket.
    (1) retired hurt 18

76. ENGLAND *v* NEW ZEALAND (Trent Bridge) 7–12 June 1990
G.A. Gooch – captain.
Match drawn.
Gooch (1) lbw b Hadlee 0

77. ENGLAND *v* NEW ZEALAND (Lord's) 21–26 June 1990
G.A. Gooch – captain.
Match drawn.
Gooch (1) c & b Bracewell 85
Gooch & A.J. Stewart (54) added 148 for 2nd wicket
    (1) b Hadlee 37

78. ENGLAND *v* NEW ZEALAND (Edgbaston) 5–10 July 1990
G.A. Gooch – captain.
England won by 114 runs.
Gooch (1) c Hadlee b Morrison 154
Gooch and M.A. Atherton (82) added 170 for 1st wicket
    (1) b Snedden 30

79. ENGLAND *v* INDIA (Lord's) 26–31 July 1990
G.A. Gooch – captain.
England won by 247 runs.
Gooch (1) b Prabhakar 333
Gooch & D.I. Gower (40) added 127 for 2nd wicket, Gooch & A.J.
Lamb (139) added 308 for 3rd wicket, Gooch & R.A. Smith
(100*) added 192 for 4th wicket
    (1) c Azharuddin b Sharma 123
Gooch and M.A. Atherton (72) added 204 for 1st wicket

80. ENGLAND *v* INDIA (Old Trafford) 9–14 August 1990
G.A. Gooch – captain.
Match drawn.
Gooch (1) c More b Prabhakar 116
Gooch & M.A. Atherton (131) added 225 for 1st wicket
    (1) c More b Prabhakar 7

81. ENGLAND *v* INDIA (The Oval) 23–28 August 1990
    G.A. Gooch – captain.
    Match drawn.
    Gooch (1) c Shastri b Hirwani 85
         (1) c Vengsarkar b Hirwani 88
    Gooch and M.A. Atherton (86) added 176 for 1st wicket

82. AUSTRALIA *v* ENGLAND (Melbourne) 26–30 December 1990
    G.A. Gooch – captain.
    Australia won by 8 wickets.
    Gooch (1) lbw b Alderman 20
         (1) c Alderman b Reid 58

83. AUSTRALIA *v* ENGLAND (Sydney) 4–8 January 1991
    G.A. Gooch – captain.
    Match drawn.
    Gooch (1) c Healy b Reid 59
         (1) c Border b Matthews 54

84. AUSTRALIA *v* ENGLAND (Adelaide) 25–29 January 1991
    G.A. Gooch – captain.
    Match drawn.
    Gooch (1) c Healy b Reid 87
    Gooch & R.A. Smith (53) added 127 for 3rd wicket
         (1) c Marsh b Reid 117
    Gooch & M.A. Atherton (87) added 203 for 1st wicket

85. AUSTRALIA *v* ENGLAND (Perth) 1–5 February 1991
    G.A. Gooch – captain.
    Australia won by 9 wickets.
    Gooch (1) c Healy b McDermott 13
         (1) c Alderman b Hughes 18

86. ENGLAND *v* WEST INDIES (Headingley) 6–10 June 1991
    G.A. Gooch – captain.
    England won by 115 runs.
    Gooch (1) c Dujon b Marshall 34
         (1) not out 154

87. ENGLAND *v* WEST INDIES (Lord's) 20–24 June 1991
    G.A. Gooch – captain.
    Match drawn.
    Gooch (1) b Walsh 37

88. ENGLAND *v* WEST INDIES (Trent Bridge) 4–9 July 1991
    G.A. Gooch – captain.
    West Indies won by 9 wickets.
    Gooch (1) lbw b Marshall 68
    Gooch & M.A. Atherton (32) added 108 for 1st wicket
        (1) b Ambrose 13

89. ENGLAND *v* WEST INDIES (Edgbaston) 25–28 July 1991
    G.A. Gooch – captain.
    West Indies won by 7 wickets.
    Gooch (1) b Marshall 45
        (1) b Patterson 40

90. ENGLAND *v* WEST INDIES (The Oval) 8–12 August 1991
    G.A. Gooch – captain.
    England won by 5 wickets.
    Gooch (1) lbw b Ambrose 60
    Gooch & H. Morris (44) added 112 for 1st wicket
        (1) lbw b Marshall 29

91. ENGLAND *v* SRI LANKA (Lord's) 22–27 August 1991
    G.A. Gooch – captain.
    England won by 137 runs.
    Gooch (1) c & b Ratnayake 38
        (1) b Anurasiri 174
    Gooch and A.J. Stewart (43) added 139 for 2nd wicket, Gooch &
    R.A. Smith (63*) added 105 for 3rd wicket

92. NEW ZEALAND *v* ENGLAND (Christchurch) 18–22 January 1992
    G.A. Gooch – captain.
    England won by an innings & 4 runs.
    Gooch (1) c Smith b Morrison 2

93. NEW ZEALAND *v* ENGLAND (Auckland) 30 January–3
    February 1992
    G.A. Gooch – captain.
    England won by 168 runs.
    Gooch (1) c Parore b Morrison 4
        (1) run out 114

94. NEW ZEALAND *v* ENGLAND (Wellington) 6–10 February 1992
    G.A. Gooch – captain.
    Match drawn.
    Gooch (1) b Patel 30
        (1) c Rutherford b Cairns 11

G.A. GOOCH IN TEST CRICKET – SERIES-BY-SERIES

SEASON	& OPPOSITION	MCH	INN	NO	RUNS	H.S.	AV'GE	100	50	CT	OVERS	MDNS	RUNS	WTS	AV'GE	B/B
1975	Australia	2	4	0	37	31	9.25	—	—	2	10	0	29	0	—	—
1978	Pakistan	2	2	0	74	54	37.00	—	1	2	6	1	15	0	—	—
1978	N Zealand	3	5	2	190	91*	63.33	—	2	1	25	9	49	0	—	—
1978/79	Australia	6	11	0	246	74	22.36	—	1	9	19	6	36	2	18.00	1/16
1979	India	4	5	0	207	79	41.40	—	2	6	4	2	3	0	—	—
1979/80	Australia	2	4	0	172	99	43.00	—	2	1	25	7	59	3	19.66	2/18
1979/80	India	1	2	1	57	49*	—	—	1	1	8	3	16	0	—	—
1980	West Indies	5	10	0	394	123	39.40	1	2	5	14	5	36	0	—	—
1980	Australia	1	2	0	24	16	12.00	—	—	—	10	4	28	0	—	—
1980/81	West Indies	4	8	0	460	153	57.50	2	1	3	33.1	6	77	2	38.50	2/12
1981	Australia	5	10	0	139	44	13.90	—	—	4						
1981/82	India	6	10	1	487	127	54.11	1	4	4	41.2	10	102	2	51.00	2/57
1981/82	Sri Lanka	1	2	0	53	31	26.50	—	1	1	7	3	27	1	27.00	1/21
1985	Australia	6	9	0	487	196	54.11	1	2	4	13	2	31	1	31.00	1/19
1985/86	West Indies	5	10	0	276	53	27.60	—	4	6	19	9	38	2	19.00	1/23
1986	India	3	6	0	175	114	29.16	1	—	5	2	1	4	0	—	—
1986	N Zealand	3	5	0	268	183	53.60	1	—	6						
1987/88	Pakistan	3	6	0	225	93	37.50	—	2	3	31	9	72	1	72.00	1/30
1988	West Indies	5	10	0	459	146	45.90	1	3	6						
1988	Sri Lanka	1	2	0	111	75	55.50	—	1	3	8	7	25	0	—	—
1989	Australia	5	9	0	183	68	20.33	—	2	4	23	4	70	1	70.00	1/26
1989/90	West Indies	2	4	1	128	84	42.66	—	1	2	18	5	69	2	34.50	1/23
1990	N Zealand	3	5	0	306	154	61.20	1	1	3						
1990	India	3	6	0	752	333	125.33	3	2	4						
1990/91	Australia	4	8	0	426	117	53.25	1	4	6						
1991	West Indies	5	9	1	480	154*	60.00	1	2	6						
1991	Sri Lanka	1	2	0	212	174	106.00	1	—	—						
1991/92	N Zealand	3	5	0	161	114	32.20	1	—	—	8	1	14	0	—	—
1975–91/92	Total	94	171	6	7189	333	43.56	16	39	94	323.3	93	800	17	47.05	2/12

Key Underlined numbers of overs/maidens represent 8-ball overs.

G.A. GOOCH IN TEST CRICKET – AGAINST EACH COUNTRY

COUNTRY	MCH	INN	NO	RUNS	H.S.	AV'GE	100	50	CT	OVERS	MDNS	RUNS	WTS	AV'GE	B/B
Australia – Home	19	34	0	870	196	25.58	1	4	11	90.2	26	218	3	72.66	2/57
Australia – Away	12	23	0	844	117	36.69	1	7	16	42	11	120	4	30.00	2/16
Australia – TOTAL	31	57	0	1714	196	30.07	2	11	27	132.2	37	338	7	48.28	2/16
Pakistan – Home	2	2	0	74	54	37.00	—	1	2						
Pakistan – Away	3	6	0	225	93	37.50	—	2	3	2	1	4	0	—	
Pakistan – TOTAL	5	8	0	299	93	37.37	—	3	5	2	1	4	0	—	
New Zealand – Home	9	15	2	764	183	58.76	2	3	10	42	16	92	1	—	1/23
New Zealand – Away	3	5	0	161	114	32.20	1	—	—						
New Zealand – TOTAL	12	20	2	925	183	51.38	3	3	10	42	16	92	1	—	1/23
India – Home	10	17	0	1134	333	66.70	4	4	15	56	15	150	3	50.00	1/19
India – Away	7	12	2	544	127	54.40	1	4	5	37.1	8	80	2	40.00	2/12
India – TOTAL	17	29	2	1678	333	62.14	5	8	20	93.1	23	230	5	46.00	2/12
West Indies – Home	15	29	1	1333	154*	47.60	3	7	17	33	8	73	3	24.33	2/18
West Indies – Away	11	22	1	864	153	41.14	2	6	11	21	8	63	1	—	1/21
West Indies – TOTAL	26	51	2	2197	154*	44.83	5	13	28	54	16	136	4	34.00	2/18
Sri Lanka – Home	2	4	0	323	174	80.75	1	1	3						
Sri Lanka – Away	1	2	0	53	31	26.50	—	—	1						
Sri Lanka – TOTAL	3	6	0	376	174	62.66	1	1	4						

G.A. GOOCH IN TEST CRICKET – GROUND-BY-GROUND

GROUND	MCH	INN	NO	RUNS	H.S.	AV'GE	100	50	CT	OVERS	MDNS	RUNS	WTS	AV'GE	B/B
Edgbaston	8	13	0	461	154	35.46	1	1	9	26	9	49	1	—	1/30
Headingley	9	16	1	469	154*	31.26	1	3	9	63	14	160	5	32.00	2/18
Lord's	17	31	1	1831	333	61.03	6	4	17	90	32	220	3	73.33	1/16
Old Trafford	6	11	0	292	116	26.54	1	1	5	—	—	—	—	—	—
Oval	9	16	1	877	196	58.46	1	7	11	23	3	78	0	—	—
Trent Bridge	8	14	0	568	146	40.57	1	4	7	19.2	7	26	1	—	1/11
TOTAL IN ENGLAND	57	101	3	4498	333	45.85	11	20	58	221.1	65	533	10	53.30	2/18
Adelaide	2	4	0	223	117	55.75	1	1	3	9	2	23	1	—	1/23
Brisbane	1	2	0	4	2	2.00	—	—	1	1	0	1	0	—	—
Melbourne	3	6	0	293	99	48.33	—	3	—	—	—	—	—	—	—
Perth	2	4	0	75	43	18.75	—	—	4	—	—	—	—	—	—
Sydney	4	7	0	249	74	35.57	—	3	8	33	9	96	3	32.00	2/16
TOTAL IN AUSTRALIA	12	23	0	844	117	36.69	1	7	16	42	11	120	4	30.00	2/16
Bangalore	1	2	0	98	58	49.00	—	1	1	4	2	3	0	—	—
Bombay	2	4	1	60	49*	20.00	—	—	1	8	1	14	0	—	—
Calcutta	1	2	0	110	63	55.00	—	1	2	8.1	1	12	2	6.00	2/12
Delhi	1	2	1	91	71	91.00	—	1	1	—	—	—	—	—	—
Kanpur	1	1	0	58	58	58.00	—	1	—	—	—	—	—	—	—
Madras	1	1	0	127	127	127.00	1	—	—	17	4	51	0	—	—
TOTAL IN INDIA	7	12	2	544	127	54.40	1	4	5	37.1	8	80	2	40.00	2/12
Bridgetown	2	4	0	206	116	51.50	1	1	3	2	0	13	0	—	—
Kingston	3	6	0	233	153	38.83	1	1	3	10	4	26	0	—	—
Port-of-Spain	4	8	1	207	84	29.57	—	1	4	2	0	3	0	—	—
St John's	2	4	0	218	83	54.50	—	3	1	7	4	21	1	—	1/21

GROUND	MCH	INN	NO	RUNS	H.S.	AV'GE	100	50	CT	OVERS	MDNS	RUNS	WTS	AV'GE	B/B
TOTAL IN WEST INDIES	11	22	1	864	153	41.14	2	6	11	21	8	63	1	—	1/21
Colombo (PSS)	1	2	0	53	31	26.50	—	—	1						
Faisalabad	1	2	0	93	65	46.50	—	1	2	2	1	4	0	—	
Karachi	1	2	0	105	93	52.50	—	1	1						
Lahore	1	2	0	27	15	13.50	—	—	1						
TOTAL IN PAKISTAN	3	6	0	225	93	37.50	—	2	3	2	1	4	0	—	
Auckland	1	2	0	118	114	59.00	1	—	—						
Christchurch	1	1	0	2	2	—	—	—	—						
Wellington	1	2	0	41	30	20.50	—	—	—						
TOTAL IN N ZEALAND	3	5	0	161	114	36.20	1	—	—						
TOTAL IN ENGLAND	57	101	3	4498	333	45.85	11	20	58	221.1	65	533	10	53.30	2/18
TOTAL ELSEWHERE	37	70	3	2691	196	40.16	5	19	36	6	1	267	7	38.14	2/12
										102.2	28				

Index